Some Assembly Required

Work, Community, and

Politics in China's

Rural Enterprises

To Mrs. Galligan,
Thank you for your guidance,
friendship, & wisdom over the
past 20 years! I wouldn't have
made it this far without AP
English – I'm afraid I broke
every rule you taught me though.

All my best,
Calvin
May 29, 2008

Harvard East Asian Monographs 302

Some Assembly Required

Work, Community, and
Politics in China's
Rural Enterprises

Calvin Chen

Published by the Harvard University Asia Center and
Distributed by Harvard University Press
Cambridge (Massachusetts) and London 2008

Printed in the United States of America

The Harvard University Asia Center publishes a monograph series and, in coordination with the Fairbank Center for Chinese Studies, the Korea Institute, the Reischauer Institute of Japanese Studies, and other faculties and institutes, administers research projects designed to further scholarly understanding of China, Japan, Vietnam, Korea, and other Asian countries. The Center also sponsors projects addressing multidisciplinary and regional issues in Asia.

Library of Congress Cataloging-in-Publication Data

Chen, Calvin, 1968–
    Some assembly required : work, community, and politics in China's rural enterprises / Calvin Chen.
        p. cm. -- (Harvard East Asian monographs)
    Includes bibliographical references and index.
    ISBN 978-0-674-02783-1 (cl : alk. paper)
        1. Rural industries--China--Zhejiang Sheng. 2. Rural development--China--Zhejiang Sheng. 3. Industrialization--China--Zhejiang Sheng. 4. China--Economic policy. I. Title.
    HD2910.Z8C4414 2008
    338.0951'242--dc22

                                                                                2007039735

Index by Eileen Doherty
♾ Printed on acid-free paper

Last figure below indicates year of this printing
18 17 16 15 14 13 12 11 10 09 08

For My Parents

Lourdes and Jack Chen

Acknowledgments

THIS BOOK REPRESENTS the culmination of a long intellectual journey. When I first started thinking about why China's rural enterprises have been so successful, I could hardly imagine that my research would take me to Wenzhou and Jinhua, two locales undergoing momentous and sometimes gut-wrenching change. Although I had not met or known any of the incredible people at Phoenix and Jupiter prior to this project, they welcomed me into their homes and treated me as if I were an old friend. I only regret that in order to protect their anonymity, I cannot thank them by name. Nevertheless, I am forever indebted and grateful to them for sharing their time, experiences, and wisdom with me. This book would not have been at all possible without them.

This book also embodies the indelible influence of my teachers. Ken Jowitt has been an amazing mentor, always offering wise counsel, inspiration, and friendship. Tom Gold went beyond the call of duty, kindly sharing his China contacts with me as well as valuable advice during fieldwork and the write-up of the dissertation. Elizabeth Perry not only introduced me to the field and study of Chinese politics but always provided unstinting moral support and invaluable guidance. Franz Schurmann continually expanded my scholarly horizons, challenging me to seek and see a deeper meaning in my work. I also thank Chris Ansell, Jyotirindra Das Gupta, Hong Yung Lee, David Leonard, Sandy Muir, and Greg Noble for their encouragement and kindness.

In China, I am deeply grateful to Professors Ying Shijie and Han Hui of the Zhejiang Institute of Asia-Pacific Studies for facilitating my research requests and visits to various enterprises. This project could not have been undertaken without them. Han Hui especially went to great lengths to ensure that my visits were successful and enjoyable. Thanks also to Ma Jinlong of the Wenzhou Economic Reform Commission, Zhong Qiushi of the Wenzhou Liaison Office, and Xiang Jianqiang in Jinhua for their help with logistics during my research visits. In Taiwan, Professors King-yu Chang and Grace Yu graciously arranged for me to use research materials at National Chengchi University.

Early financial support for this project was provided by the University of California at Berkeley's Center for Chinese Studies, Berkeley's Department of Political Science, and a Hewlett Foundation Write-up Grant. I also benefited greatly from fellowships provided by Mount Holyoke College and the An Wang Postdoctoral Fellowship at Harvard's Fairbank Center for Chinese Studies.

I thank Annie Chang, Jeff Kapellas, and Yifeng Wu for their kindness and for providing a warm and supportive intellectual home (and unlimited coffee, donuts, and nachos) at Berkeley's Center for Chinese Studies Library. Regina Abrami, Tom Bickford, Marc Blecher, Ming Chan, Neil Diamant, Jacob Eyferth, Ken Foster, Mark Frazier, Mary Gallagher, Avery Goldstein, Doug Guthrie, Bill Hurst, Ching Kwan Lee, Kun-chin Lin, Jean Oi, Kevin O'Brien, Scott Raber, Ben Read, Tia Thornton, Andrew Walder, and Susan Whiting all provided valuable suggestions for improving various aspects of the manuscript. Jeff Kapellas and Rudy Sil graciously read through multiple drafts and helped sharpen the book's argument and focus. My thanks also go to Eileen Doherty for her fantastic work on the index.

At Mount Holyoke College, I thank Steve Ellenburg, Satya Gabriel, Penny Gill, John Grayson, Sohail Hashmi, Stephen Jones, Andy Lass, Tony Lee, Jonathan Lipman, Donal O'Shea, Eva Paus, and Jon Western for their support. I am indebted to my friends at the Fairbank Center for Chinese Studies for welcoming me into one of the most stimulating intellectual environments I have ever been a part of. I will always remember my time there with great fondness because of Bill Alford, Holly Angell, Xi Chen, Martin Dimitrov, Paul

Festa, Merle Goldman, Roderick MacFarquhar, Elizabeth Perry, Bob Ross, Mingwei Song, Ron Suleski, Wen Hao Tien, Melanie Wang, Shengqing Wu, and Baoyou Xu. I am also grateful to the two anonymous reviewers of the preliminary manuscript for the Harvard University Asia Center for their helpful comments.

In addition, I am indebted to Nila Bhattacharjya, Cheng Chen, Carole Cournoyer, Peter Eldridge, Ombretta Frau, Suzanne Z. Gottschang, Peter Jones, Kavita Khory, David Kim, Xian Cao Mei, Mike Metelits, Andrés Mares Muro, Beth Notar, Becky Packard, Michael Penn, João Resende-Santos, Joshua Roth, Patricia Schneider, Holly Sharac, Craig Smith, Jane Ting, Mark Walker, Ying Wang, Cara Wong, Phillip Wong, Angela Wu, Wen Xing, Dennis Yasutomo, and Hong Mei Zhang for their friendship, graciousness, and good cheer. Rudy Sil first persuaded me to pursue graduate study years ago and has been one of the best guides and friends anyone on this intellectual ride could ever hope for.

Most of all, I am deeply grateful to my family for all their patience, love, and support. My mother, Lourdes, my father, Jack, and my brother, Irving, have always believed that I could reach any goal I set for myself. From them, I learned the importance of dedication and perseverance, values that have served me well throughout graduate school and my career thus far. I also thank them for enduring all those years of wondering when I would finish whatever it was that was consuming so much of my time and energy. That mystery has finally been solved.

C.C.

Contents

Reference Matter

Figures

Some Assembly Required

Work, Community, and

Politics in China's

Rural Enterprises

ONE

Introduction

The Emergence of China's Rural Enterprises

EVERY MORNING AT approximately 7:30 A.M., thousands of young men and women walk through the factory gates of two firms in Zhejiang province I call "Jupiter" and "Phoenix," ready to begin another day of hard work on the assembly line, amid the buzz of machinery and under the watchful gaze of supervisors. Outfitted in company-issued white and blue uniforms, these young workers, nearly all in their late teens or early to mid-twenties, chat excitedly about a variety of topics—what they just ate for breakfast, what they plan to do after work, even the results of the most recent soccer match—as they make their way to their assigned stations in the company workshops. Once there, the workers abruptly end their conversations and begin anew the process of transforming the various components before them into products that will be sold to consumers they will most likely never know or ever meet. Every day, such scenes are being repeated in more and more places throughout rural China, as industrialization transforms communities once more attuned to an agrarian way of life.

Jupiter and Phoenix, located in Wenzhou and Jinhua prefectures, respectively, are two amazing examples of rural enterprises that were

founded under dire circumstances but grew rapidly into highly successful, multidivisional firms. At first glance, these firms appear to
have little in common. Jupiter was established in 1975 as a *collective*
enterprise and today produces a huge assortment of products, including textiles, audio speakers, auto parts, and electrical relays; Phoenix
was founded in 1984 as a *private* company and churns out a dizzying
array of low-voltage electrical products, including transformers,
switches, and control panels. In spite of the obvious differences in
product lines and institutional origins, they nevertheless share some
remarkable and important similarities. Jupiter and Phoenix began as
township and village enterprises (TVEs), or *xiangzhen qiye*, a vast
category of firms with diverse modes of ownership, organizational
structures, and levels of success. During the 1990s, both underwent a
significant transition to a shareholding model of ownership and are
now considered "nongovernmental enterprises" (*minying qiye*)—in
essence, private firms. Phoenix and Jupiter are highly profitable
companies that dominate their rivals with the productivity that
comes from having approximately 15,000 workers each. Both have
nourished and continue to refine workplace institutions that encourage mutual understanding and trust among all employees. Both
are dramatically reshaping their communities by helping local residents adjust to the unpredictable rhythms of a market-driven economy and, in the process, transforming the way residents see themselves and the larger world around them. In many ways, their
reputations as leaders and role models in their respective fields are
well deserved.

Yet nearly thirty years ago, when the Chinese leadership launched
its program of economic reform and liberalization, the rise of such
companies seemed most improbable. Seeking to modernize a stagnant economy and lay the foundations for sustained, long-term economic growth, paramount leader Deng Xiaoping attempted to dis-
mantle key aspects of the Maoist model of development, a model
whose potential to effect growth seemed utterly exhausted. This new
course, which has come to be known as the "Four Modernizations,"
slowly removed many previous restrictions on legitimate economic
activity and underscored the Chinese leadership's tacit hope that
the revival of markets and commerce would overcome the failings of

China's command economy, unleash its relatively untapped economic potential, and, at long last, bring prosperity to its citizens.

What initially began as an experiment eventually coalesced into a more concerted push toward marketization and privatization. The pace and extraordinary results of China's "transition from socialism" have led many in policymaking and scholarly circles alike to begin pondering when, not if, the country will become the world's leading economic power. Indeed, recent developments appear to support such thinking. Since China's accession to the World Trade Organization in 2001, it has attracted the most foreign investment of any nation on the globe; it has amassed the world's largest foreign exchange reserves, a cache that exceeded a staggering US$1 trillion at the end of 2006; and it has established itself as the world's workshop, dominating the manufacture of many consumer and industrial goods so thoroughly that it is poised to displace the United States and Germany as the world's largest exporter by 2010.[1] American consumers have certainly noticed this change at such retailers as Wal-Mart and Home Depot. These stores and many others like them are stocked with items sporting "Made in China" tags, products whose numbers continue to grow with each passing day.

Despite the intense media attention directed toward Chinese firms like Lenovo (its acquisition of IBM's personal computer division sent shock waves through business and government circles in 2005), how and why Chinese factories became so successful so quickly remain somewhat of a mystery. In fact, Lenovo's rise obscures one of the most astonishing success stories in contemporary China, the emergence of enterprises throughout China's vast countryside. Although rural factories were more famous (or infamous to some) during the early years of reform for their inexpensive and often shoddy knockoffs of better-known brand-name products, they have since undergone a dramatic metamorphosis, especially in the past decade. Whereas they once specialized in such simple items as canned drinks, snacks, embroidered sweatshirts, toys, electric fans, and sporting goods, they now produce more complex goods like high-fidelity speakers, auto parts, ball bearings, transformers, machine tools, and critical industrial components for the Chinese and increasingly, the global marketplace.

Rural factories have undoubtedly become the new linchpins of the country's ongoing economic expansion. From 1990 to 1996, for instance, TVEs increased the value of their production output seven-fold, from 250.4 billion *yuan* to 1.77 trillion *yuan*.* Throughout the late 1990s and the first three years of the new millennium, that value rose an average of 200 billion *yuan* per year, reaching 3.67 trillion *yuan* in 2003.[2] Moreover, these companies have played a vital role in providing employment for China's vast reserves of surplus labor. In 2004, TVEs employed over 135 million workers, nearly a third of the total rural workforce and nearly 20 percent of China's total workforce.[3] Although many observers held unfavorable impressions of rural factories during the earliest stages of the post-Mao reforms, that view gradually changed. By 1987, in the midst of TVE expansion, even Deng Xiaoping himself was astonished by what rural enterprises had accomplished:

> Generally speaking, our rural reforms have proceeded very fast, and farmers have been enthusiastic. What took us by surprise completely was the development of township and village enterprises. . . . This is not the achievement of our central government. Every year, township and village enterprises achieved 20 percent growth. . . . This was not something I had thought about. Nor had the other comrades. This surprised us.[4]

It should not have. Indeed, one might argue that without these firms, the Chinese countryside would not be as prosperous or as stable (illegal land confiscations and unfair government levies notwithstanding) as it is today. Still, although countless rural factories have most certainly crumbled since the reform policies were first enacted, those that survived did so because they struggled and persevered against great odds—and triumphed. Their success prompts several questions. To what extent are their achievements, for instance, due simply to the exploitation of Chinese workers? If the growth of these factories is due to more than driving workers hard, how do peasants turned workers, considered by some scholars to be ill-suited for

---

*The *yuan*, also known as the *renminbi* (RMB), is the official name of the Chinese currency. From 1994 to 2005, the exchange rate was 8.2 *yuan* to the US dollar.

industrial work, develop such impressive skills in so short a time?[5] To what extent do the personal backgrounds, orientations, and values of employees affect the cohesion and operations of these burgeoning companies? What processes, experiences, or organizational arrangements contribute to the formation of this disciplined, industrious workforce? And how long can peasant workers sustain their efforts in the face of fiercely competitive pressures both inside and outside the workplace?

This book represents my efforts to explore and understand rural enterprise success. To be sure, success is a tricky term, a moving target of sorts that encompasses efficiency, profitability, dynamism, and staying power. To the employees of Phoenix and Jupiter, success meant all of these things and more. Although managers and workers were sometimes confused about or disagreed on what aspect should take precedence at what particular time, they almost always returned to a few common elements and themes. In this study, I adopt the definitions of my respondents and take the term to mean not only high profit margins and long-term growth but also the high levels of institutional stability that result when employees accept company policies and practices as legitimate. In studying these firms, I discovered that the resilience of these factories has as much to do with the definition and exercise of authority and the interactions of people as it does with the company's ability to generate profits. Put another way, this is a story of how Jupiter and Phoenix successfully overcame the formidable challenge of synthesizing and synchronizing the formal responsibilities and organizational routines of the firm with the disparate interests, expectations, and behavior of their employees. Although conflict resolution and interest accommodation are central aspects of any institution-building process,[6] what made Jupiter and Phoenix especially innovative was their utilization and adaptation of social networks in the course of establishing and transforming their factories. More specifically, the founders of these companies infused their operations, especially in the earliest years of their development, with what Robert Putnam calls "social capital," or the trust and reciprocity derived from the kinship and social networks in which members of both enterprises were embedded.[7]

Pushing this line of analysis further, I submit that the ability to tap, deploy, and replenish social capital at critical moments in the enterprises' histories was central to the eventual rise and consolidation of the factory as an effective, robust institution. Hence, without high levels of mutual respect, trust, and cooperation, enterprise leaders would have found it nearly impossible to improve productivity, workplace stability, and the long-term viability of their companies. With this in mind, my analysis details the origination and transformation of rural enterprises into what Philip Selznick calls institutions or organizations "*infuse*[d] *with value* beyond the technical requirements of the task at hand,"[8] a most unusual outcome in the often unsettled economic and political environment of post-Mao China.

This study is also an account of how people in the Chinese countryside make sense of and participate in the industrialization drive that has engulfed them over the past few decades. By examining almost literally the "nuts and bolts" of the factory, the work processes as well as the interactions between employees on and off the shop floor, I demonstrate how workplace dynamics can both enable and constrain the ability of workers and managers alike to attain the myriad aspirations they seek to satisfy each day. For many first-time workers especially, the work and regimen of factory life can be jarring. Having traveled for days from remote villages in China's interior, and having left family and friends behind in search of a decent livelihood, they usually do not have the luxury of easing into this new way of life. They must adjust, and they must do so quickly. At the same time, each individual brings more than just her labor, skills, and knowledge to the factory; she brings expectations, orientations, and experiences that often diverge from those of her counterparts and her employer. Disagreements over such ideas as discipline, responsibility, and fairness deeply affect how employees engage one another and how much cohesion and stability can be generated in the workplace community. How employees, especially workers, respond to and navigate the alien and sometimes treacherous terrain of the industrial workshop can make or break a company. How this process unfolds is critical to understanding not only how rural factories have grown so quickly but also why they remain so vital to China's economic development.

Approaches to Understanding Enterprise Success

How can enterprises in planned economies become dynamic and productive? At first glance, this seems like a simple and straightforward question. Conventional social science analyses suggest that the answer lies in subjecting companies, especially China's inefficient, state-owned firms, to the demands and pressures of the market. Indeed, much of the early scholarly discourse on this topic focused on how to overcome the endemic dysfunctions of socialist economic systems, specifically state-created price distortions and allocative inefficiencies that undercut economic efficiency and growth. As the noted Hungarian economist János Kornai explains, socialist enterprises are motivated by a logic very different from that of their capitalist counterparts. Whereas capitalist companies pay close attention to the "bottom line" and profit margins, socialist firms are fixated on fulfilling output targets set by bureaucratic state planners, regardless of cost or product quality. Because financial incentives to operate efficiently do not exist and because firms know they will continue to receive state subsidies despite major financial losses, a condition of "soft budget constraints" emerges. Unfortunately, such circumstances exacerbate rather than eliminate existing distortions and perpetuate chronic shortages of vital goods and a surplus of unwanted products, well before the needs and demands of consumers are satisfied.[9]

Given these dynamics, some scholars, including Kornai himself, declared that "partial reform" of socialist economies could not succeed in the long term. Continued bureaucratic manipulation of investments, interest rates, and wage structures alongside autonomous markets would only sharpen the fundamentally antithetical features and logics of plan and market. Ultimately, the solution to these problems rests on the implementation of a more radical proposal: only privatization and the complete shift to a market-oriented institutional structure can eliminate the distortions and inefficiencies of planned economies.[10] In this framework, the clear definition and enforcement of property rights are crucial to reducing "transaction costs" and generating more efficient results.[11]

This market-based approach is powerful because it demonstrates how the establishment of "correct" micro-level incentives can lead to desirable macro-level economic outcomes. For proponents of this approach, the open pursuit of private interest not only satisfies individual needs more efficiently and effectively but, more important, contributes to the broader public good. When the state sanctions such activity, the talents and potential of individual citizens, as well as innovation and progress, can be maximized. Although these insights are highly significant, critics have also pointed out that such conclusions are overly theorized and do not adequately account for the peculiar challenges and contexts of transitional economies like China's. As Edward Steinfeld notes, the approach would work well if the main economic actors in China were private individuals capable of enjoying and acting on secure property rights, as they do, for example, in North America and Europe.*[12] The problem, of course, is that despite considerable progress, post-1978 China still has little in common with most advanced capitalist economies in this respect. In fact, China is still a place where nonprivate, nonindividual actors often exhibit profit-maximizing behavior similar to that of their private, individual counterparts, even in an environment in which property rights are not always clearly defined.

Moreover, the mechanism for regulating and enforcing property rights is hardly robust. Hence, those who insist on privatization as the sole means of stimulating growth appear to be wedded more to their personal normative preferences than to a grounded understanding of China's institutional setting. In response, some China scholars have suggested that the re-examination and revision of the major tenets of traditional ownership and property rights theory are in order.[13] Martin Weitzman and Chenggang Xu, for instance, have suggested that the *informal* dimensions of economic interaction—the "cooperative culture," as they put it—may reveal why the establishment of explicit, *formal* rules may not be absolutely necessary in some institutional contexts.[14]

---

*In March 2007, the National People's Congress approved a new property law that officially recognizes an individual's right to own private assets and prohibits local authorities from seizing land for unauthorized use or development.

A competing perspective, albeit one also rooted in similar assumptions about the power and appeal of the market, stresses the benefits of gradual marketization over rapid privatization. According to advocates of this view, privatization, while preferable, need not be implemented immediately in a reforming economy like China's so long as firms are encouraged or even pressured to respond to consumer demands during the transitional period. Under such circumstances, an enterprise's behavior matters more than its ownership form. Here, what Victor Nee calls "hybrid firms" (collective enterprises) can be as competitive as private ones, at least in the short run, because their privileged relationships with local governments provide them with critical advantages not usually enjoyed by their rivals.[15] In a period of market transition, local cadres can play an important supporting role by providing immediate assistance to firms desperate for scarce raw materials, bank loans, and credits and helping them adjust to new expectations and ways of conducting business. This phase can persist until market mechanisms render such practices and relationships obsolete.[16]

Additional research on Chinese rural enterprises has confirmed a number of these assertions. Jean Oi, one of the major proponents of the local state corporatism framework, sets forth a compelling alternative understanding of local economic processes.[17] She, too, examines the consequences of economic reform, but, in contrast to other theorists, she argues that changes in central-local government revenue-sharing arrangements spurred the rapid development of rural enterprises, especially in Shandong province. More specifically, two key changes contributed to this outcome. First, new fiscal arrangements between the central and local governments have generated new incentives for local cadres to facilitate the development of factories within their jurisdictions: they can earn higher pay and promotions for helping enterprises flourish. Second, these new policies allow local governments to keep a larger proportion of revenues for local needs. Thus, some of the profits can be retained and spent on improving local infrastructure or community welfare, which further enhances the political standing and prestige of the cadre within the local community. These policy alterations essentially produced a

de facto transfer of property rights to local actors and pushed bureaucrats to behave more like private entrepreneurs.

Extending the local state corporatism approach further, Andrew
Walder likens the strategy and behavior of local governments to
those of industrial firms. In his view, government officials resemble
"the principal in a corporate structure and enterprise managers are
analogous to division chiefs or plant heads within a corporate
firm."[18] Interested in ensuring the profitability of all divisions, local
cadres carefully monitor the latest market developments and then
use their networks to provide factories with capital and technology
or assistance in navigating complicated bureaucratic procedures on
licensing, registration, and taxation.[19] Although one might wonder
whether cadres always exhibit optimizing rather than "satisficing"
behavior* or whether they simply got lucky, Oi's and Walder's point
is well taken: government officials can be just as entrepreneurial and
innovative as private individuals. In showing how the interests of
local governments and rural enterprises intersect, Oi and Walder
also draw out critical macro-level implications for planned economies in the midst of transition. The successful partnership between
cadres and firms at the local level presents the possibility that socialist institutions can be adapted to fulfill the imperatives of reform.
Rather than being jettisoned, networks developed under socialism
might be effectively used to assemble new institutions and support
more market-oriented practices, a process David Stark and Laszlo
Bruszt call "bricolage" in their analysis of the post-communist market transition in Eastern Europe.[20]

These approaches have contributed greatly to our understanding
of the importance of financial incentives, property rights, and new
contractual arrangements between central and local governments to
the success of local industries. This study, however, argues that the
politics that take place *within* rural enterprises are equally crucial to
that success. Ultimately, whether property rights are clearly defined
or not, enterprise employees must still engage in the hard work of

---

*The term was made famous by Herbert Simon; see *Administrative Behavior*,
esp. 38–41. He argues that actors are not always able to select the best available
option; instead, they are more likely to adopt the one that is simply good enough.

manufacturing products for the market. How managers and employees come together to complete this task is just as important, if not more so, than external factors in determining long-term economic success. The problem is that perspectives focusing on exogenous factors provide only a rather static view of the enterprises themselves. By blackboxing the firm, they *assume* that enterprise stability exists but do not explain how it is created and sustained. Consequently, companies often appear, in Paul Pierson's words, "frozen" or "locked in" and more inert than they actually are.[21] Factories become closed systems impervious to outside influence, when in reality they are "open" and as deeply affected by internal forces as they are by external ones.[22] Although these studies often do note how firms were founded, they seldom explain how and when authority structures evolve and why some management practices remain robust in the face of change whereas others become outmoded. In other words, they offer a limited sense of how companies change over time. Perhaps most important, they shed little light on how members of the enterprises themselves understand and respond to the strains of an industrial regimen and how they determine who will be the winners and who the losers in the debates and struggles taking place behind the factory gate.

Revisiting the Factory: Outlines of a Micro-level Approach

Examining enterprises from the inside out may recall for some the classic, "old institutionalist" accounts of organizational development as well as a number of recent pathbreaking studies of Chinese labor.[23] Certainly, my work draws considerable inspiration from these two bodies of literature and shares their view that a systematic analysis of relationships and interactions within the firm helps overcome the tired image of factories as engines of production that can be turned on or off at will. Indeed, they are so much more: they are as much sites where managers make vital decisions about a company's future as they are places where people wrestle with historical legacies they cannot ignore and myriad constraints they seek and even feel compelled to overcome. This, in part, is what makes them locations of heated contestation, places where new identities are shaped and allegiances forged and tested. In the transitional context of post-Mao China, they are also where kinship networks, native-place identities, and informal norms have re-emerged as potent social forces that often collide against the harsh logic of rationalization and impersonalism. If the formation and success of enterprises and China's economic competitiveness depend on how these forces are reconciled, it is worth exploring more carefully how and why specific management practices were created and institutionalized inside factory walls.

This book adopts an ethnographic approach to understanding the nature and trajectory of China's industrial transformation and its impact on the multitude of workers who toil on the shop floor. It builds on some recent, pioneering works on Chinese labor, which have been especially illuminating in regard to the sometimes murky world of factory work. Ching Kwan Lee's *Gender and the South China Miracle*, for example, highlights how "diverse patterns of production politics emerge as conjunctural outcomes of the state, the labor market, and differentiated deployment of gender power."[24] Her findings reveal that even as global economic forces and state objectives have dramatically reshaped work opportunities in southern China, native-place ties, age, and gender have all played a profound role in determining the control strategies managers deploy and the broader conditions of work in the two electronics plants she studied. Her ethnographic study also uncovers and explores how the personal concerns and the family commitments of the *dagongmei*, or female migrant workers, who anchor the factory workforce, at times make them more vulnerable to the machinations of their largely male superiors and how in other instances their emerging identities inspire them to defy managerial directives. By building on the testimony and experiences of her coworkers, Lee successfully uses micro-level data to demonstrate that production politics comprises a more complex, sometimes hidden set of negotiations and processes on both the individual and collective levels.

My study attempts to illuminate the complex organizational dynamics that engendered a sometimes bewildering mix of formal requirements and informal practices. To do so, I adopt the analytical approach pioneered by Ken Jowitt as a general frame for understanding the transformation of the rural enterprises on which my analysis is based. In the field of communist studies, Jowitt's work is well known for offering some of the most theoretically compelling insights into the birth, development, and death of what he terms the "Leninist phenomenon." His approach, with its focus on "elite-designated core tasks and stages of development,"[25] provides an especially powerful means of identifying not only the most essential and novel features of Leninist parties but also the dilemmas they face in attempting to transform their members, their organizations, and the external environment over a protracted period of time.

What Jowitt identified as the signature attributes and objectives of Leninism constitute an elegant distillation of the central themes in organization theory and institutional development. In many ways, those insights can fruitfully be applied to understanding China's rural enterprises. Like the leaders of Leninist parties in particular and heads of organizations in general, company founders sought to achieve key objectives through specifically tailored strategies in often turbulent environments. Through a developmental stages approach, we gain a clearer view of the complex interconnections among organizational goals, actions, and outcomes, as well as how contradictions among the three produce organizational change.

In each of the three stages—survival, expansion, and reintegration—that I lay out in Chapters 3, 4, and 5, I begin with a look at the enterprise's formal goals and structure. I examine the objectives set by company leaders and explain how these imperatives shaped production and authority. Production and authority can be studied and better understood through their more concrete manifestations: the chain of command, job descriptions and formal responsibilities, work rules and sanctions for noncompliance, and company wage scales and financial incentives. Outlining the objectives guiding the firm and the methods employed to achieve them helps us to understand why some managers seek to establish "hegemonic regimes" with near absolute authority over employees and why others reject this approach.[26] We also see why, as was the case with the firms in Mark Frazier's fascinating study, management practices are seldom as uniform and well integrated as outside observers often imagine them to be. Instead, they are layered on one another, even though this frequently results in major contradictions and confusion.[27] This is less the result of incompetence (although there is ample evidence of such) and more a reflection of the conflicting interests of diverse actors throughout the firm as well as the numerous clashes they have engaged in over time.

More is needed though. An analysis of how the informal structure, the unwritten rules and norms that can deeply influence employee behavior, either enhances or undercuts the ability of the company to attain its goals is crucial to developing a more nuanced portrait of these firms as institutions. To do this, I do not focus exclusively on one specific group within the enterprise; rather, I seek to present a more comprehensive account of factory employees, from top executives and plant managers to lower-level staff, assembly line workers, and even support staff such as members of the company canteen and custodial crew. More specifically, I show how the personal concerns and aspirations of factory personnel vary significantly by their rank within the enterprise. These differences are crucial in determining not only how workers relate to one another but also the degree to which they accept the orders of their superiors and the formal demands of the organization. I also assess the resonance of values and mindsets embodied in re-emerging group-oriented patterns of association, namely, kinship ties and native-place identities, upon a worker's willingness to comply with the rules that regulate factory activity.

By studying rural enterprises with these variables in mind, a substantially different view emerges to complement our current understanding of this institution. Juxtaposing the *formal* demands of the workplace with the *informal* expectations of employees allows us to see more clearly not only the rational intentions behind organizational design but also the points where conflict, resistance, and change may arise. The enterprise thus becomes a kind of laboratory where individuals participate in the process of defining and resolving issues of individual opportunity, collective welfare, and higher purpose. These debates on fairness and propriety are continuous and dynamic, with answers fluctuating in response to the changing conditions and imperatives confronting these firms.[28]

How much we learn about firm dynamics with this approach hinges critically on the assumptions undergirding this study. First, I see historical legacies—ecological, social, and political—as central determinants of an enterprise's and, indeed, a community's developmental pace and trajectory. Although legacies are most typically seen as constraints, I assume that they can enable economic and social activity as well. More precisely, I see collectively oriented social norms and "traditional" values and perspectives as potential facilitators of cooperation rather than permanent obstacles to it. Certainly, how such values are used depends on the actors themselves, but legacies should not be seen only as barriers to progress. Second, I assume that the ability of actors to achieve their objectives varies with the resources at their disposal and the authority of their offices as well as the choices they make. A poor decision, for example, can easily thwart success, even if, say, the company president deploys all available resources toward the attainment of a specific goal. Finally, decisions and actions can precipitate unintended but consequential effects. Their impact on interactions in the workplace, positive and negative, highlights the centrality of contingency and process in organizational dynamics.

My objective in this book, then, is to reveal and explain how these various forces and concerns are articulated and balanced against the backdrop of a broader, marketizing environment. More specifically, I evaluate how the processes of role definition and institution-building in the firm lead to the critical levels of labor stability necessary for production to proceed. As important as strong market structures and linkages to local governments are, I submit that what ultimately determines the enterprise's ability to generate profits is the degree to which members of the workplace understand and willingly fulfill the duties and responsibilities they are assigned. Without this acceptance or even begrudging tolerance to bolster the factory authority structure, the enterprise will crumble, no matter how attractive the financial incentives might be. The leaders of successful rural enterprises understand this predicament and are able to negotiate a course of action that avoids debilitating confrontation and instead promotes cooperation. As a result, they are able to transform peasants into workers.

Perhaps what is most astonishing is their unconventional approach to establishing stability within their firms. Rural enterprises thrived because the charismatic leaders of the firm successfully fused a collectively oriented, trust-based, and reciprocal social ethos with an individually oriented, profit-driven, industrial production regimen. This particular amalgamation drew on the few resources these communities possessed and created a new "historical substitute" for the patterns of industrial development that first emerged in Western Europe.[29] I further hypothesize that discontent and instability within the firm—disregard for work rules, disputes with superiors, absenteeism, and high turnover rates—reflect a profound disappointment over the divergence of formal demands from widely accepted social norms of behavior.[30] In other words, I argue that the formal structure and demands of the firm, the personal background of the individual employee, and group-oriented social norms combine to generate differing levels of labor stability within the factory.[31] The more these factors are in sync, the more likely that stability will result. Conversely, the less they are in accord, the less likely stability will follow. Balancing these often contradictory forces and concerns has been central to the lasting success of the two firms that anchor this study. Moreover, their continuing struggle to bring the formal goals of production and the informal norms of proper behavior into a workable equilibrium marks the three developmental stages I see as defining the enterprise's developmental course: survival, expansion, and reintegration. Figure 1 summarizes the approximate duration of these stages for Jupiter and Phoenix.

In the incipient stage of development, the overriding concern and the central organizational imperative for the firm's founders was the enterprise's *survival*. Working within an unstable institutional environment, firm leaders sought out employees who would be wholly committed to building the enterprise and willing to do anything necessary to keep the factory's operations running smoothly. Those who fit this profile were the people they knew best and trusted most, their closest relatives and fellow locals. With this core group, the enterprise's "heroic cadres," the need for complicated work rules and careful monitoring of work performance was low. The

Developmental stage	Jupiter	Phoenix
Survival	1975–mid-1980s	1984–late 1980s
Expansion	Late 1980s–early 1990s	Early 1990s–mid-late 1990s
Reintegration	Mid-1990s–present	Late 1990s–present

Fig. 1   The developmental stages of Jupiter and Phoenix

simple organizational structure that emerged facilitated the completion of tasks and allowed the forging of even closer personal bonds through self-sacrifice and heightened mutual commitment. Moreover, a strong sense of personal involvement by the founders and a "rough egalitarianism" pervaded the scene in this stage, cushioning members against the backbreaking burdens of factory work and assuring a crucial level of labor stability that allowed members to adjust gradually to the difficult demands of industrial production.

As the danger of firm failure diminished, the guiding motive of the next developmental stage was enterprise *expansion*. That is, in an attempt to enhance the company's competitiveness and preserve its earlier success, enterprise leaders rationalized and standardized their operations along the lines of multidivisional firms like General Motors and DuPont. In order to achieve this end, technical specialists were hired; new, uniform work routines were instituted; and a more complex division of labor was created for the factory. Even as this precipitated massive jumps in output and efficiency, social tensions and conflict increased as well. The new division of labor resulted in a steeper hierarchy of authority and status over the workforce, undermining the egalitarian spirit that had permeated the previous stage of enterprise survival. Although the new technical and managerial staff improved the overall welfare of the enterprise community, their presence created new fault lines within the workforce as well. Members of the technical staff were often nonlocals who received lucrative compensation packages and high-ranking positions within the company bureaucracy in exchange for providing specialized skills.

For the enterprise members who had been crucial during the stage of enterprise survival but lacked such expertise, this development betrayed the norms of fairness and propriety central to the kinship networks that had shaped their previous efforts. Increasingly, these changes became a source of friction within the firm.

Recognizing that profitability could not be earned at the cost of workplace peace, enterprise leaders are now in the midst of a new phase, enterprise *reintegration*. In this ongoing stage of development, they are trying to restore the camaraderie that was a central feature of the firm's earlier struggle to survive while preserving and deepening the benefits of expansion. As a result, leaders have softened many of the harshest aspects of their expanded and rationalized structure and moved toward a more flexible and decentralized managerial approach focused more on ameliorating social tensions and social distinctions in the workplace. These efforts have sparked meaningful changes in other areas as well. First, new paternalistic practices have been adopted, extending collective benefits to all members. These benefits often take the form of "red envelopes" (*hongbao*) handed out during *chunjie* (Chinese New Year), cases of soft drinks distributed during the sweltering summer months, gift items like tea sets, raincoats, and umbrellas emblazoned with the company logo, as well as more substantial retirement and severance packages and, most recently, expanded medical care. Moreover, they have moved to redefine membership in the enterprise community. So long as individual members contribute to the well-being of the enterprise, they are considered part of the enterprise "family," regardless of their background or connection with high-ranking company officials. Interestingly, this identity is being reconstructed with the help of the Communist Party, yet along different lines than those of the Maoist era. Today, the party is playing a supporting, not a leading, role in the operations and affairs of China's rural enterprises. Through *karaoke* contests, sporting events, and other public rituals, party members are helping company leaders reshape the symbolic terrain of the factory in hopes of resolving the numerous organizational and social challenges that have recently emerged on the shop floor. The local political and economic elites have once

	Survival	Expansion	Reintegration
Core task	Ensure financial viability	Rationalize production and increase scale of operations	Maintain profitability and recapture social solidarity
Authority relations	Personal and simple, based on norms of reciprocity and trust, rough sense of egalitarianism	Formal and hierarchical, greater specialization, increased reliance on impersonal rules	Bureaucratic, decentralized, paternalistic orientation mediated by party-led organizations
Workforce composition	Almost exclusively local	Somewhat mixed; locals dominate executive positions, more nonlocals in technical and line production positions	Increasingly mixed, especially in technical and administrative positions; production positions dominated by nonlocals
Level of labor stability	High—disagreements were few and resolved amicably	Low—turnover rates soared as work disputes became more confrontational	Mixed—turnover rates have stabilized but employees still frustrated by uneven enterprise policies

Fig. 2   Key attributes in the developmental trajectories of Jupiter and Phoenix

again joined forces in an attempt to ensure lasting prosperity for their local communities. Whether they ultimately succeed will depend largely on how they manage the sometimes contradictory economic and social forces that first brought them together and still occasionally threaten to tear their enterprises apart. Figure 2 highlights the critical aspects and outcomes of each stage in the developmental trajectory of Jupiter and Phoenix.

Sources and Methods

In order to learn firsthand about the internal dynamics of rural enterprises, I tried to gain direct access to such firms to interview people who worked in the factories. In the summer of 1996, I made a preliminary trip to the southern province of Guangdong, one of the fastest growing regions in China, to inquire about the possibility of doing research there. I reasoned that the enormous success of enterprises in Guangdong would encourage enterprise employees and managers to speak candidly about their accomplishments as well as the challenges they eventually overcame. By casting my examination as a serious attempt to understand their recipes for economic success, I also hoped to reduce official suspicions about the "true intentions" of my research. Although local officials accompanied me to a large enterprise in Shunde county, outside the city of Guangzhou, I was given only a short tour and brief introduction to the firm's operations and history. When I broached the issue of doing fieldwork and conducting interviews at the company, my host smiled and then summarily dismissed the possibility. "It would be too disruptive," he said, "to have someone who doesn't work here wandering around and asking questions." Anyway, as the manager of a smaller firm stated, "What is there to research? It's all very simple. If your work is good, you get paid. If your work is bad, you get fired."

Disappointed that my original plans had fallen through, I searched for other options. Fortunately, I met scholars affiliated with the Zhejiang Institute of Asia-Pacific Studies headquartered in Hangzhou, the provincial capital of Zhejiang. Through my discussions with them, I discovered that one of the institute's major research topics was the impact of the reform policies on Zhejiang's economy. In fact, some of the issues I wanted to explore in regard to factory development overlapped with their interests. It was my great fortune to develop a strong partnership with them. Before I began conducting field research, I consulted with friends at the institute about the types of firms I hoped to visit and the kind of research I wanted to undertake. I specifically mentioned that I wanted to study one private firm and one collective enterprise so as to compare their responses to the challenges of organization and production. Through intensive case studies, I hoped to observe and record the manner in which the leaders of such firms tried to shape the enterprise community and how other members of the firms responded to ever-shifting demands. In my mind, the only way I could find answers to these questions would be to talk, live, and work with factory employees. Hence, I emphasized to my friends that what I needed most was the opportunity to interview as many employees as possible and observe the workings of the shop floor.

With the help of the institute, I was finally granted permission to visit Phoenix Enterprises in southeastern Zhejiang and Jupiter Enterprises in central Zhejiang. In total, I spent nine months researching these firms: June through September 1997 at Phoenix and April through August 1998 at Jupiter. I also made brief follow-up visits to Phoenix in April 1998 and July 2004. The first few weeks at each site posed difficulties as company representatives labored to keep up with their own workloads and took on the additional burden of introducing me to the company's history and ongoing operations. When staff members were unavailable to arrange introductions and initial visits to the plants, I was allowed to examine "declassified" company documents, although I was forbidden to photocopy these materials for my own research files. These memorandums, reports, and directives provided me with significant information on the firms' history and authority structures as well as the formal regulations and procedures guiding their operations. The documents also supplied some background information on the workforce, including age, gender, education, and native-place breakdowns. Unfortunately, this information was often out of date and incomplete: employees came and went so quickly that managers barely knew the general characteristics of their workforce. Nevertheless, the information that they were able to collect provided basic profiles of each company. These profiles sharpened my focus and helped me formulate more precise questions, which I then directed to my respondents.

Both companies allowed me to shadow key managerial staff throughout their workday, labor alongside production workers on the assembly line, and eventually to conduct multiple interviews with various personnel. My extended stays provided numerous opportunities to ask key questions about the genesis and implementation of company policies as well as the sources of resistance to them and their eventual evolution. More important, the data I collected prompted me to revise my initial hypotheses regarding the necessity of clearly defined property rights for ensuring enterprise profitability and efficiency. None of this could have been accomplished without the generous help of a great number of people I have come to know so well. Every one of them patiently answered my seemingly point-less queries, and each one of them helped deepen my understanding of the world in which they live. I was privileged to share countless conversations with them, most often in their offices or on the shop floor, but also over dinner, over tea, and even on pedicab rides through both townships. For the purposes of this book, however, I rely chiefly on the information provided by 135 respondents, 105 from Phoenix and 30 from Jupiter. I also benefited from discussions with a handful of scholars and local officials as well. Their insights added considerably to my understanding of the broader regional dy-namics—economic and political—in which Phoenix and Jupiter were enmeshed.

The obvious disparity in the number of respondents at the two firms reflects the unavoidable challenges of field research. At Phoe-nix, I was fortunate enough to live in the employees' dormitory com-plex, where a mix of workers, technical specialists, and managers resided. Just below my room, on the first and second floors of the building, were the company canteens, one for production line work-ers and the other for managerial and technical staff. Both canteens provided opportunities to interact with employees from different of-fices and factories and find out firsthand about the day's events. More important, Phoenix's executives graciously granted me nearly unlimited access. Although the company's 43 plants were scattered throughout the far reaches of the township (making many virtually inaccessible), I was able to visit and study twelve of the longest-running factories, all of which were clustered around the company's headquarters. I was given complete freedom to roam the shop floor and investigate any aspect of the operation I wanted. Managerial and technical staff were cooperative and supportive and even al-lowed me to work on the production line. I assembled on-off switches and an assortment of indicator lights, almost none of which passed quality control, much to the amusement of my fellow work-ers. I also wrapped and packaged relays and transformers, a much simpler task, at least until I was asked to switch to stacking them neatly on pallets and help move them to the warehouse. Although I turned out to be a rather unproductive worker, my direct experi-ences on the line in several plants over many weeks gave me a new perspective on how the demands and pace of work affected the views and behavior of factory employees.

In contrast, the situation at Jupiter was more restrictive. First, my base was a local hotel, not company dormitories. Most of the dorm complexes (I knew of at least five) were dispersed throughout the township and located much farther away from the plants I studied, distances that were considerably farther than those I faced during my stay at Phoenix. The hotel was closer to the places I needed to be and served as a better base for extended interactions with enter-prise members. Second, three months prior to my visit, Jupiter had experienced a case of industrial espionage. A foreign spy posing as a graduate student stole a set of closely guarded blueprints from one of the company's plants. In response, the company tightened security considerably, limiting full access to a select group of high-ranking company officials. Despite these restrictions, I nevertheless received clearance to study five of the company's major divisions. At one of the plants, I was able to engage in participant observation and make arrangements to talk with respondents more intensively after work hours. Occasionally, I stayed for overtime shifts in the workshops as well. I was also given the opportunity to attend other company events, including a meeting of the company's Communist Party members, as part of my research. So although the situation at Jupiter was, in some ways, more restrictive than that at Phoenix, I still came away with a thorough overview of the company's operations. I tried as much as possible to adapt to the situation at hand, juggling my schedule and quickly taking advantage of opportunities to engage employees in conversation as they unexpectedly arose. In many ways, my experience at Jupiter reflected the successful application of what Thomas Gold has called "guerrilla interviewing" techniques.[32]

The methodology I employ in this study is qualitative in na-ture. That is to say, I aim to provide as "thick" a description of the enterprise and its members as I can and locate them within their specific historical and institutional contexts.[33] Yet unlike more traditional ethnographies and case studies, I attempt to use a "holistic approach" to explain how a number of factors together, not in isolation, lead to labor stability within the firm. This process of discovery is predicated on the view that multiple conjunctural causation provides a stronger basis for evaluating and understanding social phenomena.[34] It also suggests that data drawn from the micro-level of the firm can contribute to our understanding of macro-level issues of rural development in China as well as China's political economy.

Still, questions about the conclusiveness of this kind of study are not easily dispelled.[35] Scholars may justifiably question the representativeness and reliability of my respondents' testimony. To be sure, my respondents may not constitute an ideal sample of enterprise employees, but the number of people I interviewed and their varied backgrounds and positions within the firms lend important insights into the formation and conduct of company operations. Many of them had intimate knowledge of work routines and the evolution of managerial practices and provided this information to me in a series of long discussions. My interviews were semi-structured yet open-ended so as to allow me to explore interesting leads and unanticipated topics. Even so, I was aware that respondents might embellish their stories or provide self-serving testimony. I tried to minimize this by separating specific events and processes from their understandings and assessments of them. As much as possible, I also attempted to corroborate events and actions with the testimony of other respondents and my own observations. In addition, I hoped my refusal to pay for the testimony and my insistence on keeping their identities confidential further reduced incentives to provide false information. Although I cannot guarantee the absolute veracity of all their statements, I do believe I have a strong collection of truthful responses on which to base a study of rural firms in China.[36]

Others might wonder whether the two firms I analyze here can be seen as representative of China's myriad rural enterprises. The large size of both firms and their location in a relatively advanced coastal province, some would say, disqualify them as subjects from which we can draw more far-reaching conclusions.* Although such points are well taken, they also miss some crucial aspects of the Chinese situation. Both firms began as small-scale enterprises and grew in size only after years of continuous struggle and operation. Furthermore, their location in remote and resource-poor areas of Zhejiang decreased the possibility of their benefiting from significant governmental investment and assistance in comparison to rural enterprises in other provinces.[37] As a result, enterprise leaders relied largely on their own networks and resources in organizing and maintaining a competitive work organization.

Although the two cases that anchor this study are not typical in a conventional sense, both firms confronted and overcame common organizational challenges facing all enterprises in highly turbulent environments. More specifically, their lack of resources and relative isolation parallel the situation in which the vast majority of factories in the Chinese countryside find themselves today. Consequently, firms in interior regions of China seeking to escape their own difficult circumstances may learn a great deal about the process of building an enterprise from the rich histories and experiences of Jupiter and Phoenix. In this sense, I hope this book provides an empirical foundation for a broader theory of rural enterprise development and deeper insights into how individual Chinese fare once they step inside the factory gate.

Overview of the Study

The following chapters take up specific aspects of the developmental course taken by rural enterprises and show the linkages among the various parts of my argument. Chapter 2 examines the specific historical legacies of southeastern and central Zhejiang. In looking at these features, I try to show how broader ecological, economic, political, and social constraints influenced the strategies enterprise leaders eventually adopted.

———

*I readily acknowledge that a study of failed enterprises would offer an important contrast and enhance the findings of my study. Of course, the problem was that once such firms went bankrupt and shuttered their operations, there was no way to interview their personnel or investigate their organizational dynamics.

Chapters 3 through 5 concentrate on the processes and experiences of the industrial workplace, describing in finer detail the main processes that defined each of the developmental stages the enterprises underwent. Chapter 3 explains the institutional origins of Jupiter and Phoenix and highlights the strategies employed by enterprise leaders that allowed the firms to endure. I point out especially how the personal charisma and commitment of firm founders and the informal norms of trust and reciprocity enhanced accountability and a sense of common purpose, which, in turn stabilized shop floor dynamics. Chapter 4 focuses on the leadership's plans to expand and rationalize enterprise operations and how the growing divide between formal objectives and informal expectations created new conflicts and a new identity crisis among the workforce. I break down the varied backgrounds and concerns of enterprise members and show how resentment over new, rationalized work procedures and growing status distinctions among the workforce eroded labor stability in the factory. In Chapter 5, I evaluate enterprise efforts to deal with the newly emerging conflicts and fissures that emerged during enterprise expansion and the impact of growing bureaucratization on both firms. Specifically, I appraise enterprise strategies to restore earlier levels of labor stability through an expansion of paternalistic practices and the adoption of a more inclusive, "enterprise family" orientation, efforts supported by the Communist Party, which was surprisingly called back into the enterprise to assist in overcoming internal dissension. In the final chapter, I discuss the implications of the experiences of rural enterprises and evaluate not only their future prospects but, just as important, their legacy for a dramatically altered Chinese countryside.

TWO

Seeds of Transformation
Ecology, Society,
and Politics in
Two Townships

ZHEJIANG OCCUPIES A storied place in the Chinese popular imagination. Since the twelfth century when Hangzhou, the current provincial capital, served as the seat of government for the Southern Song dynasty, Zhejiang has been considered a place of unmatched taste and refinement, a land of fine silks, fragrant teas, and timeless beauty. More recently, efforts to restore Hangzhou's architectural splendor have only heightened expectations among both residents and tourists alike of a return to the city's former grandeur. Indeed, the city is moving forward quickly and reinventing itself as one of the region's most economically and culturally vibrant centers. The old adage "Above there is heaven, below there are Suzhou and Hangzhou" (*shang you tiantang, xia you Suhang*) is perhaps as fitting today as it was in ages past. For many, it is an equally apt description of all Zhejiang as well.

Such notions have been fueled by the province's accelerating industrial growth in the post-1978 reform period. In 2004, for example, its industrial output was valued at 939.5 billion *yuan*, making it the third largest province in terms of production of manufactured goods, behind Guangdong and Jiangsu.[1] Given these developments, it is not surprising that some scholars view Zhejiang's post-1978 industrial success as a natural and even inevitable outcome of the favorable circumstances it has seemingly enjoyed through the ages.[2] Like Guangdong and Jiangsu, the two provinces with which Zhejiang is often compared, it is situated on China's eastern seaboard and benefits from a temperate climate, extensive trading opportunities, and a sophisticated and robust economy.

Although this depiction is historically accurate, not all of Zhejiang's communities have been equally blessed. Far from Hangzhou, far from the prosperous port city of Ningbo in northern Zhejiang, the local situation was often radically different. In the remote mountain and coastal regions of central and southeastern Zhejiang, life has been and continues to be considerably more precarious. Like others elsewhere whose livelihoods depended primarily on agriculture, residents of Jinhua and Wenzhou prefectures struggled each day to make ends meet, for their meager incomes seldom sufficed to ensure economic survival. From this harsh environment, Phoenix and Jupiter eventually emerged to become two of contemporary China's great successes.

In this chapter, I examine the impact of ecological, political, and social legacies on the developmental paths of Phoenix and Jupiter. In taking ecology into account, I am by no means arguing that the physical environment predetermines a region's chances for long-term economic success or the behavior of a region's inhabitants. Rather, like Elizabeth Perry in her study of peasant rebellion in China, I submit that "the natural setting simply provides certain limits and parameters to human activity."[3] For the inhabitants of Wenzhou and Jinhua prefectures, the respective homes of Phoenix and Jupiter, the surrounding physical environment offers few natural resources for industrial development. Furthermore, what commodities these communities did produce prior to the reform era were not widely marketed, nor were these areas historically well integrated with other regions in the way that the Su'nan area in Jiangsu and Shanghai were and still are today. Consequently, they remained, until the post-1978 reform era at least, comparatively desolate places on the periphery of economic and social life within the province.

These ecological constraints limited the survival strategies area natives could adopt and, in the process, stalled efforts toward self-sustaining economic and social development. Even after the Chinese Communists ascended to power in 1949 and implemented new policies, locals continued to eke out a subsistence living: farmers did not produce a consistent surplus and were compelled, in their spare moments, to engage in sideline activities in order to supplement their meager earnings. As demographic pressures in the area increased, more residents migrated elsewhere in search of opportunity. Resource poor and largely neglected by central authorities, neither Jinhua nor Wenzhou experienced steady social progress; both lagged well behind in the broad educational and technical skills that many scholars consider vital to effecting industrial take-off. In fact, in contrast to what happened in South Korea and Taiwan after World War II, such constraints seemed more likely than not to erode the motivation and determination of area residents to improve their situation.[4]

Political considerations further complicated prospects for industrial development. In the post-1949 era, party leaders saw Zhejiang as one of the nation's most prosperous provinces and consequently extracted more resources from it than the central government invested in return. It also appears that political conflict between the Chinese Communist Party and the Guomindang, or Nationalist Party, on Taiwan also impacted Zhejiang's developmental trajectory. As Alan Liu has pointed out, Zhejiang "suffered from serious political discrimination under Mao, due partly to Zhejiang's status as the home province of Chiang Kai-shek."[5] Moreover, the leadership feared that Wenzhou's proximity to Taiwan made it a likely military target in any potential conflict with the rival Nationalists. To them, investing in such a vulnerable area made little practical or strategic sense. These decisions, however, proved disastrous for Wenzhou and Jinhua. Provincial and central authorities committed few resources to developing vital communications and transportation links, let alone local industry. Both locales thus lagged behind more economically advanced regions in China along several developmental dimensions and for the most part were left to find their own solutions.

Despite these shortcomings, Wenzhou and Jinhua are now two of the most dynamic industrial zones in the province. How did this come about? Ironically, the combined effects of ecological, social, and political constraints in these two areas strengthened the capacity for self-reliance in both communities.[6] Physical isolation, a poor material resource base, inadequate economic and social development, and governmental neglect—these factors compelled local residents to rely on one another. In many ways, the vast networks of family and friends that made these communities so tightly knit filled the voids left by government and facilitated the eventual exploitation of the new economic opportunities that grew out of the post-1978 reform policies. These social connections served as the ultimate source of both the material and the organizational resources necessary for building successful factories in the Chinese countryside.

Location, Location, Location: Ecological and Social Legacies

Zhejiang province is a land of stark contrasts. Situated on China's seaboard, Zhejiang occupies approximately 102,000 square kilometers, or 1 percent of the country's total land mass.[7] Roughly equal in size to the state of Indiana, Zhejiang is China's smallest mainland province.[8] Historically, the province has been renowned as the "land of rice and fish" (*miyu zhi zhou*), an area of lush landscapes and fertile fields. Despite Zhejiang's relatively small size, its agriculture has been productive enough to sustain an ever-growing population, which in 1998 totaled over 44 million.[9] This vast population has been one of the province's greatest strengths and the source of innumerable scholars and officials. In fact, during the Ming and Qing dynasties, the province was so renowned for the number of imperial officials it produced that Ping-ti Ho dubbed Zhejiang a "talent-exporting" province.[10]

However, this image masks starker disparities in local developmental conditions. The highly romanticized image of Zhejiang is drawn almost exclusively from the north and northeastern portions of the province, where the flatter terrain is highly productive and communication and transportation are facilitated by a network of roads and canals, including the famous Grand Canal. It does not apply to life in the central and southeastern regions located farther away from the core. Hence, although the cities of Hangzhou, Shao-xing, and Ningbo elevated the province to new commercial and cultural heights, the inhabitants of other regions of Zhejiang had to struggle to survive and rarely attained the levels of wealth or comfort of their northern counterparts, at least until more recent times.

In many ways, Wenzhou represents the antithesis of the urbane and cultured north. Although it is the province's only major southern port, it is by no means Ningbo.[11] Ningbo was home to a class of prosperous merchants similar to those who dominated nineteenth-century New England; in contrast, Wenzhou was the base for marauding bands of pirates and smugglers, whose activities in ages past forced imperial authorities to close the port for extended periods of time.[12] Not surprisingly, much of the area's success as a haven for illicit activity was connected to its rugged terrain and relative inaccessibility. Nearby mountain ranges run from the northeast to the west and south, hemming the area in and preventing easy access and interaction with other parts of the province. Zhejiang is often described as a land consisting of "seven parts mountains, one part water, and two parts land" (*qishan yishui erfendi*), a perfect place for avoiding unwelcome attention from government authorities.

Unfortunately for Wenzhou residents, however, the physical surroundings offer few resources on which to build a thriving economy. The local mountains, for example, contain no appreciable amounts of valuable minerals such as coal or gold, just ordinary rock that is today commonly blasted and carted away for use in construction projects. Residents have nevertheless survived by raising crops on limited amounts of farmland. However, the per capita amount of cultivated land has dropped precipitously since the founding of the People's Republic. In 1949, the average in Wenzhou was 1.16 *mu* of land; six years later, it had slipped to 1.0 *mu*.* By 1990, well after the Household Responsibility System had restored family-based farming, the figure declined to 0.41 *mu*; and in 1994, it fell to

---

*A *mu* is a Chinese unit of measurement equivalent to 1/6 of an acre. The amount of farmland a village committee allocates to each farming household can vary considerably because of household size as well as the overall population of the community itself.

0.37 *mu*, compared to the current provincial per capita average of 0.55 *mu*.[13]

Nevertheless, scholars like Christopher Bramall argue that a closer examination of natural conditions in Wenzhou suggests that the area was not significantly worse off than many other developmentally challenged areas, even if it was not as well endowed as Hangzhou and Ningbo.[14] To be sure, as Bramall notes, juxtaposed against Gansu, Guizhou, or Tibet, Wenzhou appears to possess considerable advantages. If Wenzhou is set in a larger comparative context, however, there is no escaping the fact that local ecological conditions were unpropitious at best, adverse at worst. Although the climate in Wenzhou is indeed more temperate than that of China's border areas, even Bramall points out that the area's annual rainfall, so vital in determining the planting season, is unevenly distributed throughout the year and typically concentrated during the summer months. Without well-developed irrigation systems to deliver cheap and abundant water consistently, local area farmers would be just as vulnerable to the vagaries of nature as are others elsewhere.

When I first began conducting research in the area during the summer of 1997, for example, local farmers were desperately hoping for an end to a dry spell that had lasted for weeks. Rumors abounded that local authorities had tried unsuccessfully to induce rain through cloud seeding; those who had grown more desperate simply prayed at local temples for divine intervention. Without relief, crops began to wither, the next planting was in jeopardy, and enormous financial duress seemed inevitable. When the rains finally arrived, they came in the form of typhoons that quickly flooded the small parcels of land that farmers tilled, nearly ruining their harvest. Although this example is a rather extreme one, it is nevertheless instructive. When the unpredictability of Wenzhou's ecology is taken into account, Bramall's analysis actually underscores the grave ecological challenges Wenzhou natives face each day.

In addition to straining agricultural production, persistent population pressures have intensified demands for employment and public services. With a current population of over 6.6 million, Wenzhou is the most densely populated prefecture in Zhejiang (the province itself ranks third nationally in this category, after Jiangsu and Shandong). Historically, this high population density created demographic pressures that forced Wenzhou natives to pursue a number of different survival strategies. One approach was to produce handicrafts like umbrellas and shoes; another was cotton spinning.[15] Although such activities contributed to a growing industrial tradition in Wenzhou proper, this drive was prematurely undermined by foreign competition and worldwide economic depression during the interwar years. These developments severely hampered long-term investment and stalled the advance of deeper economic linkages between Wenzhou proper and its surrounding environs.[16] As a result, residents who were not engaged in agriculture or industry often moved into petty trade, peddling local products even in distant regions like Shanghai. Still others adopted out-migration as a survival strategy, moving to other regions of China and even other continents in search of work. These *tongxiang* (fellow natives), individuals who settled in new places and even those who temporarily migrated to more urban areas as temporary workers, later played a crucial role in building up Phoenix during its earliest phase of development.

Because of this "tradition" of movement among Wenzhou natives, most Chinese consider them to be perhaps the country's premier and most intrepid pioneers. Indeed, Chinese often joke that "if there is a Chinese anywhere, he [or she] must be Wenzhou native."[17] Even during the tumultuous Cultural Revolution decade, nearly 300 Wenzhou natives managed to leave home and settle in the more remote expanses of Xinjiang. Today, that initial number has grown to an astounding 80,000 residing in the region.[18] People from Wenzhou are present in all of China's major metropolises, from Beijing to Shanghai, and also constitute the largest contingent of the overseas Chinese community in Europe, especially France. These early migrant waves radiating out from Wenzhou eventually became the foundation for influential business networks; in fact, the first Wenzhou business association outside Wenzhou was established in Kunming, the provincial capital of Yunnan, in 1995. By 2000, 23 more associations had come into existence to represent and promote the interests of their members.[19]

Even with such high rates of out-migration, the situation at home remained desperate. Because of this stagnant, if not shrinking, economic base, there was little surplus for the local state to devote to public works projects. In fact, the area's infrastructure remained dilapidated well into the post-Maoist era. For example, many roads just on the other side of the Oujiang River, across from Wenzhou municipality, were unpaved, dusty, and bumpy paths well into the late 1990s. When I went to Phoenix for the first time in April 1997, a newly paved road connecting the interior counties to dock facilities along the river had just been completed, and many hoped this would reduce the transportation bottlenecks that plagued enterprises located farther away from the city. Unfortunately, the docks remained in a sorry state. In addition, Wenzhou's first airport was completed only in 1990 with large infusions of private funds; direct rail links with Jinhua and the rest of the province were not established until mid-1998. Nevertheless, the pace of infrastructure development has picked up in the past few years. As the number of private automobiles in Wenzhou and China has soared, local authorities have launched massive highway building projects to accommodate the growing traffic.

Even as party officials have touted the completion of these projects as evidence of the benefits of reform and local state effectiveness, they have conveniently forgotten that their plans were greatly delayed by past policies. Indeed, at the beginning of the reform period, basic electricity and gas utilities reached only a limited number of households outside Wenzhou municipality. In fact, one of the favorite pastimes of locals was recounting how the electricity always seemed to stop at the most inopportune times, when, for example, one was reading or even eating dinner. At Phoenix, collective groans could be heard in many offices during the late 1990s when the electricity went out just as the office staff had finished typing an important office memo (without saving it). Even the company's backup generators provided little protection against such power outages.

The social sphere was afflicted by similar considerations and difficulties as well. Although in the twelfth and thirteenth centuries the Wenzhou region was home to the famous Yongjia school of Ye Shi,[20] the scholastic tradition in contemporary Wenzhou is a pale reflection of its glorious past. In fact, secondary schools suffered greatly from state neglect, as did institutions of higher learning such as vocational schools (*dazhuan*) and universities (*daxue*). At the primary and secondary levels, Wenzhou experienced severe difficulties not only in attracting and retaining qualified instructors but also in graduating large numbers of students from local high schools. Students often left school before completing their middle-school education because their families simply could not afford the fees that schools demanded. More important, families desperately needed the supplemental income that even their youngest members could provide through odd jobs like shoe shining or tailoring.

Many promising students thus sacrificed their education in order to satisfy more immediate economic needs, a reality captured in educational indices. In 1982, for example, only 3 percent of the Wenzhou population held high school diplomas, and only 36 percent had completed a primary school education. In 1990, illiterates or semi-illiterates (*wenmang banwenmang*) constituted 19.63 percent of the total population, down from 27.1 percent in 1982.[21] Those age 15 or higher, the group that serves as the backbone of the workforce, accounted for 28.08 percent of those falling into this category. The figures for adjoining counties were not much better. In 1990, the illiterate/semi-illiterate rate in one county, for instance, had dropped but remained at a stubborn 18.77 percent.[22] Unfortunately yet not surprisingly, women fared considerably worse than men. In nearly every county within Wenzhou prefecture, the illiteracy/semi-illiteracy rate for women was 40 percent or higher.[23] Although this did not automatically or forever condemn locals to lives of poverty, it clearly limited their formal ability to absorb new skills and knowledge that could help them compete in China's new marketplace.

At the post-secondary level, Wenzhou University could hardly rival better-endowed institutions like Zhejiang University in Hangzhou or Fudan University in Shanghai. Although it remained important as a place of higher learning, it did not play the role that Stanford and Berkeley or the Massachusetts Institute of Technology did in providing highly educated, technically skilled labor for their respective regional economies.[24] In 1982, for example, the number of college graduates per 100,000 residents of the Wenzhou area was an anemic 25. Even though this average more than doubled to 63 graduates per 100,000 people in 1990, it continued to lag behind

provincial and national averages.[25] As more private schools are established in Wenzhou (in the late 1990s, 92 percent of the city's
pre-schools, for instance, were privately run),[26] locals are cautiously
optimistic that the area's educational shortcomings can be arrested
and reversed.

However, education was not the only sector to suffer from state
incapacity and neglect. Other social services such as public health,
care for the elderly, and poverty alleviation also lacked sufficient
government backing, which added to the already heavy burdens
borne by local families. Not until the early 1990s, over a decade after the post-Mao reforms were initiated, did these trends begin to
shift as more revenues became available for investment in social services. Some notable breakthroughs in the delivery of medical services
occurred between 1992 and 1994 when several children's hospitals,
a burn center, and other specialized treatment facilities were established with the help of outside investment.[27] These, however, were
exceptions to the more typical pattern of establishing clinics for
those most in need of basic care. During the same period, the provincial government approved a plan to set up small-scale enterprises
in low-income areas within Wenzhou prefecture and use the profits
for poverty alleviation.[28] Although the impact of this particular initiative remains unknown, it is telling that such programs were
launched in a period of growing prosperity primarily by nonstate actors, the inhabitants of Wenzhou prefecture themselves.

For most of the post-1949 period, Wenzhou prefecture was a remote and highly inaccessible locale, which languished on the periphery of the province. With overwhelming physical obstacles to
overcome and little to offer in production or trade, Wenzhou was
largely forgotten and left to develop on its own, much like an out-of-
the-way frontier town. This state of affairs reinforced a perception
among outsiders that Wenzhou natives were extremely parochial or
"inward-oriented."[29] Even today, such sentiments among nonnatives
are in part influenced by the distinctiveness of the Wenzhou dialect,
which, according to a 1955 report, "was understood only by those
living within a 34-mile radius of the city radio station."[30] Yet this pa-
rochialism was not necessarily the result of an inherent or natural
animosity toward outsiders. The tight social bonds that existed

among area residents were a crucial survival mechanism that grew out of efforts to overcome Wenzhou's difficult physical milieu and, later, political attacks from the center. Closed off from the outside, locals had no one to trust but one another, at least until new opportunities for engagement and cooperation finally arose.

In many ways, the physical setting of Jinhua prefecture is similar to that of Wenzhou. Although Jinhua does not lie close to a major seaport or waterway (and is considerably hotter and drier as a result), its topography is also rugged. In fact, nearly 80 percent of the local terrain is hilly and unfavorable to expansive agricultural production. The township in which Jupiter is located lies in a secluded valley, ringed on all sides by a chain of mountains. These mountains hinder nonresidents from intruding on this community and constrain area natives from building durable linkages with the outside world.[31] Even in 1998, just one major road cut through the mountains to the outside. This was the only channel and lifeline for an otherwise landlocked and forsaken place.

As in Wenzhou, local ecological conditions did not provide a strong foundation for highly diversified economic activity. Although the land in the basin below the mountains was considerably flatter and more suitable for agriculture, the average amount of land an individual farmer tilled totaled 0.53 *mu*, only slightly better than that of his Wenzhou counterparts.[32] But with Jinhua's population totaling over four million and the population of the township in which Jupiter is located exceeding 700,000, the prefecture faced demographic pressures similar to those in Wenzhou, ones that forced residents to increasingly pursue sideline activities outside farming as a means of survival. Residents of the area have traditionally relied on carpentry, silk weaving, and ham curing to supplement their incomes. Still, notwithstanding the fame of Jinhua ham throughout China, these vocations did not typically provide the income necessary to overcome persistent economic pressures, leading large numbers of area natives to migrate out of the prefecture in search of better opportunities.

Despite national restrictions on population movement, Jinhua residents continued to migrate to other parts of China during the Maoist period. Some left to attend college or serve in the military; others worked in distant locales in such diverse sectors as construction, mining, and the steel and machine industries. Some Jinhua area natives left for such faraway places as Inner Mongolia and Xinjiang from the late 1950s through 1969, and others ended up in Hong Kong and Macao. In fact, the number of people leaving the area in search of employment reached a jaw-dropping 29,431 in 1981, 58,132 in 1984, and 69,438 in 1988.[33] This accounted for 9.01, 16.93, and 18.54 percent of the area's total labor force, respectively. In short, such figures highlight both the dearth of employment opportunities and the enormous economic burden the area shouldered for decades.

Jinhua also resembled Wenzhou in terms of its limited physical and social infrastructure. Local roads were poorly maintained, as were levees and bridges on area waterways. Not until the late 1980s and after years of constant flooding, for example, were the banks of a local tributary shored up with funds contributed by Jupiter. The low educational level of area residents was also painfully obvious. Although Wen-hsin Yeh points out that Jinhua could at one time boast of a tradition of scholarship that reached a climax between the twelfth and fourteenth centuries, this tradition extended only to the area's former gentry elite and has been in serious decline ever since.[34] In 1982, for instance, only 37.85 percent of the population had completed primary school. Moreover, the illiteracy/semi-illiteracy rate for the county where Jupiter is located stood at 21.78 percent, a painfully high level although a significant drop of nearly 15 percentage points from the 1964 rate of 36.33 percent.[35] Although the local gazetteer notes that this was only 1.9 percent lower than the national rate for 1982 and 5.35 percent lower than 1982 rate for Zhejiang province as a whole, relatively few Jinhua natives completed a college education. In fact, there were only 259 college graduates per 100,000 people, compared to a provincial average of 468 and a national average of 617.[36] Although this average is over ten times that of Wenzhou's, one can clearly see that even the area's famed legacy of erudition played a negligible role in local development during the Maoist era. Not until the 1980s did more educated natives begin returning to the area, albeit in small numbers.

In time, Jinhua came to share Wenzhou's fate. Jinhua was saddled with numerous obstacles that made "economic take-off" extremely difficult.[37] Tucked away in a remote pocket of the province, the area remained rather insulated from the outside, preventing the community from rising above subsistence levels of economic development. Here, too, residents were forced to rely increasingly on one another in order to ward off extinction. In the process of fighting for survival, these tight social bonds became more than just a means of self-reliance: they became the emotional and social pivots on which community action turned.

The Limited Reach of the State

Although ecological factors profoundly influenced prospects for economic growth and the nature of social interaction in Wenzhou and Jinhua, they were not the only important variables. In addition to ecological, economic, and social constraints, one must also consider the role of the Chinese state. Whereas the state intruded on and dominated critical aspects of citizens' lives in urban areas, it assumed a comparatively smaller role in the two communities I studied.[38] This view meshes with Vivienne Shue's analysis of the post-1949 Chinese state. For Shue, the state's developmental strategy, embodied in communes and locally based development projects, reinforced the cellular nature of rural society, preventing full administrative and normative integration of center and periphery.[39] In rural communities, the situation this created was precisely the opposite of what the party intended: over time, it became more difficult to penetrate these communities and ensure a lasting socialist transformation. For Wenzhou and Jinhua, historical legacies, limited state resources, and strategic calculation combined to undercut state domination in these areas.

Since the early days of revolutionary struggle, Chinese Communists have found it difficult to create and maintain a consistently strong presence in Wenzhou. According to Yia-Ling Liu, the CCP established itself in the area in 1924 and soon thereafter began organizing local peasants to oppose local landlords. However, communication with and direction from the party leadership, then based in Shanghai, were intermittent at best because of Chiang Kai-shek's Communist suppression campaign. Consequently, "Wenzhou communists were from the first basically self-guided and self-supplied."[40] Although some contact was re-established with the party during the Long March and at the start of the Sino-Japanese War in the mid-1930s, the continuing struggle against Chiang Kai-shek's Nationalists and the invading Japanese army cut off the Wen-zhou party branch, forcing it to operate on its own.

Communists in Wenzhou thus confronted a highly unstable situation, one that compelled them to adapt to the prevailing mores of the local environment. As much as the party needed to gain the confidence and support of the local population, its leaders also realized that considerable time, effort, and resources were required to overcome local suspicions, raise peasant consciousness, and, ultimately, generate support for the party's policies. If Wenzhou's Communists were to win public trust, they needed to implement not only policies that the local community would accept but also ones that did not betray their socialist vision. This realization resulted in the indefinite postponement of more radical actions like land reform and, more interestingly, prompted cooperation with local commercial interests. By helping local elites do business in Communist-held territories, the party won the goodwill of local powerbrokers and access to crucial supplies of ammunition and weaponry. For the disenfranchised of the area, cadres reduced tenant rents and abolished "oppressive taxes and debts owed by peasants" in order to lay the groundwork for a future political awakening.[41] These actions inspired confidence among the populace by demonstrating that party and community interests were not entirely antithetical and that, in fact, they could be united for the benefit of all.

These relationships were vital to the party's eventual victory in Wenzhou in 1949. Unlike many other areas in China, local Communist guerrillas successfully seized and "liberated" Wenzhou before the arrival of Mao's troops. This rare instance of "self-liberation" gave local cadres and military leaders a stronger presence in the newly established government, in contrast to other areas where nonlocal army veterans assumed key governmental positions. Local cadres sympathetic to the plight of fellow compatriots were thus well positioned to thwart central directives in favor of local interests when necessary. Much like the cadres who helped villagers hide their harvests from central authorities in the post-1949 period, Wenzhou officials often colluded with local residents to create an illusion of compliance with state policies.[42] This "tradition" remains alive and well today and was vital to creating the political space necessary for area enterprises like Phoenix to become firmly established in the local economy.

Although this strong sense of localism made central-level governance of Wenzhou in the post-1949 period a major challenge, CCP policies did little to ameliorate the difficult situation in the area. In agriculture, for example, opposition to collective farming was so fierce that area officials, siding with the local populace, defied the central authorities and initiated China's "first experiment with the household contract system in agriculture" in 1956.[43] When party officials insisted that their policies be fully implemented, they were forced to expend prodigious amounts of energy and resources to achieve compliance, most often through the dispatch of work teams to the area. Yet once political pressure from above abated, locals often reverted to their previous survival practices, such as small-scale trading, even smuggling, that ran counter to central government policies. Wenzhou's recalcitrance and lawlessness infuriated party-state officials and led to continued calls to bring order and ideological conformity to Wenzhou.

The party's industrial policy for Wenzhou also left a negative imprint. Although state-owned factories were in operation intermittently in Wenzhou, they never became a vital part of the local economy. In fact, by 1978, state-owned enterprises were responsible for only 35.7 percent of the municipality's total industrial output value and for considerably less in adjoining rural areas.[44] Moreover, government policies during the Maoist period reinforced a turn away from industry by dictating that residents commit themselves more toward expanding agricultural output than toward furthering industry or commerce. Even under these circumstances, Wenzhou natives continued to surreptitiously operate smaller-scale, private workshops at great personal risk. Such activity, coupled with experimentation in contracting agricultural production to the individual household, reinforced the image of Wenzhou as deviant and insufficiently "red," drawing the ire of central government leaders in Beijing. Not surprisingly, Wenzhou became the target of political attacks during the 1950s and especially the early phase of the Cultural Revolution. Wenzhou's private workshops were characterized as "tails of capitalism" (*ziben zhuyi de weiba*) and were forced to shut down by zealous rebel groups committed to rooting out capitalist tendencies.[45] Despite such overwhelming political pressures, area residents remained unrepentant and simply went underground with their private initiatives until the post-1978 reforms slowly allowed them to re-emerge.

The impact of these differing policies on local industrialization trajectories is especially striking when other rural locales are considered. As Susan Whiting points out in her illuminating comparative study of Chinese rural development, the industrial output of Yueqing in 1949, a county within the jurisdiction of Wenzhou, was higher than that of Songjiang, a county outside Shanghai. Yet by 1978, its production was only one-third that of Songjiang's. Although state support for rural industry in Songjiang was sometimes inconsistent, it was more substantial than that provided to Wenzhou. In addition to easy access to capital in the aftermath of the Great Leap Forward, Songjiang enterprises developed strong ties with Shanghai factories. Such linkages not only accelerated the exchange of critical material inputs, technology, and expertise but, more important, ensured a ready market for the goods produced by Songjiang factories.[46]

The reality of ineffective governance was often overshadowed by Wenzhou's proximity to Taiwan. Located across from the island on the Taiwan Strait, Wenzhou lies within immediate range of any potential GMD-led military assault. Indeed, China's periodic shelling of the Nationalist-controlled islands of Quemoy and Matsu during the 1950s and 1960s and Chiang Kai-shek's insistence on reunifying China under his leadership seemed likely to lead to a resumption of hostilities. Given the persistent threat of war, the CCP considered Wenzhou a front-line (*qianxian*) battleground that would probably be reduced to rubble. Consequently, provincial and central leaders refused to invest any appreciable amount of resources in the area's development, especially its infrastructure. To them, it made little sense to devote precious funds and energy to building up the surrounding area only to have it decimated in a military confrontation. In short, Wenzhou was simply not a good long-term investment.[47]

Under these conditions, Wenzhou's military vulnerability provided political justification for the central state to concentrate on fulfilling other objectives. State officials, realizing that they did not have enough resources to extend their control over every community, instead focused their energies on selective development. Other parts of China such as Jiangsu and the northeast were critical to the realization of national developmental goals in ways that Wenzhou was not. As China mobilized for rapid development under Mao, it also began the painstaking process of developing the country's interior at the expense of the coastal regions. This shift resulted in a major reallocation of resources and a 7 percent decline in gross industrial output value in the coastal provinces from 1952 to 1980.[48]

The decision to concentrate developmental efforts elsewhere dovetailed with the central leadership's view of Zhejiang province as a whole. Central authorities shared the popular perception of Zhejiang as a comparatively affluent province and believed it was better to extract its resources for the development of other areas in greater need of outside assistance. In carrying out these plans, the party leadership also exacted a measure of political revenge on the province, the *laojia*, or native place, of archenemy Chiang Kai-shek. Under the tight control of outsiders who staffed the highest echelons of the provincial leadership, Zhejiang and especially Wenzhou became net losers in the developmental process under Mao's reign.

In contrast to Wenzhou, the Communist presence in Jinhua prefecture was somewhat stronger, but it, too, suffered from inconstancy and general weakness. The party was active as early as 1927 in the county I researched, and it plotted to seize control of the area in 1935. However, Nationalist authorities discovered these plans and ended the plot by rounding up and executing insurrection organizers.[49] Although the CCP sent agents to the area to re-establish its presence a few years later, ongoing Nationalist campaigns to suppress the Communists greatly reduced the likelihood of achieving this goal. Furthermore, the occupation of the area by Japanese troops in 1942 virtually eliminated any remaining hopes for consolidating Communist control of the area. Instead, party cells were forced to retreat to nearby counties, where they began coordinating efforts to harass and defeat Japanese forces.

Unlike their Wenzhou counterparts, Jinhua Communists were so preoccupied with resisting the Japanese that they could not seriously contemplate the enactment of basic socialist policies. Because they did not hold clear, exclusive control over a bounded area, they were thus unable to experiment with different policies, as was the case in Wenzhou and the Communist stronghold of Yan'an in the north. Still, the guerrilla campaigns launched by local Communists became a critical means of solidifying bonds among area residents. Working with the local population to defeat the Japanese, party operatives drew on and deepened their social alliances in the same way their Wenzhou counterparts did. After Japan's defeat, the spirit of cooperation that emerged during the war expedited the expansion of Communist influence throughout the area. Although local forces did not independently "liberate" Jinhua, they did facilitate its eventual takeover by the People's Liberation Army.

After the Communist ascension to power in 1949, socialist programs took root in Jinhua more quickly and less painfully than in Wenzhou. Agricultural collectivization was completed by September 1958, and commune and brigade enterprises based on local handicraft industries were started as well in an effort to stabilize the local economy.[50] However, this promising beginning eventually fell apart in much the same way it did in Wenzhou. Although Jinhua was much farther away from any potential Nationalist military assault, the region nevertheless suffered from the critical decision of national authorities to invest more heavily in other parts of the nation rather than in Zhejiang. Public works projects were scaled back drastically, as was support for enterprises started under collectivization. In 1962, for example, government resources were redirected toward the construction of a sorely needed local reservoir but unfortunately the area's overall budget was slashed by 62 percent.[51] Many years passed before other projects garnered any appreciable governmental assistance.

This policy change also inhibited the development of the region's economic capabilities right when the foundation for it could and should have been laid. Although numerous enterprises were established in the 1950s to produce agricultural implements and process agricultural products, nearly all such enterprises in the county I visited were shut down because of low efficiency and massive financial losses in the mid-1960s. Thus, contrary to the picture some scholars have painted of commune and brigade enterprises (CBEs) as highly successful precursors to today's rural enterprises, the history of such enterprises in Jinhua at least does not confirm their role as catalysts of industrial development.[52] In fact, this early experience with CBEs left a negative legacy in the sense that it failed to impart critical management skills or the ability to organize workers in the local community. As some of my respondents described it, the "software" (*ruanjian*) that was critical to the smooth functioning of enterprise "hardware" (*yingjian*) was glaringly deficient. These early failures dampened enthusiasm for industrial projects for a long time as locals remained convinced that prospects for industrial success were dim.

Interestingly, from 1949 through 1970, in contrast to Wenzhou, little collusion between Jinhua residents and local officials materialized to ease the pressures of their desperate economic circumstances. One possible explanation for this is the different personal backgrounds of the individual officials. During this period, all party secretaries and vice-secretaries for Jupiter's county were natives of Shandong province: not a single cadre hailed from the region he was assigned to oversee.[53] These officials were veterans of the People's Liberation Army who stayed in Jinhua after the Communist triumph, and as nonlocals, their allegiances were first and foremost to Chairman Mao and the party, not the local population. In contrast to their Wenzhou comrades, they were more determined to carry out central directives even if such actions impinged on local interests. This development strikingly recalls the "law of avoidance" under the old imperial system, which forbade magistrates from overseeing their home districts in order to forestall possible collusion with the local population. In a way, this absence of state sympathy and assistance accelerated the growth of local solidarity. For area natives, these developments confirmed what they had always suspected: if they wanted to escape from their suffocating predicament, they would have to develop the strategy and the means of doing so themselves. The state would not provide them with a viable way out.

Actualizing Self-Reliance

So far in this chapter, I have tried to demonstrate that the natives of Wenzhou and Jinhua enjoyed few of the prerequisites scholars deem necessary for effecting economic take-off. In both locales, poor ecological circumstances provided at best a weak material foundation on which to base a thriving economy. Furthermore, the harshness of the physical milieu limited the economic options inhabitants could pursue, leaving some to engage in sideline activities such as handicrafts and small-scale trading and others to search for new opportunities elsewhere. These conditions further arrested social development and lessened the likelihood of a developmental breakthrough. Clearly, Wenzhou and Jinhua were sliding slowly but unequivocally into economic and social decline.

With the rise of the new Communist regime, citizens hoped for substantial improvements. Unfortunately, in Jinhua and Wenzhou, these dreams were soon dashed, as the Chinese party-state was both unable and unwilling to commit the material, financial, and human resources necessary to initiate self-sustaining development. It did not possess the organizational capacity to start and uniformly implement new projects throughout the vast expanse of the Chinese countryside. With the threat of war with the Nationalists always looming on the horizon, state officials made a strategic decision to shift critical aid from Zhejiang to other parts of China, compelling the people in these areas to fend for themselves. It is indeed one of the great ironies and tragedies of the post-1949 period that these poor communities, which so needed infusions of aid, received the least amount of assistance from the Chinese party-state.

In highlighting the various constraints on human action within these communities, I am simply pointing out the nature and scale of the challenges faced by the founders of Jupiter and Phoenix. In so doing, I want to emphasize that my argument is by no means one of strict path dependence. All communities certainly enjoy different physical and social endowments, but such conditions alone do not decide their ultimate trajectory or developmental fate. If it were so, one could not explain Wenzhou's and Jinhua's eventual breakthrough to prosperity. Although neither community initially possessed the material components or the immediate qualities critical to economic success, they nevertheless shifted successfully to another track, an outcome scholars like Douglass North would not have predicted.[54]

To be sure, the legacy of self-reliance I have described is in and of itself insufficient to explain the eventual rise of Jupiter and Phoenix. Though significant, communities elsewhere in China have also developed similar survival strategies and yet have not achieved commensurate levels of growth. What, then, separates Wenzhou and Jinhua from other locales? One major distinction is the social ethos that enveloped these two communities. In contrast to the inhabitants of other areas, Wenzhou and Jinhua residents not only understood and accepted risk as a part of everyday life but exhorted one another to take bold action. Although most would-be entrepreneurs realized that their chances of succeeding were low, they never seemed paralyzed by the thought of failure. In this sense, their understanding and handling of risky new projects share striking similarities with the entrepreneurs of California's Silicon Valley. According to Annalee Saxenian, in Silicon Valley, "not only was risk-taking glorified, but failure was socially acceptable. There was a shared understanding that anyone could be a successful entrepreneur: there were no boundaries of age, status, or social stratum that precluded the possibility of a new beginning; and there was little embarrassment or shame associated with business failure."[55] In Wenzhou and Jinhua, residents seemed to truly detest only those who made no effort whatsoever to improve their station in life by chasing dreams of becoming "their own boss" (*dang laoban*). Such intense pressures to transform their lives generated an unusual zealousness, even an overeagerness to launch the next great venture. Indeed, Wenzhou natives are well known, even legendary, throughout China for their willingness to take on projects with an almost utter disregard for what others think of their prospects for success. This fearlessness and drive propelled residents forward at the very time others were still deliberating and hesitating to begin any new initiative.

Even among such intrepid souls, the founders of Jupiter and Phoenix displayed a particularly acute form of this risk-taking orientation. As with many Horatio Alger–type, rags-to-riches entrepreneurs, their stories are ones of daunting challenges, tenacity and courage, and eventual redemption and triumph. Although the stories that have been told and written about them by respondents and the Chinese media sometimes border on hagiography, it is nevertheless clear that both possessed an uncanny ability to inspire others to heed their calls. Both men were considered unusual by local standards: they possessed superior intellectual ability, strong leadership and problem-solving talents, and prodigious amounts of energy, qualities which convinced many that they could succeed at almost anything. Unfortunately, neither individual was able to develop his talents further in the formal setting of schools. Because their families' financial situations were so unstable, both were forced to leave school prematurely, well before they could complete their high school education or consider vocational or college training. Instead of attending classes, Jupiter's founder worked alongside his father, tilling the fields; the founder of Phoenix roamed the streets of Wenzhou, shining and repairing shoes.

Looking back on these events many years later, both men insisted that these actions were absolutely necessary to ensure family survival. They felt they were simply doing what other filial sons would do. Both founders endured intense personal suffering and devoted themselves entirely to a larger purpose, replacing their educational training with years of punishing physical labor and "real world" experience. To others, these acts were noble instances of self-sacrifice. In addition, Jupiter's founder was forced to endure political persecution during the tumultuous Cultural Revolution. As a Communist Party member and commune official, he tried to improve the operations and the revenues of the commune. For his efforts, Red Guards accused him of being a "capitalist-roader," a charge he vehemently denied. As he put it, "To give commune members enough to eat; to have enough money to use; what's wrong with that? To fix bridges and construct roads; to engage in public service; is this also wrong? . . . Is socialism poverty? Isn't that just like the 'old society'? What's wrong with being prosperous?"[56] This stubbornness infuriated the Red Guards further and forced him to go into hiding for some time. Yet after the Cultural Revolution ended, locals lionized him for his dedication to the community's well-being. They considered his level of caring and commitment to be exceptional, even by their own lofty standards.

Although stories of personal sacrifice and political persecution are quite common in many communities throughout China, the responses and actions of these men during this period of intense deprivation reinforced perceptions that they were truly extraordinary. In the face of adverse circumstances and personal suffering, most people were more apt to avoid risk and perhaps eke out a quiet, unassuming existence. However, the founders of Jupiter and Phoenix did precisely the opposite. Their determination to establish these enterprises and bring prosperity to their communities did not waver, but instead deepened in the face of colossal adversity. They had withstood arduous trials and were even more convinced that they were destined to fulfill a higher mission. Even though the direction of the country's reform program was far from settled at this time, both men were nevertheless prepared to pursue these risky undertakings, ones that, if they turned out badly, could potentially end with imprisonment, even death. The selflessness, sacrifice, and grit they displayed were reminiscent of "heroic cadres" but with a critical difference: these men were dedicated to fulfilling the needs of their families and communities, not the demands of the party.

Although Jupiter's and Phoenix's founders lacked extensive personal experience in enterprise management, the force of their personalities and their personal histories eventually drew their relatives and friends closer to them. They were, in almost every sense that Max Weber described, charismatic leaders.[57] They successfully laid out a vision of a better future and, more important, helped their relatives and fellow villagers believe they were capable of achieving what seemed improbable, even impossible. As they rallied their partners to tackle this new challenge, they created and spread the "faith" that Alexander Gerschenkron considered crucial to breaking out of economic backwardness. This was the "faith, in the words of Saint-Simon, that the golden age lies not behind but ahead of mankind."[58] In a most fundamental and essential way, these men provided vital leadership at a most crucial time. Instead of settling for less, they inspired others to join the far more complicated and challenging task of building an enterprise together.

As they continued to move forward, they also revealed a talent for satisfying the difficult organizational requirements on which factory success hinged. Both recognized the valuable resources contained within their social networks and came up with innovative approaches to using them. Not only did they systematically mine their personal networks to an unprecedented degree, depending on them to supply start-up capital, information, technical expertise, and even physical labor, but they also grafted social harmony and mutual trust to the institutional machinery of the factory. They were able to counteract many of the harsher aspects of the industrial regimen they introduced, ones that threatened to wear down even the most committed of enterprise members. More important, they helped others see the benefits of collaboration and solidarity. In short, the genius of these two individuals rested on their ability to meet and contain contradictory organizational and social imperatives that would have and often did tear apart other firms.

The theoretical significance of these developments is clear. These efforts at enterprise-building diverge unmistakably not only from the state-led developmental approach highlighted by Alexander Gerschenkron and, more recently, the local state corporatism framework advanced by Jean Oi but also from the path of the individual utility-maximizing entrepreneur.[59] In Wenzhou and Jinhua, the state played a negligible role in creating the framework in which these enterprise founders eventually flourished. Instead, the basis of enterprise success rested with societal forces, not the state. It was rooted in the effective use of collective social ties—specifically, kinship and native-place relationships—rather than state-allocated resources as the trigger for economic advance. Thus, the founders of Jupiter and Phoenix recognized the potential of "social capital," reconfigured it, and then deployed it in the new context of the industrial workplace.[60] As lightning rods, or what Malcolm Gladwell calls "connectors,"[61] these men recognized that their closest associates possessed a vast reserve of knowledge and initiative that could help them launch successful factories. What they did better than anyone else was to define a challenge and create an outlet for the aggregation and concentration of these resources in a remarkably flexible and effective manner. What this suggests is that in situations of high uncertainty and imperfect information, drawing on multiple perspectives and expertise rather than relying predominantly on the particular vision or perspective of state officials may, in fact, produce an equally satisfying, if not better, outcome. In a critical sense, Phoenix and Jupiter underscore how success can be achieved through collectively oriented social relationships, not in spite of them.

Concluding Remarks

In contrast to the general impressions many have of Zhejiang province, the ecological, social, and political circumstances surrounding the residents of Jinhua and Wenzhou in both the pre- and post-1949 periods offered few viable opportunities for making a sustained developmental breakthrough. Although there were brief pulses of industrial change on the horizon, especially in Wenzhou municipality during the first half of the twentieth century, these were snuffed out first by war and later by political considerations and tensions largely beyond the control of area natives. It was under these conditions of isolation and state neglect that the people of Wenzhou and Jinhua adopted modes of self-protection, refined strategies of self-reliance, and eventually applied them to the much grander ambition of enterprise-building.

Yet those strategies in and of themselves did not guarantee success. Undergirding their self-reliance approaches was a daring sense, even celebration, of risk-taking that was rarely approximated elsewhere. That individuals in Jinhua and Wenzhou were eager and encouraged to realize goals others were hesitant to even dream of fueled their willingness to experiment with different types of products and ventures. Strong leadership was crucial here, for without the dynamism and charisma of Jupiter's and Phoenix's founders, it is hard to imagine either company generating and sustaining the level of solidarity and cooperation central to their emergence, especially in the earliest stage of their development. In a vital way, their leadership served as a catalyst for the eventual take-off of both firms.

In focusing on vision and leadership, I want to emphasize that I am not suggesting that the founders were all-powerful individuals who possessed some sort of spellbinding power over their kinsmen and friends. Far from it. Like other would-be entrepreneurs, they had their share of faults and weaknesses. Yet what separated them from their rivals was an ability to see their situations in ways others did not and then devise innovative solutions to their organizational predicaments. They provided an overarching objective, a sense of purpose, which reassured others that joining such an undertaking was worthwhile rather than sheer folly. By projecting hope and confidence, the founders were eventually able to utilize a wealth of resources and, perhaps more significant, what James Surowiecki calls "cognitive diversity," the collective wisdom generated from a wide range of perspectives and experiences, a wisdom already embedded in their social networks.[62]

How the challenges of organization were overcome and how high levels of solidarity and mutual commitment were eventually "manufactured" were largely determined by the efforts of Phoenix's and Jupiter's founders and those of a small, close-knit staff who became the vital core of the enterprises' respective management teams. In the following chapters, I detail how this process unfolded as these enterprises emerged and analyze specifically how the needs of enterprise members were continually balanced against the unavoidable pressures affecting the firm from within and without. The manner in which these opportunities and pitfalls were navigated prompted the rise of a powerful institution and changed the dynamics and terrain of these small communities, generating not only new wealth but new understandings of work, trust, and commitment.

THREE

Enterprise Survival
Ensuring Industrial
Success

In general, township and village enterprises have few connections with
local government. . . . TVEs are like cows: we have to find our own food,
and we have no one to give it to us. State-owned enterprises are more dependent: they're like piglets.

—Respondent #103, personal interview, June 18, 1998

As REFORM POLICIES were enacted and gradually took
hold during the 1980s, new business opportunities slowly appeared
throughout the Chinese countryside. Although some responded
cautiously to these initial impulses by engaging in trade or other
small-scale economic activities, others set out to launch riskier but
potentially more lucrative ventures such as businesses to produce
consumer goods. Rural entrepreneurs, long prohibited from participating in such projects, were eager to explore the openings offered
by a burgeoning market. Yet despite policy changes at the national
level that heralded a new direction in Chinese economic strategy,
the success of rural enterprises was far from inevitable. Formidable
obstacles still stood in the way of an enduring breakthrough.

As I noted in the previous chapter, some of these obstacles were
ecological; others, social and political. None, however, were more

critical than the nagging, practical issues of amassing the necessary resources and establishing an effective organization. Where were these ambitious self-starters to look for and secure initial start-up capital, material inputs, and equipment so that they could begin operations? Who would work on the shop floor and how would the new members of the enterprise handle the demands of industrial life? What kind of authority structure should be instituted to keep factories running smoothly and efficiently? How would enterprise management handle possible meddling from local cadres? In short, could the enterprises withstand the multitude of internal and external pressures that would inevitably bear down upon them?

This chapter examines how leaders at Jupiter and Phoenix addressed these concerns in the earliest stage of development, a phase I call "survival." For Jupiter, this period roughly spanned the years from 1975 to the mid-1980s; for Phoenix, the period lasted from 1984 through the late 1980s. During this initial stage, the core task or central imperative of enterprise founders was to ensure the economic viability of the firm. Although Jupiter and Phoenix had no contact with each other during this time, the manner in which they developed exhibits striking similarities. At both firms, kinfolk and fellow natives played a decisive role in the early success of these companies. Leaders at Jupiter and Phoenix not only raised capital and acquired technical expertise through their social networks but also mined these networks extensively to staff company ranks and form the heart of the enterprise labor force. This decision proved to be extremely wise: the founders were able to draw on the extensive reserves of "social capital" contained in these networks to increase organizational stability and enhance their overall competitiveness. According to Robert Putnam, social capital consists primarily of norms of reciprocity and trust, guidelines of behavior that are deeply embedded in day-to-day interactions among relatives and close acquaintances.[1] These norms are valuable precisely because they enable sustained cooperation and deter cheating and malfeasance. In the parlance of economists, they reduce "transaction costs" and make it easier to do business. By extension, social capital makes the management of factory affairs considerably easier and allows the workforce to focus more intensively on turning out products that consumers want.

In addition to highlighting the significance of social organization, this chapter presents an analysis of the work regimen and physical environment, the actual demands and conditions of production, under which all employees labored. I demonstrate how the inability to predict demand and to standardize operations at this stage forced both firms to adopt and maintain a "heroic storming" mentality. This mobilizational approach to production worked well initially because the technical demands of production were low and because the requirements for effective enterprise coordination were simple. When, for example, a production problem occurred on the shop floor, technically skilled personnel were always present in the workshop, ready to offer guidance and encouragement. In other instances, even the managers themselves worked alongside the rank and file to complete an order when a deadline was especially pressing. It is not surprising that the strong sense of mutual commitment between managerial staff and workers that grew out of laboring under these stressful conditions, coupled with less hierarchical patterns of authority, served to harmonize relations on the shop floor.

The final section of the chapter discusses how each firm's relationship to local government was redefined. In contrast to scholarly accounts emphasizing the direct role of local cadres in guiding and nurturing enterprise success, this work argues that the leaders of Phoenix and Jupiter were more critical in determining enterprise direction and growth than were local officials, who assumed a secondary, supporting role. In return for the autonomy to manage their own affairs, enterprise leaders provided increased tax contributions, help with achieving policy objectives, and, occasionally, both tangible material and intangible political benefits for cadres. Both parties ultimately realized that neither could succeed without the other. Thus, for these entrepreneurs and local officials, the important question was not who gained the most from the relationship but how both parties could benefit from it. In Jinhua and Wenzhou, this was a dynamic process of continual redefinition and a major factor in the spectacular growth of both firms. Indeed, it set the basis for the transformations of Jupiter and Phoenix into two of the largest conglomerates in their respective areas.

Enterprise Beginnings

The impulse to engage in industrial production at Phoenix and Jupiter arose from a combination of pressing economic need, bold risk-taking, and entrepreneurial spirit. For the residents of these neglected regions of Zhejiang, business in general and manufacturing in particular held out the promise of becoming vehicles for overcoming economic stagnation. As population density increased, even advances in agricultural production could not overcome the natural, physical constraints of the land or the absence of job opportunities. Increasingly, peasants realized that they had a greater chance of survival off the land than on it, and rural enterprises became a new outlet for their energies. More immediate financial pressures, however, accelerated this push. At Jupiter, the situation was particularly urgent, for the state-owned enterprises that had previously purchased the raw silk produced by local peasants could no longer do so because they were embroiled in the final stages of the Cultural Revolution.[2] As production in urban factories stalled, these peasants faced the real possibility of starvation if no new takers for their raw silk could be found. By starting a silk-processing factory, the primary goal of Jupiter's founder was to cut the financial losses peasants would incur as a result of canceled orders.[3]

Similar concerns led to the establishment of Phoenix. Phoenix's founder, barely twenty years old when he opened the company's first workshop, recalled later that at the time he certainly "wanted to have better food, nicer clothes, a more comfortable home" for himself, but he was even more motivated to help his family, since his father was recovering from a debilitating illness and could not work to support them.[4] For him, starting an enterprise offered a greater chance for a steady income than did the shoe shine and shoe repair jobs he had been forced to take on the streets of Wenzhou during his adolescence. Indeed, his family's long-term survival would have been seriously jeopardized had he remained in that line of work. It should come as no surprise, then, that the originators of these firms eventually came to see factories as a more effective means of fulfilling their needs and dreams. Although these decisions were certainly adaptive responses to their particular predicaments, they also required a high degree of creativity, courage, and fortitude.

Although dire economic circumstances seemed to justify bold action, the decision to move forward with new enterprises still represented a considerable risk. Neither founder knew for sure that his factory would endure. In Jinhua prefecture, all factories established under the auspices of the commune had failed, and Jupiter's prospects of success were no better. In addition, the Cultural Revolution had not yet ended in 1975, when Jupiter's first factory was established. The possibility of leftist attacks for taking the "capitalist road" loomed large for Jupiter, as it would for Phoenix in 1984. Although Deng Xiaoping had charted a new course of economic reform, the numerous small-scale, private operations in Wenzhou remained vulnerable to the machinations of party conservatives, who saw their emergence as a serious challenge to the socialist vision.[5] To complicate matters, Phoenix's status as a private enterprise did not afford it even a minimum of official legal protection. The vulnerability of both enterprises was masked only temporarily by cautious efforts to maintain a low profile and by local party leaders' relative inattention to small-scale business.

Nevertheless, to begin operations, these factories required critical resources—capital, basic material inputs, a physical plant, and equipment—as well as personnel and technical expertise. Consequently, the founders of both firms moved aggressively to bring these elements together as quickly as possible. Although they initially consulted local cadres, it was clear that party offices could offer little sustained assistance. Local cadres did, however, contact potential partners and clients and provide some ideas on setting up a factory, but little more. Although Jupiter's first factory was initiated under the auspices of the commune, it was never considered an official commune project, and local authorities did not take the lead in its development. Likewise, leaders at Phoenix did not expect cadres to promote industrial transformation: they understood that they were responsible for their own fate. Thus, in Jinhua and Wenzhou, local governments assumed a more passive and complementary role vis-à-vis local enterprises.

Undaunted by the relative passivity of local government offices, the entrepreneurs pressed forward. One manager at Phoenix described it this way:

People often say Wenzhou people can really endure hardship and work hard. But they aren't any different from other Chinese—all Chinese are this way. Wenzhou people are special for a different reason: they have an independent spirit. They want to be pioneers and pathbreakers and will endure hardship so that their dreams can be realized. They are out to reshape the world.[6]

One longtime consultant at Phoenix pointed out that a personal element needed to be included in any accurate portrait of rural enterprise development: "There is intense pressure to succeed among entrepreneurs. They feel extremely embarrassed if they fail. Profit is a guiding motive but so are personal responsibility and reputation."[7] Indeed, it appears that their persistence, their tenacity, was one of the intangible factors that sustained these projects at their most critical moments. Another respondent at Phoenix echoed this sentiment:

The company's success is due to our chairman and founder. Just think, he has no more than a middle school education: he comes from a peasant family. . . . He has always looked for more ways to improve the operations of the company. He is open to new ideas and is not afraid to seek help when he doesn't know something. He really has the right attitude.[8]

The ambition to succeed drove the founders to seek help from all possible sources, but ultimately they relied most on relations and other inhabitants of their communities.

Utilizing family ties to achieve economic ends is, of course, a well-established practice throughout the world.[9] Students of Chinese economic development have pointed out how relatives, often living overseas, played a crucial role in the meteoric rise of Guangdong's economy. In Wenzhou and Jinhua, too, relatives living elsewhere were central in providing kin back home with financial and moral support. Yet what distinguishes both of these firms from other cases is the extent to which they relied on their networks to provide vital goods and services. Whereas one might reasonably expect relatives to supply a portion of the firm's needs, few would expect them to do so on such a vast scale. What makes Phoenix and Jupiter even more unusual is that kinship networks simultaneously resolved "technical" and "human" dilemmas.* Here, relatives and fellow locals provided capital, information, expertise, and labor at high levels over a *protracted* period of time. These elements were critical in sustaining the firms' operational processes, literally the nuts and bolts of production. More important, the participation of family and friends introduced norms of trust and reciprocity into the workplace, reducing the sting of the occasional disagreements and confrontations among enterprise members. Their familiarity with one another reinforced the idea not only that cooperation was necessary but also that it would bring financial rewards. They were confident, as Mark Granovetter has argued, that those closest to them would behave honorably and not cheat them.[10] And in contrast to the experience of many other firms, the imprint of these relationships remained strong at Phoenix and Jupiter, even after the companies had become well established.

Lineage and village members provided significant portions of the initial start-up capital for both firms. Scholars studying the rise of Zhejiang in general and Wenzhou in particular have noted the importance of capital provided by kin and natives to the area's economy. For instance, the well-known Chinese sociologist Fei Xiaotong estimated that if each Wenzhou native working outside Wenzhou sent home 100 *yuan* (about $12) per month, up to four billion *yuan* (ca. $488 million) in venture capital could be injected into the Wenzhou economy per year.[11] Although the estimate appears unrealistically high, there is little doubt that the pace of development throughout the area would have been substantially lower without such cash infusions.

Amassing these funds was no small accomplishment, since any remittance represented a considerable personal sacrifice on the part

---

*By "technical" I mean the aspects most directly associated with production, namely, the means (capital, equipment, plant facility) and ability (technical expertise) to manufacture goods. By "human" I refer to the manner in which individuals in the factory interact with one another. My definitions follow but differ slightly from those used in Schurmann, *Ideology and Organization*, 231–35.

of the sender. Relatives often denied themselves small comforts in order to send money home each month. Some respondents recalled that they could not bring themselves to buy snacks or other non-essential items: the inevitable feelings of guilt would have been too much for them to bear. Even with such assistance, raising capital was and remained an arduous undertaking. In the case of Phoenix, raising the initial 10,800 *yuan* from relatives was a herculean task, all the more so because the founders did not make use of the financial brokers or rotating credit associations that eventually emerged throughout the area.[12] At Jupiter, despite an eventual 240,000-*yuan* bank loan, the factory still needed an additional 50,000 *yuan* to begin production. This final infusion of cash was secured only by pleading with relatives and fellow villagers for help.*[13]

Given the difficulty of capital formation, it is not surprising that enterprise founders were extremely careful about investing these funds. This raised another problem: what kinds of goods should these enterprises produce? Although these entrepreneurs clearly looked to turn out goods that consumers desired, they also wanted items that were easy to manufacture. Initially Phoenix considered smaller items like the cigarette lighters, buttons, and shoes popular among their rivals throughout Wenzhou; eventually it settled on low-voltage electrical products. To a lesser extent, these issues concerned Jupiter's founder as well. Although the needs of local peasants determined Jupiter's first product line, executives had difficulty deciding whether the factory should concentrate on making bolts of silk, move to the production of silk garments, or when to make the transition. Ultimately, this decision hinged on consultations with members of their personal networks.

The large numbers of out-migrants from both areas over the years proved to be an unexpected asset. Relatives and fellow natives working in other parts of the country, especially in Shanghai, drew on their familiarity with urban tastes and markets to provide their rela-

---

*Although the bank loan represented considerable assistance from the local state, it alone would not have jumpstarted Jupiter's operations. My point here is not to denigrate the contributions of local cadres to enterprise building but to show how kinsmen and local villagers provided the crucial missing link.

tives back home with important information about consumer trends and product feasibility. That is, they provided critical market research analysis for these firms, a service Jupiter and Phoenix could ill afford even in more secure economic times. In this way, they helped ensure that the products manufactured in their native places were in high demand and easily sold. Hence, these "strong ties," as Mark Granovetter calls them, became a conduit for valuable information on trends outside Wenzhou and Jinhua, a development usually associated with "weak ties," or acquaintances, as was the case in Silicon Valley's computer industry.[14] For Silicon Valley, AnnaLee Saxenian has demonstrated how entrepreneurs created tight personal bonds with one another on the basis of their common educational backgrounds and informal socializing. These connections facilitated "collaboration and the sharing of information" and eventually propelled Silicon Valley companies to the forefront of the industry.[15] This dynamic was evident at Phoenix as well. One Phoenix administrator, a native of Anhui province and an outsider, describes the company's rise with some admiration:

Wenzhou people are very smart, and they look at what others are doing. Many people here look at Shanghai as a really advanced place. In fact, lots of Wenzhou natives live there today. They looked around and thought about making some type of product but something like the electric fan seemed to be too complicated at the time. But an on/off switch: that seemed feasible. From there, indicator lights and other types of switches seemed like logical extensions.[16]

Although somewhat simplistic, this characterization captures the essence of how Phoenix broke into the low-voltage electrical products industry. The decision sprang not from an exhaustive, rational, and calculated study of all available options but from incomplete albeit reliable information from their relatives. Despite the desire to find the most "optimal" product, neither Phoenix nor Jupiter possessed the resources to undertake such an analysis. As a result, Phoenix and Jupiter ended up with unglamorous, "satisficing" solutions that ultimately proved highly profitable.[17] This process was similar to that found in other townships outside Zhejiang province. Ding Yuan Zhu, for example, describes how one enterprise director decided to manufacture fishing gear after reading an account about the product's market potential. In similar fashion, Rong Ma details how another enterprise director shifted to the production of disposable needles after numerous friends who worked in city hospitals told him about the needle shortages that occurred in the aftermath of hepatitis A outbreaks in 1988.[18]

Interestingly, neither Jupiter nor Phoenix took the traditional handicrafts industry as the foundation of their firms. Despite the long histories of woodcarving in Jinhua and umbrella making around Wenzhou, both firms opted to establish very different product lines. In large part, this was a pragmatic move, unavoidable in a way because few members of the original founding group possessed the artisanal skills necessary to make these products in large quantities. Training a large workforce would require not only a relatively large number of skilled masters (*shifu*) to teach them but also a significant learning period. One senior craftsman at Jupiter's woodworking factory (opened nearly ten years later than the silk-processing factory) said that traditionally, "training took a long time, sometimes up to three to four years . . . [whereas] now, when a worker arrives, the training period is only six months."[19] And even by the end of the training period, no one could be sure these skills would translate into profits. Umbrellas, cloth, and other products native to the Wenzhou region suffered from similar limitations. So long as such goods were made by traditional methods of production, opportunities for survival and eventual expansion would remain limited.

Once the enterprise's overall direction was set, the only major challenge remaining was technical in nature; this, in turn, was closely intertwined with the task of personnel recruitment. Because the founders of Phoenix and Jupiter had little experience in factory management, they desperately needed to learn the details of production: product specifications, equipment requirements, and manufacturing processes. Although both enterprises needed workers of different skill levels and capacities, technically skilled personnel were crucial to their plans, for only they could provide the expertise necessary to keep the production process moving smoothly and efficiently. Again, the leaders at both firms plunged deeply into their networks for help. In a now-famous episode that would be repeated many times in the future, Jupiter's founder contacted a skilled fellow native who had lived near Dongyang in central Zhejiang province and pleaded with him to return home and join the new start-up. The founder so desperately needed his experience and knowledge that he even promised the engineer a salary higher than his own. "I'm imploring you," he said, "please help us this time."[20] The engineer finally accepted the offer after much importuning from the founder. Most of Phoenix's technically skilled staff faced the same choice: either take a chance and return home or maintain their precarious status as workers in distant city factories. Since few of them held an urban *hukou*, or permanent worker designation, they fell instead into the temporary or contract worker category, a status that consigned them to lower wages, negligible benefits, and little job security.[21] Returning home offered them an opportunity to overcome these inequities and potentially improve their own situation in one bold stroke.

This homecoming of skilled personnel allowed both firms to adopt two very distinct approaches to production. In Phoenix's case, the initial strategy emphasized imitation and incremental modifications over radical innovation. A member of the enterprise would begin this process by securing samples of an item they eventually hoped to produce, like an on/off switch, for example. Once the samples were in the workshop, several members would disassemble the article slowly, noting the composition and measurements of each individual component. With this information in hand, the designated technical "expert" could draw up a crude blueprint and include any modifications suggested during this process of "reverse engineering." Personnel at Phoenix would then assemble their own version of the switch and test it. If the model worked, full production would soon follow. If not, members of their networks could be consulted to help improve the design. In other instances, their products were based on specific requests from a client. These customers provided feedback and direction on what production adjustments were necessary. By relying as much as possible on their own ingenuity and calling on others only when they themselves could not resolve a problem, they hoped to avoid delays that could cost them lucrative orders.

In contrast, Jupiter's urgent needs and different technical requirements forced enterprise leaders to adopt a different strategy.

Rather than focus on mimicry and the development of its own production process, Jupiter was compelled to acquire a complete, functional plant from the beginning. Obviously, this move was a significant financial risk, but the founders felt it was the only viable option. Still, even with a turnkey operation, no one at Jupiter knew much about silk processing. If anything went wrong with operations on the shop floor, they needed someone to step in, analyze the problem and solve it, and most important, ensure continuous production. Rather than imitating the products of other companies and finding alternative ways of manufacturing them, Jupiter's objective was to preserve its considerable investment in equipment and transform raw silk into salable goods. All this planning and preparation finally led to the most important task of all: production.

Initial Work Conditions

Since their inception, Jupiter and Phoenix have been deeply affected by constraints in the external environment. In addition to the limitations already mentioned in Chapter 2, the enterprises faced an undeveloped market structure. Without a stable customer base, neither company could fully control the number of work orders it received and, consequently, the structure and pace of the work process. In fact, during this stage of enterprise development, neither Jupiter nor Phoenix possessed enough resources to offer a diverse line of products. That would have required not only sufficient reserves of working capital but, more important, reasonable assurances that their manufactured goods would be purchased. Unfortunately, neither could be guaranteed. Their initial inability to find takers for their products was further compounded by their relative obscurity, for few companies inside or outside Jinhua and Wenzhou knew of them, and fewer still felt they could be trusted as reliable partners or producers. It was up to the members of Jupiter and Phoenix to establish their firms in their respective markets.

Employing a number of different tactics, both firms actively sought out orders from new clients. Their most basic strategy of customer outreach entailed personal visits to the offices of potential customers with samples of their goods in hand. As Barry Naughton points out, smaller firms in the post-Mao reform era typically targeted more established and sometimes even state-owned firms for contracts and work orders.[22] Although potential customers were unfamiliar with Phoenix and Jupiter, they might be more inclined to purchase products once they understood the advantages of working with a flexible and reliable partner. These early sales visits were undertaken precisely to convince potential customers of this fact. When they were rebuffed, representatives of both firms remained undeterred and would visit other firms or return at a later date. In addition to fostering closer ties, these personal visits allowed the firms to gather information on what customers desired, data that were then incorporated into future product designs. Using this information, company representatives persisted in their rounds until clients were finally won over.

Moreover, their outreach strategy extended beyond their immediate community. Despite the limitations of the local state, representatives of both firms asked local government offices for assistance in establishing links with others located in the more isolated pockets of the prefecture. This turned out to be one of the tasks local officials executed rather effectively. Relatives working in other locations also played a significant role in the pursuit of clientele. Whenever possible, they showed their superiors different product samples and lobbied them to swing an order to Phoenix or Jupiter with assurances that goods unavailable elsewhere could be produced quickly and inexpensively at these rural factories. If they succeeded, an initial test order would be placed. The strategy of courting enterprises closest to them first and then more distant ones permitted both firms to utilize the knowledge and ties of locals in various parts of the country to build and extend their customer base.

This approach also allowed Jupiter and Phoenix to maximize their limited resources. Once orders had been secured, they could purchase additional material inputs with reasonable confidence that they were not endangering themselves financially. Sunk costs related to production were minimized, and a fast turnaround led to quick profits and reduced overall risk. As a result, inventory rarely accumulated in factory stock rooms. Unfortunately for workers, this also meant tight limits on wages. Enterprise leaders were reluctant to raise employee salaries for fear of losing their competitive edge in pricing. Any thought of wage increases would have to wait, at least until the stream of work orders grew and stabilized. At Jupiter, most of the managerial staff earned only 36 *yuan* per month for the first three years of the factory's operation.[23] In contrast, in 1984, workers in Wenzhou's few state-owned enterprises made roughly 105 *yuan* per month and workers at other firms earned as much as 200 *yuan* per month.[24] Wages at Phoenix did not even come close to these levels. In fact, workers often shouldered the burden of the factory's precarious finances by accepting delays in wage payments. It was not uncommon for either Phoenix or Jupiter to owe workers several months of back wages. When workers were finally paid, their income rarely exceeded that of agricultural laborers. Without the patience and support of workers, both enterprises could not have wrestled any contracts away from their competitors or stayed in business for long.

For potential customers, the terms of this arrangement were nearly ideal. By placing small orders, they could gauge the quality of the workmanship at minimal financial danger to themselves. If product quality was acceptable, the relationship would continue, even deepen; if it was substandard, the relationship would end. The flexibility of this arrangement allowed both parties to engage one another, build credibility, and diminish the risks involved. Some scholars have likened this arrangement to steering a "small boat" (*xiaozhou*), concluding that such a high degree of flexibility allowed companies to evade financial danger. They suggest that without this quality, few if any rural factories could have survived. Indeed, their nimbleness allowed them to minimize risk and forge strong links between producers and clients.

However, the unsteady stream of work orders made a deep impression on the physical work environment. Factory work conditions in this early phase of enterprise development were spartan, even dismal, just as they were in other national and historical contexts at a comparable stage of growth.[25] Although the founders would have preferred a spacious, well-designed facility from the beginning, the practical reality of limited finances and enormous risk made this impossible. Instead, like most other small-scale, family-based operations, Phoenix and Jupiter focused simply on starting their operations in whatever capacity they could and deferred expansion plans to the distant future.

Space was at a premium, and the physical layout of the workshops was small and cramped. These workshops often began in rented spaces, and any inefficiency only increased operating costs and the burdens on the enterprise founders. At both firms, the workstations where most of the final processing or assembly was completed took up the greatest amount of space. Typically, they were arranged in rows or along one long table so as to ensure the greatest freedom of movement and efficiency. These workstations occupied the center of the workshop, with other equipment placed along the periphery, most often along the walls of the factory. This arrangement was designed to allow workers greater freedom in procuring needed materials and in moving completed items out of the way for later inspection. Sitting side by side, workers could also consult with one another if questions regarding work tasks arose. In other workshops, the workstations were separated like individual desks in a classroom and arranged in one direction, offering workers only views of the coworkers' backs. Incoming parts and materials, processing equipment such as presses and lathes, and outgoing inventory were placed in the remaining available space in the workshop. As much as possible, items were labeled and separated for easy identification and handling, but often materials just piled up around the workshop as work demands increased, creating an intricate labyrinth that workers eventually learned to navigate. Phoenix's first workshop resembled the ubiquitous "store in front, factory in back" layout that characterizes most family-centered businesses in Wenzhou.

This shop floor design holds for the vast majority of small firms that exist alongside Phoenix and Jupiter. In the township where Phoenix is located, for instance, many of the narrow lanes in the commercial section are still home to small, family-owned shops, which seemingly operate at all hours of the day. Unfortunately, conditions at these businesses do not appear to have improved significantly since reforms were first initiated twenty years ago. In 1997 and 1998, I noticed that lighting remained minimal, ventilation poor, and work spaces tight. Amid the metal shavings and grease

and constant hum of running machinery were workers with black-
ened faces and clothes, much like coal miners emerging from a mine
shaft. The small industrial operations in Jupiter's township tended to
be larger than their counterparts in Wenzhou, but they could be just
as stifling and oppressive despite fledgling attempts to improve the
work environment. Although the focus was on silk spinning rather
than assembly, early work at Jupiter was carried out under similar
conditions, despite the larger initial capital outlay.

In some respects, the difficult circumstances that besieged Phoenix and Jupiter plagued smaller firms to an even greater degree. Most
of these small-scale entrepreneurs hoped that, as profits increased,
they would have greater resources to devote to facility upgrades. Yet
improving work conditions meant higher costs for individual owners, a price most were unwilling or unable to pay. With just the
thinnest of profit margins, they were operating at the brink of economic collapse. In recent years, these firms have grown increasingly
unstable, especially with the changing composition of the workforce.
One administrator at Jupiter who is in close contact with these local
firms explained it in this way:

Most of the workers in these private firms are outsiders [nonnatives of the
area] because [the owners] can give them lower wages. Occasionally, serious
labor conflict emerges. . . . Because cash flow is tight, the owners sometimes
might delay the payment of wages. Of course, outsiders feel they are not being treated with respect. They feel that they will have a problem feeding
themselves. At this point, arguments sometimes turn into fights. This becomes very serious, and they [the owners] try to stop it before it gets this
bad. They try to resolve economic problems before they become social
problems. Sometimes there are even workers who are so desperate, they
threaten to kill the owners.[26]

By no means are these challenges peculiar to Wenzhou, Jinhua, or
Zhejiang alone. Other small-scale operations throughout China
share similar features. A small garment manufacturer in Guangzhou
that I visited in 1996 also bore the impact of financial and spatial
constraints. Production was confined to one large processing room.
A small number of workers cut fabric in one corner, while the majority of workers sat in front of rows of sewing machines, piecing

the final product together. The fabric cutters often stood on bolts of uncut fabric or on the tables because new shipments of materials were strewn around their work area. In spite of the obvious discomfort and inconvenience, it was the only way they could complete their work assignments.

Under these trying circumstances, factory operations were sustainable only because work processes were relatively simple. In this early period, a high degree of work specialization did not exist, nor was it necessary as compared, say, to the assembly of more complex products.[27] Although workers in rural enterprises focused most of their energies on particular tasks, they often took on other duties that ranged from assembly to quality control to packaging to transport. It is important to point out that these early workers assumed these additional responsibilities because there were so few of them in the factory. Phoenix began with a total of five workers, including the founder, in the workshop. With 238 employees, Jupiter's ranks were considerably larger, but only a handful of them had received training in silk processing (from a plant in the provincial capital of Hangzhou).[28] Because the skilled personnel focused on fulfilling the most technically demanding responsibilities, the remaining workers were forced to shoulder a heavier workload and endure longer hours in order to complete the day's scheduled chores.

These pressures engendered a positive but unanticipated development. The ability of each worker to undertake a broad array of responsibilities benefited the factory by boosting the worker's familiarity and versatility in tackling production. For example, a worker at Phoenix was required to collect the various components of a product from the storage area and bring them to his or her workstation before beginning assembly. Each worker assembled the entire product from start to finish, a process that might involve anywhere from ten to thirty steps. After completing a batch of switches, the worker would take them to another station for quality control tests. If no problems surfaced, the products would be packaged and readied for delivery. Substandard products were returned to the worker, who then rechecked them and made the necessary adjustments. At Jupiter, workers were not responsible for as many work steps as the assemblers at Phoenix, but they nevertheless moved around the workshop in similar fashion. After the cocoons were prepared, the filaments were ready for reeling. Workers not only tended the reeling machines but also inspected and packaged the final product. Given the constraints under which the factory operated, workers were "jacks-of-all-trades," capable of nearly all work tasks except those that required the most advanced technical skills.[29]

Undoubtedly, the situation was grueling for laborers on the shop floor. To make matters even more difficult, none of them knew ahead of time what the workday would be like. In the absence of work orders, workers were not scheduled for work and would not be paid. This time off allowed workers to stay home and rest or pursue other activities. At other times, especially when work orders with short turnaround times poured in, workers were not only expected to work longer but were asked to sustain an intense production pace to meet impending deadlines. This concentration of routine work into short, furious bursts of production broadly paralleled the mobilizational approach used in Soviet factories under Stalin and Chinese factories during the early years of the People's Republic.[30]

For a limited time, all enterprise members exceeded the qualities exemplified by the label "jack-of-all-trades" and became "organizational weapons." According to Philip Selznick, the organizational weapon is a person who is not only committed but also competent, a person who could be trusted to act in strict accordance with established values and practice.[31] Under these circumstances, what enterprise members lacked in technology, they attempted to make up for in discipline and dedication. Their objective was to ensure the enterprise's continuing existence, and they used any means to secure their chosen ends.[32] Like the Stahkanovites in the Soviet Union, enterprise members were asked to be innovative in resolving production problems.[33] If workers discovered better and more effective methods for assembly, they were encouraged to make full use of them and bring them to the attention of their superiors so others could utilize them as well. Although workers were not asked to overfulfill production targets, in every other sense, enterprise employees exceeded their superiors' expectations. At a time of great urgency, they became Phoenix and Jupiter's most valuable assets.

Worker Profiles

In the face of these intense pressures, hardly anyone expected peasants to become effective, long-term workers. Prominent scholars of labor politics have suggested that peasants are not well suited for an industrial way of life and are unlikely to shed their ties to the land or their agrarian mindsets. Charles Sabel, for instance, argues that peasant workers engage in factory work for short-term economic gain. In comparison with skilled workers, "the peasant worker has no pride of accomplishment in factory work. . . . Even when the peasant worker does work, furthermore, he is indifferent to what he does."[34] Observers often point out that agricultural and industrial work are two distinct worlds, with few commonalities. Peasants sometimes articulate this view as well. One worker at Phoenix from a village in neighboring Anhui province explained the key difference in terms of control over time: "If you are a farmer, you have a lot of free time and you can decide what you want to do. There is a lot more free time to rest. [At the factory] we have to be on time each day and can't stay home just because we are tired."[35] However, this understanding of time-discipline can also be deceptive. Agricultural work requires discipline too, as evidenced by the comments of another worker at Phoenix. For her, factory work conditions were actually an improvement over work in the fields:

Getting here at 7:30 A.M. is easy. Back in the village, I got up at 4:00 in the morning each day to avoid the heat. It didn't help much because I still worked late into the night. I like working [in the factory] much better than working the fields. I never want to go back there again. Do you know how hard that work is? When you must work all day under the hot sun, it's unbearable. At least I'm not under the sun here.[36]

The British historian E. P. Thompson also argues that farmers are not totally out of sync with an industrially oriented regimen: "The entire family economy of the small farmer may be task-oriented; but within it there may be a division of labour, and allocation of roles, and the discipline of an employer-employed relationship between the farmer and his children."[37] In the same article, Thompson raises another crucial point that sheds light on the early work dynamics at

Phoenix and Jupiter. Agricultural work patterns, he suggests, are inherently irregular and result in "alternate bouts of intense labour and of idleness."[38] This is precisely the situation most workers, especially those employed at Phoenix, faced. Peasant workers were already accustomed to intense work rhythms well before they walked through factory gates. In other words, the emphasis on mobilization and "heroic storming" was not as shocking to them as one might think. The irregularity of factory work orders only transferred these already familiar work rhythms to the workshop.

Moreover, peasants possessed not only the ability to work in rural factories but also the motivation to succeed. Although incomes from industrial work were meager and inconstant, factories like Phoenix and Jupiter offered local villagers, especially less-educated, younger residents, an opportunity to help out with family finances while gaining practical experience. Staying at home precluded this chance at personal improvement and amounted to only marginal aid to household members already engaged in agriculture. After all, if the labor of these sons and daughters were truly needed, say around harvest time, they could lend assistance after their day jobs ended or even be excused from work if the family was especially shorthanded. This desire to bolster income drove others to assume nearly impossible work schedules. "I worked my land," said one of the plant administrators at Jupiter, "at 3:00 or 4:00 in the morning and came to work in the factory at 7:30. After work, I returned home to work on my land again. I was totally exhausted. Even after the harvest, you have to pick new seeds, apply pesticides, and clear land."[39]

For many, factory work was appealing because of the enterprise's close proximity to their homes. Nearly all the workers could reach the factories by foot or bicycle; only a handful needed to ride a bus to work. This short commute reduced costs across the board; workers did not incur the additional expenses for housing, food, and long-distance travel involved in working in faraway places such as Shanghai or Guangdong. Instead, the savings could be spent on personal goods or saved for future large-ticket items. It became increasingly common for young workers to stroll the township's streets on weekends, buying sweets, clothing, and other small things with their newly earned disposable income.

Income aside, important social considerations were in play as well. Many relatives and locals felt obliged to help their kin and neighbors succeed in their endeavors in any way possible. Some felt obliged to repay debts for help received in the past; others feared the potential strain their refusal would place on their social relationships. Whatever their motivation, enterprise managers expected them to put forth their best efforts. Undoubtedly, these expectations were strongly influenced by prevailing norms of reciprocity and social trust. This type of interaction also lessened parental worries about the welfare of their children on the shop floor. These young workers, even their parents if need be, could speak directly with factory officials if they felt dissatisfied. Many did so with ease. These meetings were not simply exchanges between employer and employee; rather, they were discussions between familiar parties who interacted socially outside the workplace. A stronger sense of mutual commitment and understanding bound them together, not to mention the fear of violating prevailing norms. Such a relationship stands in stark contrast to the ties between many migrant workers and their nonlocal factory employers. Parents were consumed with dread and often opposed their children's move to faraway factories for fear that they would be forced to endure backbreaking, oppressive work conditions.[40] Absent kinship or native-place ties to the employers, parents felt there was nothing to shield their children from exploitation.

Clearly, then, industrial work was not necessarily alienating or antipathetic to peasants. In fact, many of the new workers demonstrated a strong ability to contribute to the growth of the factory. Some workers even developed a stronger sense of self-esteem and efficacy as a result of their success. In turn, enterprise management's flexibility and eagerness to help them adjust to the new work regimen made the transition smoother than one might expect. They established an institutional framework within which the collective energies of all enterprise members could be channeled toward enterprise survival and stability. By choosing to operate in accordance with traditional mores and practices, they paved the way for a relatively smooth transition from tending fields to laboring in industrial workshops. Without this, the nature of relations in the rural factory would likely have been considerably more distressing and contentious.

Authority Relations in the Factory

The less than ideal work conditions at both firms created a situation in which discontent and unrest could potentially cripple the production process and relations within the factory. Surprisingly, at Jupiter and Phoenix, slowdowns, strikes, absenteeism, and sabotage—the most typical expressions of worker dissatisfaction—were rare. Indeed, what stands out so prominently in the early history of Phoenix and Jupiter is the relative lack of conflict and high degree of cohesion and social harmony among the members of the enterprise. In contrast to factories where severe disagreements often broke out, both enterprises in this study were able to contain and prevent disputes from turning into major confrontations. This outcome rested largely on how factory authority relations were defined and structured.

The ability to achieve a high degree of stability within the firm stemmed from the significant overlap between the factory's management system and the norms and practices guiding interaction among kin and fellow natives. By incorporating familiar social elements into the institutional framework, enterprise members came to invest the authority structure with more legitimacy than employees of other companies did in theirs. In this early formative stage, the managerial signature emphasized a collectively oriented spirit of cooperation as well as the wide-scale sharing of benefits. Piece rates were eschewed in favor of fairly equal wages that reflected the continuing influence of an "eat from one big pot" mentality (i.e., an egalitarian wage system). This approach also relied heavily on persuasion over coercion in eliciting higher levels of work performance from employees. On the whole, it was a system flexible enough to accommodate differing levels of skill, ability, and commitment yet strong enough to focus diverse interests and viewpoints toward the common purpose of enterprise-building. In short, enterprise resilience emerged from the amalgamation of a personal, more egalitarian system of authority and a more rational (albeit weak) industrial production regimen.

The factory's authority structure was simple and easily understood by all members of the enterprise. Authority—the decision-making power over work content, work schedules, and work pace—rested in the hands of the enterprise founders and an inner circle of "heroic cadres" who assisted in overseeing production tasks. The founder held ultimate responsibility for the direction of work; in his absence, these lieutenants, many of whom were skilled in technical matters, were entrusted with keeping operations running smoothly and efficiently. The remaining factory personnel were expected to follow their example. In many ways, the manner in which these rural factories were managed paralleled that of the American entrepreneurial firm in the nineteenth century. In both post-Mao reform China and late nineteenth-century America, factory founders were personally involved in almost every facet of factory activity. In the words of Stephen Hyman, they "saw everything, knew everything, and decided everything."[41]

The personal presence and direct participation of firm leaders in shop floor activities served a number of important functions. First, it afforded them an intimate understanding of almost every aspect of production. With this knowledge, leaders could identify and help correct a problem before it grew more serious. In this way, they shared and reduced the demands placed on the firm's skilled personnel, who were often preoccupied with other important work tasks. Their ability to intervene successfully was further enhanced by the small scale of these early operations and the limited number of production facilities. Leaders could easily oversee work if they had to be concerned only about one or two workshops rather than several.

More important, the personal presence of the founders on the shop floor served to inspire workers and strengthen the bonds between members of the factory community. When workers saw their superiors working side by side with them, engaged in tough, manual labor, worker perceptions of factory work changed dramatically. They gained a new sense of dignity and self-respect, reasoning that if the founders were not averse to staying late and getting their hands dirty, neither should they be. Management's willingness to take on any work task also reduced potential charges of neglect or abuse by disgruntled relatives or fellow natives. By putting in long hours, the employers signaled their willingness to make personal sacrifices for the enterprise's survival and, by extension, the welfare of all members. Their example of commitment assuaged the perception of social distance between worker and administrator and became a critical means of solidifying enterprise solidarity.

For these managers, fostering camaraderie and "human feeling" (*renqing*) seemed like the most natural and effective way to oversee factory affairs. Managers were well aware that public embarrassment and poorly timed disciplinary action could destroy morale and undermine the sense of community they had worked so hard to achieve. A plant manager at Phoenix, widely regarded as one of the most caring and upstanding men in the managerial ranks, explained his approach this way:

I don't like to use a tough, cold approach. If I have a problem with a worker, I call that person into my office and we talk. I discuss the problem and ask how the worker feels. It's a discussion, not a scolding. I would never discuss anything in the workshop. The worker would "lose face" [*meiyou mianzi*], and this would cause serious emotional problems. I try to treat people in such a way that if they leave the factory, they leave on good terms. It's impossible to work without some "human feeling." . . . If you think the worker is here to serve the factory and the factory has no need to serve the worker, the factory will eventually fail. You can't go around ordering people to do whatever you want them to do.[42]

At the same time, this approach placed a great deal of responsibility on the managers to assess a situation and take appropriate action. Despite their commitment to "human feeling," their responses to the unfolding situation could still lead to tension. To correct work performance without disrupting factory harmony was the ultimate challenge, and to do so consistently depended on anticipating and adjusting to the responses of factory personnel. For one of the plant administrators at Jupiter, this ability is what separates successful enterprises from unsuccessful ones.

Management is not a dead science; you don't follow the rules in every case. A manager needs to be flexible and understand that workers have very different personalities. For some employees, you have to explain what they did wrong and be courteous. They'll listen because they want to improve and feel embarrassed. Others won't listen at all unless you scold them. They won't be motivated unless there is a chance they'll lose their jobs. We have to realize that workers aren't stupid and that we cannot treat them like robots. They work very hard, and we have to respect their work.[43]

Although the operations of the factory relied heavily on the personal direction of its managers, this did not mean decisions were whimsical or arbitrary. Standards were needed, if only to make work routines easier to remember. Hence, work rules were created, but in sharp contrast to those established during the later stage of expansion, they were few in number and circumscribed in scope. The ones in force tended to focus on the prevention of accidents and damage to machinery rather than proper procedures for work. In production areas where grease or oil could be found, for example, managers at Phoenix prohibited smoking to guard against the outbreak of fire. In other instances, female workers were asked to tie up their long hair to prevent it from being caught in running machinery. Workers were not fined if they violated these rules, but they were reprimanded and cautioned. Supervisors hoped that the embarrassment and the danger of injury would be sufficient to elicit a change in behavior. Unfortunately, oral warnings were not always enough to drive the point home. Rules were not widely posted throughout the factory, nor were workers given a handbook prior to the assumption of work duties, and workers sometimes forgot to take precautions, creating dangerous openings for accidents.

In comparison, the approach taken by a producer of machine bearings in the Wenzhou area, which I call Sparta Enterprises,* was radically different. Sparta's management likened the company to a military regiment and argued that a strict code of work rules and vigilant enforcement (even surveillance!) was necessary to the proper molding of their employees' characters. Tobacco was perhaps the most dramatic case in point. No one at that company, from shop floor workers to the enterprise president, was allowed to smoke. To create a smoke-free environment, the enterprise instituted draconian rules

---

*Although I wanted to conduct a more in-depth study of Sparta, I was allowed to take only a brief tour of the facilities and speak to only a few employees. Nevertheless, it was clear that Sparta's heavy emphasis on control and discipline contrasted sharply with the more relaxed approach adopted by managers at Phoenix and Jupiter.

and discouraged workers at every turn from developing this habit. The company's manager of administration told me:

> At first, if you were caught smoking, you would be assessed a 20-*yuan* fine. Now the rule is even tougher. If you are caught smoking anywhere, you will be fined 200 *yuan*,* and your supervisor will be fined 50 *yuan*. No administrator is allowed to smoke either. When they go to meetings or banquets, they are allowed to offer cigarettes only to guests, but they are not allowed to smoke with them. If anyone is caught, their names will be announced to the entire company.[44]

Sparta's management thus decided that worker lifestyles and company safety were closely interconnected. For the sake of the company and their jobs, workers were compelled to give up smoking, and few seemed to mind. Most seemed to feel that this policy not only saved them money but improved their overall health as well. Interestingly, Phoenix imposed a similar ban on smoking in 2003 after a fire that started with a lit cigarette butt caused major damage to a large workshop.

On the whole, enterprise managers at Phoenix and Jupiter were not overbearing. Although decisions could be illogical, even contradictory, enterprise leaders were not consumed by the need for complete control over workers. In fact, some of them viewed rules in this early stage as more a hindrance than an aid to effective administration. Compared to other industrial workplaces, their demands were minimal. Indeed, they cared less about the conduct of work and more about its actual completion. So long as the product was reliable and work was completed with a reasonable amount of professionalism, few restrictions were placed on workers. At this point, they did not expect a "fully" committed workforce and were satisfied with a "partially" committed one.[45] Coming from an agriculturally based community, they knew the importance of the harvest and even rearranged the factory work schedule so that workers could return home to assist with work in the fields. Because managers understood the happenings and rhythms of their communities, they sel-

---

*For the average full-time worker, a 200-*yuan* fine was equal to one-sixth of his monthly wages.

dom exercised their authority in the harsh manner reminiscent of the "foreman's empire."[46]

Consequently, a rough sense of egalitarianism and fairness emerged within the enterprise. Much of this grew out of the direct interaction between personnel, for all the workers experienced close and frequent personal contact with their top leaders. Rarely did they go through long stretches of time without some form of contact. Although everyone clearly understood the chain of command, few felt formal authority or the status of office to be the guiding force behind their relationships. Instead, their bonds were more informal and extended well beyond the confines of the factory walls.* In fact, enterprise members often socialized a great deal outside the industrial workshop. Enterprise members felt they were tied together in a common cause, a family (literally) linked together by the larger purpose of survival and the dream of wealth. In the crucible of the workshop, these ties were further strengthened, as was their sense of discipline. Members offered one another vital support, but the uncertainty of success prevented the rise of an "indulgency pattern" that, to them, would have destroyed any chance of enterprise survival.[47] When I asked the older workers about their earliest experiences in the workshop, many of them related stories about how they worked frantically into the night completing a batch for shipment the next morning. Despite the strain of work, workers often looked back fondly to this period as the "good old days." Many employees at Phoenix also expressed admiration for the company founder during our daily lunches in the company canteen. They often exclaimed, "Look, he's not arrogant and even eats the same food we eat."

At the same time, there is a danger of romanticizing these tight social bonds. In the classic study *Work and Authority in Industry*, Reinhard Bendix cautions against this tendency, for as he aptly notes, "Intimate personal contacts can be every bit as unbearable as

---

*The statement of a mechanic at an American gypsum plant nicely captures the nature of relationships at Jupiter and Phoenix: "The bosses associate with the men. They will drink with them at the saloon or restaurant, and there is a fine sentiment. That's something you don't see in other plants. . . . They're sociable that way. They hunt and fish together" (Gouldner, *Patterns of Industrial Bureaucracy*, 39).

the impersonality of the market place."[48] Moreover, "paternalistic benevolence and ruthless oppression often made use of exactly the same managerial devices."[49] Hence, the flexibility and informality of the factory authority structure did not mean dissatisfaction was non-existent. Workers grumbled about unpaid back wages and the long overtime hours they were asked to work. When they approached factory managers with these concerns, most were counseled to be patient. Wages would be eventually paid out, they were told. After all, relatives would not betray the trust of one of their own, although it appears that they nearly stretched this trust beyond its breaking point. Consequently, most workers stayed on the job so that they would not end up with nothing if they left (*baizuole*) and gave their relatives another chance to make amends.

In addition, the tensions and frantic pace engendered by tight deadlines often set everyone on edge. It took only one flippant remark or one dirty look to ignite a confrontation that threatened to upend the social stability of the workshop. Despite the close ties of blood and friendship that bound members together, rifts occasionally surfaced. For the most part, the disputes resulted in catharsis: once pent-up frustrations were aired, grievances were quickly forgotten. At other times, the disagreements were more serious. In the heat of the moment, employees would sometimes come to blows. Such action was grounds for immediate dismissal, regardless of family connections. At other times, employees chose the "exit" option on their own rather than stay in an unhappy situation.[50]

No exact figures on worker turnover rates for this initial stage were available for either Jupiter or Phoenix. Enterprise leaders were unconcerned with documenting these conditions, training their energies instead on other aspects of firm survival. Although inconclusive, many of the older managers and workers stated that, from what they remembered, turnover was rather low, staying within the range of 10–15 percent. However, how many left because of actual work dissatisfaction remains unclear. Managers allowed employees to leave for personal reasons—illness and family matters being the two main causes of departure—while always leaving the door open for their return. Even workers who had left on bad terms could return if they rededicated themselves to following the prevailing norms and practices of the enterprise community instead of "losing their cool" (*hunao*). What resulted from this volatility, then, was a temporary leave of absence rather than a permanent exit from the factory community. In hindsight, labor turnover in the enterprise was more a release valve than a symptom of deeper troubles, as it would become in later years at both Phoenix and Jupiter.

Refashioning the Enterprise-Cadre Relationship

As Deng Xiaoping and other reformers moved to stimulate the growth of more rural enterprises like Jupiter and Phoenix, they realized that lasting success necessitated the curtailment of, if not an outright end to, the divisive political struggles that previously paralyzed factories throughout China, especially during the tumultuous decade of the Cultural Revolution. Party leaders recognized that a greater unity of purpose and action among all enterprise members was crucial to their quest to revitalize the rural economy. They ultimately concluded that the duties and responsibilities of their own agents, the local-level cadres, would have to be redefined drastically if market forces were to reach and transform the countryside. To facilitate this process, they gradually replaced cadres dedicated to the realization of the lofty aims of revolution with a more professional but less intrusive corps of officials committed to integrating the mores of commercial and industrial activity into the rhythms of village life.[51]

Despite the potential gains of increased economic activity, these policy changes represented a major shift in policy direction, a development that was not well received by some party members. Leaders of the party's conservative wing such as Chen Yun decried the shift to household production over collectivized agriculture and the growing enchantment with markets and capitalism. They feared the promise of material wealth would undermine China's long-term commitment to socialism. For Deng Xiaoping, though, it was not simply a choice between socialism or development, "red" versus "expert": he wanted China to be both but without the high costs that Mao had exacted through political campaigns and mass mobilization. For the villages especially, Deng's reform program tacitly acknowledged that "too large a dose of socialism had been imposed upon too backward a countryside."[52] Instead, he hoped that new incentives would prompt citizens to worry less about demonstrating their political fitness and to concentrate more on improving their standard of living. His solution to this dilemma was to bypass the debate altogether and simply assume that citizens could be both "red" and "expert" rather than limited to one or the other. This clever redefinition allowed previously marginalized actors to participate in his broader efforts to modernize China and eliminated one of the most critical points of contention in recent Chinese history.

In a more practical vein, implementation of Deng's proposal required strong determination as well as innovation. Because the policy sought to reduce the power of cadres and, in some cases, eliminate them outright, cadre hostility and resistance were expected. Lower-level cadres needed to be convinced of the reform policy's benefits, but their conflicting roles made it all the more difficult. Like the scholar-gentry elite of China's imperial past, local cadres performed contradictory functions in the jurisdictions they oversaw: they not only served as agents of the state but also derived a livelihood from those communities. The unique roles they played as policy implementers and community guardians made them the focal point "where political power, economic control, and social status all converge."[53] The fused power of cadres led them, in their better moments, to extend policy deep into the reaches of the countryside and, at other times, to help local communities survive daunting economic challenges. At their worst, cadres could subvert the policies they were supposed to uphold and engage in corrupt, domineering, and even criminal actions.

Given these circumstances, party leaders reasoned that by limiting the discretionary powers of local cadres, they might contain and even control abusive cadre behavior. Indeed, the decision at the Third Plenum in December 1978 to shift responsibility for agricultural production from teams to individual households set this process in motion by significantly curtailing the monitoring and coordinating functions local cadres fulfilled under the old commune system.[54] Although the narrowed scope of formal cadre authority was welcomed by many local communities, it did not immediately put an end to cadre improprieties. One respondent at Jupiter, himself a former local cadre, felt frustrated by local officials even after the reforms had begun to take effect.

A lot of cadres still have not changed their thinking. To be honest, there are just too many people in government offices, and the worst thing is that they all feel self-important. When they go to inspect a factory, they always want a free meal and they want to play *mahjong* or cards afterwards. The factory manager, of course, will feel obligated to do so but will also feel resentful because he can't do more important things. This strains relations between local government and the enterprise. These government bureaucrats feel they aren't receiving enough respect, but they don't realize that their salaries depend on successful enterprises.[55]

Although the original intent of the policy change was to rein in local state agents, these efforts could often result in political emasculation. Well-qualified cadres, even ones who possessed useful administrative or management skills, were forced out of office in areas that might have benefited from their continued service, whereas less-qualified ones remained entrenched in their positions. As Richard Latham has noted, in some instances the reform program "not only deprived grass-roots party leaders of prestige and political advantages but also left cadres at an economic disadvantage and imperiled their normally secure leadership positions."[56] Some were even forced to return to tilling the land to survive, a rather ignominious end to their official careers.

On the whole, these incidents were rare. In most communities, the process unfolded along the contours and needs of local circumstances. Some cadres, recognizing that the new limitations often shackled them from initiating new projects, struck out on their own and established themselves as successful entrepreneurs. Others, however, stayed in government offices and tried to harness local state resources for the development of new enterprises throughout the Chinese countryside. Their uneven success on this score reflects the vast range of cadre capabilities. This partially explains why some local governments are deeply involved in enterprises in their jurisdiction and others are not.

Leaders at Phoenix and Jupiter clearly understood the political ramifications of their plans. Although they believed local cadres could not help them in the day-to-day running of the factories, to aim for their full ejection from the enterprise environment would have been unrealistic and indeed counterproductive. In fact, even as they sought to achieve their ultimate goal of "separation of government and enterprise" (*zhengqi fenkai*), these entrepreneurs realized they had to reassure local governments that factory autonomy was in the best interest of all parties instead of an attempt to subvert government authority. Like Deng, the originators of both firms continually reaffirmed this position in an attempt to avoid potential political backlash.

For them, this debate was not about property rights in the sense it has been debated in scholarly circles. Enterprise leaders simply assumed they possessed these rights and acted accordingly. They often found it amusing when I asked about this, attributing this interest to an American fascination with legal rights. To them, the creation of a legal system would do little to enhance the security of property rights. Instead, property rights operated on a more informal basis in accordance with local codes of proper behavior. In Wenzhou especially, leaders at Phoenix believed the legacy of cooperation between cadre and citizen provided better guarantees against government interference in enterprise affairs. Personal honor and trust were central to these relationships, and failure to fulfill one's promises was viewed as personal betrayal. Shared social norms thus served as an alternative means of enforcing agreements; informal sanctions substituted for formal, legal punishments.

Nevertheless, securing political approval was unmistakably one of the most critical tasks facing Phoenix. Despite the new tolerance for economic experimentation, the firms in the Wenzhou area were overwhelmingly private in ownership form. In the existing economic order, not only were private firms denied access to various inputs, but they were also vulnerable to political attack as the embodiment of a capitalist revival. Officials could and often did harass them and exact fees in exchange for the cessation of raids and surprise inspections. Although Phoenix began as a small, kin-based assembly operation and offered few opportunities for rapacious cadres, its growth in the late 1980s eventually sparked greater attention and opened the door to harassment from the authorities. In a pre-emptive move,

Phoenix "donned the red hat" (*dai hongmao*) and registered as a fake collective (*jia jiti*). This action not only provided political cover for the company but also forced local cadres to stay in line and even assist the firm on some occasions. With Phoenix's new but false status, cadres could gain more by helping the firm than by harassing it.

In contrast, Jupiter's process of spinning itself off from government control proved to be more contentious but equally consequential. The major issue with Jupiter was its clear origins as a commune and brigade enterprise. During the early 1970s, Jupiter received crucial backing from area officials, who protected the enterprise and its founder from leftist accusations that they were "heading down the capitalist road." When Jupiter's president pushed hard for independent management of the enterprise in response to changes in national policy, local officials were stunned and angry. To them, the proposal heralded the abandonment of socialist institutions and symbolized a breach of their strong relationship.

Their steadfast opposition was broken only through the expenditure of considerable political capital. Jupiter's president, the local party's general secretary when Jupiter was first created, gave his personal assurance that his only goal was to enhance the firm's flexibility and its profits. In decisive terms, he reiterated that Jupiter and the proceeds it generated were the common property of the community. This pronouncement marked a tactical change, not a substantive one. In order to secure cadre acceptance of Jupiter's autonomy, the president even appealed to pride in their native place, stating flatly that his life has been dedicated to improving the welfare of the entire community and that he was not about to stop now. In a confrontation with the man most responsible for the area's recent economic success, most cadres could only grumble but few could actually oppose his plan.

Yet for both Phoenix and Jupiter, the most crucial factor in their successful attempts to ensure enterprise autonomy was their willingness to engage in old-fashioned horse trading. Through their numerous encounters with officials, entrepreneurs knew that the political status of the factory was only one and not necessarily the most important issue for cadres. Personal ambition and desires also motivated local bureaucrats. They wanted to show higher authorities

that they were increasing local tax coffers, improving local infrastructure, and promoting economic prosperity in their jurisdictions.[57]
At the same time, they watched others—with some alarm—become
increasingly prosperous and were concerned that they and their
families might be left out of the economic boom. If enterprises like
Phoenix and Jupiter could help cadres allay these concerns, their relationship would assume a more stable footing. This assistance sometimes took the form of hiring a cadre's relative or acquaintance (or
even the cadre!) or of secret financial payoffs. So long as such arrangements did not interfere with the enterprise's operations and
long-term viability, there was no opposition from company leaders.
After all, it was clear that an antagonistic relationship would only
prevent both parties from achieving their objectives. Although no
formal written agreement was drawn up, this logic underpinned the
process of negotiation and bargaining between firms and local governments in these two areas of Zhejiang.

This new pact worked on the premise that each party could provide the other with what it wanted but could not secure on its own.
Through cooperation, the enterprise and the local government
could overcome constraints by engaging in this symbiotic relationship. For example, in addition to increasing tax revenues, both firms
offered expanded employment opportunities to fellow residents,
mitigating to some degree government obligations for welfare provision. In turn, local government offices helped firms navigate complex labor regulations and other bureaucratic procedures in addition
to providing key contacts with suppliers and banks. Although the
terms of the relationship were subject to periodic evaluation and negotiation, the nature and logic of the relationship had clearly shifted
to one of mutual benefit.

Concluding Remarks

The founders of Jupiter and Phoenix accomplished what no
one in their respective areas could: the establishment of a profitable,
industrially oriented enterprise. It was not an easy task by any measure. In Jinhua and Wenzhou prefectures, few natural or governmental resources could be utilized to start these businesses, forcing the
leaders of both firms to look elsewhere for assistance. Fortunately,

they were able to tap into extensive networks of kin and fellow natives that radiated from their places of origin to major metropolises in China. In their time of most desperate need, their relatives and friends provided them not only with hard-earned money to launch the business but also critical information and technical skills they could not obtain elsewhere. Without them, neither Jupiter nor Phoenix could have been started in the first place.

Yet in analyzing the early history of both firms, what stands out as the most crucial element in their success was the ability to ensure a high level of stability and social harmony within the firm. By fusing the shared trust and collective orientation of their communities with the impersonal regimen of rural industry, by maintaining a sense of flexibility and demonstrating their unflagging commitment to making their enterprises successful, the founders built the outlines of a new community, one that bound together peasants and entrepreneurs. They even convinced local cadres that, for the sake of local community welfare, it was best that they possess the autonomy to direct the affairs of the factory as they saw fit.*

As Jupiter and Phoenix entered their next phase of development, some of their most cherished assumptions about work and authority would be questioned and challenged. For the first time, enterprise leaders confronted a serious potential for social conflict within the enterprise community, a development they hardly expected. As they moved to defuse these tensions, they were forced to address some difficult questions. Could, for instance, mutual trust and norms of reciprocity be established with people who were not members of their networks? How does a company balance the need for expertise and the status distinctions that result from growth and success with the sense of community it so desperately wants to preserve? These are the issues that marked the experiences of both firms as they entered the stage of expansion, the subject of the next chapter.

---

*In short, what Franz Schurmann (*Ideology and Organization*, 230) observes regarding Japanese business during the Meiji period applies equally well to Jupiter and Phoenix: these enterprises were successful "amalgams of the modern and the ancient."

FOUR

Enterprise Expansion

Mass Production
and Centralization

YEARS OF ARDUOUS work and careful management at Jupiter
and Phoenix had laid strong cornerstones for enterprise stability and
future expansion. Although the immediate threat of enterprise failure
had receded, company leaders did not rest for long. As the pace of reform quickened in the 1980s, they raced to prepare for the new opportunities and the emerging threats looming on the economic horizon.
In order to earn even greater profits and keep old and new rivals at
bay, enterprise leaders believed they could and should transform their
small factories into larger, more rationalized firms. Realizing this
objective became the new core task of expansion.

In this chapter, I analyze Jupiter's and Phoenix's efforts in the late
1980s and early 1990s to expand and improve their production capabilities. Although executives at both companies initially responded
to skyrocketing customer orders by enlarging their operations and
hiring more workers, they soon realized that the broader organizational environment was changing dramatically. Rival firms increasingly employed newer, more efficient production techniques that
improved both output and product quality. Intensifying competition
forced enterprise executives to conclude that the approach they had
used during the survival stage, with its emphasis on "heroic storming," was too haphazard, too unsystematic, to be effective. If their

companies were to flourish, the old, small-scale, batch-oriented production techniques would have to be jettisoned for more rationalized, mass-production methods.

The transition, however, was neither easy nor smooth. At every turn, Jupiter and Phoenix faced major challenges and constraints that prevented the full implementation of this new production approach. Some of these obstacles stemmed from technical and financial limitations over which they had little control; others arose directly from the social antagonisms the new strategy engendered. Clearly, the new strategy was a radical departure because it emphasized above all else greater specialization, adherence to impersonal rules, and increased managerial control over enterprise activities. In their attempts to create multidivisional firms in the tradition of DuPont and General Motors, enterprise leaders moved away from the norms of reciprocity, social trust, and collective well-being that had been integral components of the company's previous strategy.[1] Any difficulties, they believed, would be temporary and easily overcome as new routines became customary and profits increased.

Yet instead of unqualified support for management's plans, what emerged were unprecedented levels of social conflict that threatened to torpedo the social foundations of both enterprises. Feeling a deepening sense of ambivalence and even seething resentment regarding management's new direction, enterprise members clung even more tenaciously to the social norms and values that had been melded into the enterprise's authority structure. To workers, the new plans represented their growing marginalization in the work process and the factory hierarchy. Hence, harmony and commitment, the two hallmarks of the enterprise community prior to expansion, could no longer be assumed or guaranteed. The tight-knit community the founders had worked so hard to create was now jeopardized by rapid change and the demands of expansion. The rough sense of egalitarianism that had previously existed was soon replaced by an ever-widening gulf between the skilled and the unskilled, the managers and the managed.*

----

*As much as leaders thought they could avoid such an outcome, the growing fissures in Jupiter and Phoenix stemmed directly from their assumption that the firm

As expansion proceeded, Phoenix and Jupiter experienced ever-greater degrees of fragmentation. In addition to the oppressive weight of new production demands, longtime employees felt increasingly alienated from their new coworkers. The new workers performed the same tasks, but they were strangers. Indeed, these new employees differed from area natives in personal background, experience, and, most important, native-place allegiance. Although these "outsiders" (*wai-diren*) provided invaluable services to these firms, their presence aroused major suspicions that were not easily dispelled. Could outsiders be trusted if they did not belong to the closed networks of kin and familiar acquaintances? Would such divided loyalties hinder the enterprise's ability to generate wealth for the benefit of all? In short, expansion created new questions of individual and group identity and opened major social fissures in the enterprise. The entire enterprise community was forced to re-examine fundamental organizational and social issues and decide if and how they should adapt "old" values to "new" goals.* For both firms, expansion proved to be more challenging than they had imagined.

A New Production Approach

Trends and developments in their respective industries convinced enterprise leaders at Jupiter and Phoenix that the adoption of rationalized, mass-production techniques was critical to enterprise growth. Through fact-finding tours of leading enterprises in Jiangsu, Guangdong, and Shanghai, senior executives saw what other firms were doing and recognized the dangers posed by their rivals. Despite the earlier success of their firms, they continued to fear extinction and remained deeply concerned that everything they had struggled so long and hard for could disappear in an instant. Stories about the sudden rise and fall of enterprises in contemporary China are com-

---

as an "institution" would remain intact as they wrestled with revamping its "organization"; see Selznick, *Leadership in Administration*.

*In facing these challenges, both Jupiter and Phoenix more closely resembled Kikkoman than DuPont at a similar stage of enterprise development. For an analysis of how family ties and other social factors initially hampered the development of Kikkoman into a large-scale enterprise, see Fruin, *Kikkoman*.

mon,[2] and Phoenix and Jupiter did not want to become the latest examples of this alarming trend. As a result, leaders at both firms imi-
tated their rivals, adopting as quickly as possible production and
management techniques used elsewhere.[3] This in turn also led to a
major shift in how managers viewed other members of the enterprise.
As they gained wider exposure to managerial practices at other firms,
they increasingly deplored the "backwardness" of their workforce and
were determined to reshape workers' habits and values along more
"rational" lines. Gone now, at least in the upper echelons of the enterprise, was the hope that sheer force of will could overcome the
demands of an intensely competitive market environment.

By incorporating the latest innovations into their operations,
both firms sought to become competitive, modern, and progressive
(*xianjin*). Throughout my stays at Phoenix and Jupiter, for example,
managers frequently and proudly pointed out their ISO 9000 certifi-
cations,* emphasizing that even though they were rural enterprises,
they were employing the latest and most effective production and
management methods. These efforts offered major payoffs in public
relations. Both firms earned "advanced enterprise" (*xianjin qiye*) ac-
colades from the government and press as well as enhanced reputations in the marketplace as stable and reliable producers. The impact
was immediate and tangible: a number of Jupiter's factories used
this status to win new clients and customers, some of whom, for example, are major firms in the international audio speaker industry.
To company executives, these changes meant they were joining the
ranks of elite Chinese companies and adopting the standards used
by leading Western firms. These developments heralded the rise of
rural enterprises as serious economic competitors on the Chinese
economic scene.

Still, the grand design adopted by firm leaders diverged markedly from previous operational practices. In the past, employees had
been jacks-of-all-trades, performing multiple tasks in completing a

---

*The International Organization of Standardization (ISO) headquartered in
Switzerland has set forth voluntary standards regarding production. ISO guidelines
are designed to promote greater efficiency in production as well as greater confidence among businesses.

product. As part of the expansion process, enterprise managers sought to increase specialization and coordination in their operations. Greater specialization would create a more efficient division of labor by breaking the work down into simpler chores and allowing workers to apply their skills for maximum effectiveness while minimizing their individual deficiencies; greater coordination of the enterprise's various activities would reduce redundancies and lock in higher efficiency. Thus, through the clearer delineation of work tasks and better control of enterprise activities, management hoped to increase productivity and improve profitability.

What distinguishes both enterprises at this stage from other firms is the scope of their ambitions. Leaders at both companies wanted and expected major improvements almost instantaneously. Whereas other companies introduced what Richard Edwards calls technical and bureaucratic control sequentially, Jupiter and Phoenix introduced them concurrently and expected a quantum leap in the scale and quality of production.[4]

The first part of this strategy called for major improvements in the physical work environment. As production demands intensified, Phoenix and Jupiter began to outgrow their cramped, poorly lit workshops and needed more spacious and better-equipped facilities. Both firms moved quickly to acquire additional land and construct new plants. Both also began outfitting these factories with new tools and machinery. Although such changes required large amounts of capital and posed enormous financial dangers, company leaders believed that such investments were worthwhile and would contribute to the enterprise's long-term development.

These new facilities were also valuable because they helped justify the imposition of centralized authority over their remaining workshops. By standardizing the work regimen, management hoped workers would devote less time to thinking about such issues as where materials were located and what job they should be performing and instead concentrate on producing more and better-quality goods. One of the most notable features of the new system was the designation of work spaces on the basis of specific tasks. This was a great departure from the previously disorganized and more chaotic setup of the workshops. Now, a supply room for product components, a quality control area for the testing of goods, a warehouse for finished products awaiting shipment, and a main area devoted solely to production were clearly delineated. Moreover, these workspaces designated specific locations not only for material goods but also for factory personnel as well. Workers and managers no longer labored side by side; rather, workers remained in the assembly room, and the managerial staff was sequestered in offices away from production areas. In real and symbolic terms, the categorization and physical separation of enterprise personnel embodied the growing social stratification of employees, a development that did not escape the attention of numerous enterprise members.*

Nowhere were changes more apparent and dramatic than in the main production room. As enterprise managers attempted to establish a new production system that would make better use of the workers' energies and talents, production assumed a more linear orientation, with neat rows of workstations or an assembly line dominating the workspace.[5] Where conveyor belts were introduced, workers performed only specific, repetitive tasks. Linked together, they became tenders of the *liushuixian*, or assembly line, and worked collectively to meet production quotas determined by management. "Fordist" methods of production had arrived in the Chinese countryside.

As carefully thought out as these plans were, realizing them remained a daunting task. The process of financing and constructing new production facilities was complicated and protracted, involving complex negotiations among factory representatives, government officials, and local peasants. Debates on the proper direction of local development never ceased and grew especially acute during my research stint in Wenzhou in 1997. Phoenix's proposed plans to build a massive industrial park containing its entire operations were defeated because peasants in a nearby village, despite pressure from

---

*The creation of separate administrative offices at Phoenix and Jupiter during this stage did not yet elicit the kind of jealousy or resentment among workers as it did in the factories in Guangdong studied in Ching Kwan Lee, *Gender and the South China Miracle*, 113. Most of the offices in my study were rather bare and did not give a sense of being "a world apart from the hot and humid shop floors." Only later, when office conditions were upgraded, did workers begin to harbor a sense of resentment.

local cadres, rejected the firm's financial package. Increasingly concerned that their long-term security was being sacrificed to the demands and growing influence of local industry, the villagers are said to have enlisted the intervention of provincial-level cadres to ensure the project's demise. However, their opposition forced Phoenix only to slow, but not to abandon, expansion of its facilities.*

In contrast, Jupiter was more successful in securing long-term land leases and establishing new plants because of its apparent willingness to make concessions and strike deals. For example, Jupiter often agreed to contracts stipulating not only that the enterprise pay annual royalties to the peasants who leased their parcels to the company but also that it reserve small patches of land near the plant entrances for peasants to grow subsistence crops, thereby providing local farmers with a safety net in the event factory revenues plummeted. When I asked plant management at Jupiter about this development, most of them sympathized with local farmers, even though they wished these plots could be moved to a less noticeable spot. Nonetheless, they believed these plots were a small price to pay to acquire the land. In fact, the plots served as a constant reminder of the economic struggles the local community had only recently overcome. Although this image of crops growing next to a factory gate is curious, it graphically illustrates the external constraints both firms faced even before they turned to rationalizing their production lines.

Often, both firms were either forced to settle for renting buildings nearby or tailoring existing ones to their growing needs. As a result, the new plants were located in different parts of the township, far from one another. Storage and transport of finished products became major logistical challenges, intensifying the need for smooth information flows and coordination among the various divisions at a time when the institutional structure was not able to fulfill such functions. The new locations also posed problems for workers, since many lived a considerable distance from the new facilities, and they struggled to arrive on time each day. The relocation of one of Phoe-

---

*Phoenix eventually prevailed and in 2003 began operating in the industrial park it had wanted earlier.

nix's factories, for instance, lengthened some workers' commute by as much as thirty minutes.

Moreover, the large expenditures on construction and renovation greatly strained the finances of both firms. Management at both enterprises soon discovered the costs of purchasing new production technology to be prohibitively high. Consequently, enterprise leaders were forced to delay the adoption of new technology and instead make smaller investments in their existing operations, such as the introduction of electric screwdrivers, which enhanced productivity enormously in comparison to regular screwdrivers. Improved lighting and ventilation also contributed, albeit indirectly, to better worker performance. Under these conditions, workers could assemble a product more efficiently yet expend less energy in doing so.

Cost constraints aside, company executives eventually realized the assembly line orientation was not universally applicable or effective. Because the majority of their products were based on technical designs from the 1970s, they were less, not more, amenable to assembly line manufacturing. At Phoenix, for instance, many of the transformers and relays the company produced contained small screws and bolts that made their insertion into compact spaces more difficult and time-consuming. Assembly line methods could, and often did, result in bottlenecks at critical stations on the line, leaving some workers idle while others struggled furiously to keep up. Technical specialists were extremely hard-pressed to adapt such designs to the demands of mass production and could offer only minor solutions that failed to satisfy enterprise leaders.

At Jupiter, the decision to introduce assembly line production techniques rested on similar considerations. Yet the problem for Jupiter's textile operations was that such methods were not appropriate for the specific conditions and demands of production. Only the first stages of garment production—the preparation, cutting, and bundling of cloth—stood to benefit (and only marginally) from the application of these techniques. The task of sewing various pieces into pants and sweatshirts rested with the individual worker operating the sewing machine and could not be broken down further. Hence, employees could work only as fast as their energy, skill, and experience allowed. It should not be surprising that in this case, management tailored work regulations to encourage increased output through individual performance-based incentives rather than teamwork.

Although financing and technical limitations severely inhibited the adoption of mass-production techniques, securing adequate supplies proved to be an even greater problem. In order to maximize gains from mass-assembly techniques, the multitude of components used in the final product must also meet standardized criteria. Problems surface when the supplied components are the wrong size or shape, for even a millimeter's difference in the size of a screw can bring the line to screeching halt. A technical chief at one of Phoenix's plants that assembles relays analyzed the situation in these terms:

Our product quality has been fairly consistent, but sometimes our subcontractors create problems [for us]. Sometimes they cut down on the copper content, or they reduce the thickness of some parts. This creates problems when the electricity is turned on. It changes the performance capabilities of the products, and it's because they "cut corners" (*tougong jianliao*) and think they can make a little more [money] this way. It's difficult for us to control this because we use lots of different parts. It would take too long to check all these parts, so we just spot-check them when [new shipments] come in. Sometimes we receive bad ones. . . . We can only complain and hope our subcontractors improve the quality of their output.[6]

For some subcontractors, variability in product quality was arguably unavoidable, for the technology employed in manufacturing the components was also outdated and unreliable. Given their precarious finances, it was nearly impossible for them to upgrade their capabilities without external assistance. If managers at Phoenix and Jupiter decided to use the supplied parts anyway, the costs and risks of doing so multiplied.

Under the direction of their superiors, production workers regularly adapted substandard parts for use in production. During my short stints working on the line, I saw just how much this decision slowed work. The extra work they were assigned typically added two to three hours to the workers' workday. One female assembler remarked, "When we tell management [about the parts], they say, 'Just slice off the extra plastic. There are too many parts like that, and we can't return them all.'"[7] Such policies not only led to a waste of time and money but, more important, affected the safeguards and quality of the products. However, managers often had no other recourse. Even when lower-ranking staff explained the costs and dangers of using substandard components to senior executives, they were overruled and ordered to continue with production. In such instances, the desire to maintain a competitive pricing advantage overtook the need to improve product quality, despite the potential damage to both firms in revenue and reputation if they maintained such practices. When I asked why management did not seem to feel a greater sense of urgency, one employee at Phoenix explained:

The major problem we encounter is that of pricing. We can't raise our prices or else we lose customers. . . . What happens then is that factories begin substituting inferior parts for better ones. This may save money, but it also goes against the original specifications. . . . If we normally have a filament that can handle 200 watts and we replace it with one that has a capacity for 180, the bulb will burn out before 200 watts is reached and we're blamed for having a shoddy product.[8]

As one might expect, the replacement costs and losses often turned out to be overwhelming. During my stay at Phoenix, I noticed that numerous employees at various levels were forced to devote a substantial amount of time and effort to dealing with irate customers and their complaints about low-quality products. Numerous staff members at Phoenix's central office, as well as factory personnel, were constantly engaged in answering customer demands for replacements and damages incurred because of poorly assembled transformers and panels. In fact, not one day went by during my stays in 1997 and 1998 without at least one staff member from the administration office being summoned to the customer service desk in Phoenix's main lobby to deal with a complaint. Although staff members never revealed the details of the final settlement terms, it was clear they included replacement of the faulty product, as well as compensation for damage to machinery and other property and unfortunately in some cases, injuries to personnel.

Despite the immense pressures of market competition, these technical problems have a critical social dimension to them as well. Specifically, kinship relations were intimately linked to the issue of substandard components because the suppliers were often relatives of key enterprise personnel seeking to profit from the company's success. A technical parts designer at one of Phoenix's newer factories highlighted the essential dynamic driving the relationship:

I know that much of their collective success is based on involving as many family members in the enterprise as possible. They may not all work at the same factory, but if they need a part for their product, they'll order from the wife's side of the family or from a cousin. Later on, they may part ways but only after they've made some money.[9]

For reasons of familial harmony, managers accepted these components, even though they knew product quality was and would continue to be poor. According to a factory-level quality control chief, managers will "approve a bad batch of products, ones that have not passed quality control, because they earn a share of the profit. They don't care if things work or not—they only want the money."[10] At least initially, most managers tried to ignore these problems and hoped they would eventually fade away as suppliers gradually upgraded the quality of their products. Unfortunately, this problem did not disappear, at least not as quickly as personnel at Jupiter and Phoenix would have liked. "How can the founder [of Phoenix] argue with the subcontractor," one plant official cracked, "that guy's his uncle. How do you tell an elder that his factory is turning out low-quality products?"

The problem was further exacerbated by the outright refusal of some relatives to cooperate. Even one of the senior members of Phoenix's Quality Control Department admitted this was not an easy problem to solve: "Kinship ties are generally something that must be overcome. It can be a problem because you can't order relatives to do things they don't want to do nor can you break relations with them entirely."[11] At Phoenix, for example, workers once discovered roughly 25 percent of a components shipment to be substandard. When these parts were returned to the subcontractor, they were not replaced or discarded. Instead, the owner instructed his workers to place one of the returned substandard parts in each new, outgoing bag of one hundred. If Phoenix still found problems with the "new" shipment, the supplier could at least claim that the ratio of defective parts had decreased dramatically, thus reducing the chances of Phoenix making a complaint and demanding replace-ments. More important, the relative would not incur a financial loss and harmonious social relations (or at least a façade of harmony) could be maintained in the short term. Still, enterprise executives remained troubled by the prevalence of shoddy components in their products, for they were ultimately responsible for defects and subject to potential lawsuits. In this sense, kinship ties deeply impaired and compromised production at Phoenix and Jupiter and exposed both firms to major financial and legal risks. Hence, even though these relationships initially served as the foundation of cooperation *within* the enterprise, they later created problems *between* companies that adversely affected Phoenix's and Jupiter's ability to improve their production capabilities. As economic interests and kinship became more tightly intertwined, implementation of a rationalized produc-tion strategy became ever more difficult.

Another factor hindering realization of the assembly line ap-proach in some plants was worker opposition. Workers sensed that the new production orientation ran counter to the norms of worker initiative and control to which they had grown accustomed. When the new production methods were implemented at a Phoenix con-trol switch plant, workers remained suspicious even as the manager extolled the possibility of higher wages and the benefits of being "re-sponsible for only a few tasks." Some workers saw this as a ploy to cut their wages and feared that they would have to work harder to make up for the deficiencies of their coworkers.[12] They were espe-cially worried about workers near the front of the line slowing down or holding up the rest of the group and delaying completion of the day's work and thus reducing their compensation. Despite some positive results when the experiment was first conducted, such fears persisted. The assembly line in this factory lasted only two months before the manager reverted to the old individual assembly orienta-tion. He lamented that "we just don't have a sense of teamwork or collective effort here." "They care only about themselves," he added, "there isn't any human feeling (*renqing*) anymore. Workers will do what you ask if it doesn't affect them financially. If it does, they be-come selfish and complain."[13] He was surprised and disappointed that workers did not embrace changes designed to ease their work-loads and improve their welfare.

Although I could sympathize with the manager, I could also un-derstand the workers' gripes because I once stopped an assembly line while working at Jupiter's audio speaker plant in 1998. My job was to glue small, donut-shaped magnets to other speaker components coming down the line and put them back on the conveyor belt so that others downstream could finish assembling the product. Al-though the pace was brisk, I managed to keep up, at least until I dripped hot adhesive on my hands and glued a magnet to myself. In between the howls of laughter (and my yelps of pain) and the efforts to clean me up and make sure I did not need to go to the hospital, the assembly line came to a complete standstill. Without me, the workers further down the line could do nothing. Although everyone was deeply concerned about me, they understandably did not want to extend an already lengthy workday. Not five minutes had gone by before they began clamoring for the line to start up again. A work-shop director quickly moved another worker into my place, and al-most instantly production resumed as if nothing had happened at all.

If we situate these responses against the work conditions that ex-isted during the survival phase, it becomes clear that what is moti-vating worker behavior is not solely economic self-interest but the persistence of what might be termed a "heroic storming" mentality. That system at least allowed workers to retain a significant measure of personal initiative and control over the work process. They could determine how and when work was to be completed; this decision-making power controlled both machines and managers rather than vice versa. The assembly line scheme, in contrast, restricted workers' decision-making authority and even physical mobility. Such con-straints increasingly led to the deterioration of the social bonds among workers, ties that especially during the survival stage were renewed through continual interaction in the workshop. In being positioned at a specific place on the assembly line, workers lost the ability to initiate work and had less opportunity to socialize with others. One result was that workers increasingly lost interest in their work. One young female worker who had worked at Phoenix for three years complained that her "work is boring. It's always the same stuff over and over. We can't talk. . . . We can't even turn around. That's why the time passes so slowly here."[14] In this context, worker recalcitrance does not simply underscore a desire for self-enrichment, as several managers argued; instead, it also highlights a preference for and commitment to personal initiative. Workers could exercise their own judgment and still contribute to the collective good.

Thus, for many of the factories at Phoenix and Jupiter, only some of the advantages of mass production could be instituted and enjoyed since managers were hampered in their attempts to fully implement the new strategy. Technical and social constraints allowed for only the partial and incremental adoption of mass-production techniques. This generated a diverse set of production practices that appeared chaotic and illogical on the surface but in reality grew out of myriad organizational concerns and challenges these firms faced each day.

Refashioning Authority Relations

For enterprise leaders, rationalizing production techniques was only one component in their overall plan. Improved control over production meant little to them unless it was also accompanied by greater control over the workforce. To achieve this end, they applied the same processes of specialization and coordination to the management of their employees. In other words, the pattern of authority relations at Phoenix and Jupiter emerging during the period of expansion was defined by greater specificity of roles and responsibilities and more formal rules regarding performance and behavior. Both organizations assumed stronger hierarchical overtones with more decision-making authority vested in a growing managerial class, a class also responsible for enforcing worker compliance with executive directives and company policies. These efforts culminated in the creation of a central management structure to oversee and direct the activities of the various factories. In the fullest expression of rationalization, the top echelons of management created specialized departments devoted exclusively to the coordination of enterprise activities.[15] In this sense, the previously loose conglomeration of individuals was quickly assuming the profile of a deliberately de-signed machine.*

Like the changes inaugurated in the production arena, the new authority structure represented a major departure from previous norms, especially in terms of management's perception of workers. During the survival phase, company founders were more tolerant of worker shortcomings, more patient in helping workers adjust to the demands of industrial work. Unfortunately, success bred less tolerant views. With a mass of job seekers waiting outside factory gates, man-agement became ever more selective and fussy. Now, instead of management adjusting to the talents and foibles of workers, workers were obligated to fulfill the terms that management set. Neither firm was satisfied with a mere willingness to labor: both wanted workers to commit themselves entirely to achieving the goals laid out by en-terprise executives.

This sentiment was strongly evident in the companies' changing recruitment policies. Decrying the "low cultural backgrounds" (*wen-hua beijing di*; i.e., lack of education) of their employees, both compa-nies raised the bar for entry into the factory. All workers were now re-quired to have more education. Shop floor workers, for example, were required to "have at least a middle school education [three years of secondary schooling in addition to six years of primary education]. Without that, it's really hard to train workers. They won't have the ability to adjust to new procedures."[16] Applicants with only an ele-mentary school background were no longer accepted. For nonproduc-tion posts, the educational requirements were even more stringent. Candidates were required to hold a vocational school (*dazhuan*) de-gree, if not a university (*daxue*) degree. Enterprise leaders believed that the more educated workers on the shop floor were, the more effi-cient and effective they would be. This would ease pressure on the managerial staff by reducing the time and energy they normally ex-pended in explaining rules and procedures to new employees.

———

*Richard Scott sees these features as the defining marks of what he calls "ra-tional systems." This conception sees the organization as mechanical and suscepti-ble to deliberate manipulation, precisely the view that management at both firms shared. For Scott's full discussion, see *Organizations*, chap. 2.

Still, fulfilling these initial requirements only exposed the new employee to management's next level of evaluation and control. This stage was marked by the new employee signing a short-term contract to work for the enterprise for two to three months under comparatively harsh terms. First, a deposit of 200 to 500 *yuan*, the equivalent of two to four weeks' wages paid as a lump-sum or through monthly installments, was required of all workers as proof of their commitment to staying and working hard for the company. The deposit would be returned to the worker after two or three months unless she decided to leave before the terms of the contract had been fulfilled. In addition, new workers were paid lower wages than established, full-time workers. The typical amount rarely exceeded 500 *yuan* per month and, in extreme cases, consisted only of subsistence pay, approximately 300 *yuan* per month or 10 *yuan* per day, to cover living expenses.[17] In comparison, most full-time production workers averaged approximately 700 *yuan* per month.

Once on the shop floor, the new apprentice learned the production routine from a more experienced worker or "master" (*shifu*), who also assisted factory management in assessing the candidate's potential and progress. During this time, each worker tried various tasks, hoping to find a suitable one. A worker regarded as promising would be offered a longer-term contract of a year or more; otherwise, the worker was unceremoniously released at the end of the trial period.

Interestingly, gender significantly influenced management's understanding of job suitability. In a Phoenix plant that produced large circuit breakers, for instance, one administrator explained that the employees were "mostly male because the size of the product means we need stronger workers to lift it. Less than 15 percent of the workers are female. They perform tasks such as wiring and securing the covers that do not require heavy lifting."[18] An administrator at Jupiter expressed similar sentiments: "Most of our workers are female and young—this has nothing to do with their being more obedient. Women are just more patient with this type of work [assembly]."[19] Given their dexterity, it is not surprising that in such plants women commonly made up over 60 percent of the workforce. This development was not simply a reflection of managerial preferences or assumptions about the desirability of female workers but also the result of placement tests that each job applicant took. Indeed, during these trials, the women repeatedly beat the men in both speed and efficiency of assembly and made it easy for managers to hire them.

As important as authority over entry into the factory was, the essence of managerial authority pivoted on control of the work process. The shift in work initiative that began with the introduction of new production techniques was completed under the watchful eyes of the managerial staff. The manager and his (sometimes her) coterie of assistants became the sole catalysts of work, deciding when work would begin and when it would end. They planned the day's schedule and determined the volume and pace of work on the basis of orders and inventories. One of the workshop directors at Phoenix described her responsibility in this way: "My main duty is to set the [daily] production target. I look at the number of orders the factory has received and past records and then assign the quota. So if I assign a quota of 3,000, I sign off on a form for the first worker on the line to pick up 3,000 parts from the supply manager. Then I notify others on the line too."[20] Despite a punishing regimen under which workers generally labored twelve–sixteen hours a day for twenty-two–twenty-four days a month, managers could also schedule overtime as they saw fit, bringing the total of work days at many Jupiter factories to twenty-eight days a month.*[21] In addition, factory management actively kept watch over the production process. Workshop directors in particular focused on preventing potential problems from stalling production. This critical role was underscored in the comments of another young female workshop director at Phoenix:

Each day I spend some time filling out a number of forms. We keep track of which parts were brought in, how many products were made, how many were taken from inventory, and how many were left over. I also must make sure that workers on the line have enough supplies. There are twelve workers per line, and if one of the first eight workers [the first eight assemble the product; the remaining four check quality and package the product] is short on materials, the whole line is affected.[22]

---

*This clearly violated the stipulations of the 1994 Labor Law but was a common occurrence in most rural factories.

Although authority was disproportionate to the size of the staff (staff rarely exceeded 10 percent of the total employees in a workshop),* it was clearly expressed in the power to force workers to meet pre-set levels of performance through the enforcement of formalized rules. Through the clever manipulation of incentives and sanctions, managers believed they could truly reshape their workers into more efficient and committed employees. No longer inspiring workers through the force of personal example, these onetime "heroic cadres" increasingly resembled ordinary supervisors. They now followed routines they had once disdained as overly restrictive.

As is typical of such systems, the rewards for acceptable performance were overwhelmingly defined in financial terms. The new schemes both firms utilized not only gave the worker greater responsibility for his earnings but more clearly distinguished outstanding workers from less productive ones. Piece rates (*jijian*), which compensated workers for each product completed, were preferred and instituted over timed wages (*jishi*) in the vast majority of plants at both firms. Piece rates usually varied according to the difficulty of product assembly but averaged ten *fen* (0.1 *yuan*) per piece. According to an assistant manager at Phoenix, such rates yielded a monthly income ranging "from a low of 500 to 600 *yuan* per month to over 1,000 *yuan* per month. With overtime, some workers can earn as much as 1,600 to 1,700 *yuan* per month."[23]

Ironically, one of the company officials instrumental in effecting this policy change at Phoenix also doubled as the chairman of the enterprise labor union. He repeatedly stressed that piece rates actually benefited workers. He explained that "most of the managerial staff received differentiated pay, but there was no way to give workers a chance to earn more. We didn't want to be like the state-owned enterprises where you receive the same pay whether you do a little or a lot of work. By introducing piece rates, workers now had

---

*Phoenix's 1:10 supervisor to worker ratio compares favorably with those of firms elsewhere. In the United States, the ratio in medium and large companies is typically 1:7. Under Vice President Al Gore's Reinventing Government Initiative during the 1990s, the federal government sought to cut the ratio to 1:15 in all of its departments. The goal was to cut the proportion of supervisors from over 14 percent to approximately 7 percent of total federal employees.

an opportunity to earn more based on their own ability and hard work."[24] Indeed, many workers tried to maximize their wages by working at a feverish pace and, on occasion, requesting higher quotas. Although they were well aware of possible physical and mental exhaustion, these young men and women were attracted to the possibility of high earnings. In some factories, the most productive workers received additional cash awards in recognition of their exceptional performance, further solidifying the enterprise's policy of rewarding the individual rather than the group.

However, other factories added a collective element to this individual-oriented approach. According to an administrator in Jupiter's building materials subdivision:

All employees are given additional incentives and pressure to improve performance. [Ours] is a reward and punishment system. Eighty percent of an employee's wages are fixed as part of their basic pay. The remaining 20 percent is set up as a floating bonus. If the year's profit target is met, everyone receives a bonus, even the regular workers. If only 80 percent of the target is reached, for example, then everyone receives 80 percent of the bonus. If the company made no profit or took a loss, no one receives a bonus.[25]

Although basic wages still differed among workers, Jupiter hoped to at least dampen individual rivalry among workers by making their bonuses dependent on mutual cooperation and teamwork. This approach also offered the additional benefit of easing pressures on individual workers to perform. By simply looking at gross financial figures, managers determined whether workers as a group should be given bonuses, thus providing some reward and cover for those employees who could not match the performance of the company's best employees. It was only after profit targets had been reached, however, that factory management would consider "sharing the wealth." Taken together, these two variations represent a clear break with traditional norms of collective responsibility. The emerging "managerial ideology" shifted the burden of welfare from the enterprise to the individual worker.[26] If workers were dissatisfied with their earnings, management believed workers had no one to blame but themselves.

Despite the appeal of financial incentives, leaders considered rewards alone to be insufficient in effecting lasting change. Without the threat of fines and sanctions, managers felt workers would still possess too much individual discretion and would never abandon bad habits. Many managers expressed exasperation with their employees, stating flatly that without the possibility of punishment, workers would end up turning out shoddy work and becoming unruly. Said one administrator in Jupiter's central offices: "Most of the workers are peasants, and they don't have strong educational backgrounds. Although many have worked here for some time, you must be tough on them or else they become spoiled. They'll slack off."*[27]

Efforts to prevent slacking off and self-indulgence were neatly contained in work regulations that laid out a sliding scale of fines for various infractions. Minor infractions such as not wearing identification badges, being sloppily dressed, or combing one's hair during work time usually resulted in fines of two to five *yuan*. More serious offenses, especially those involving work safety or product quality, drew heavier levies. For instance, regulations at one of Phoenix's transformer panel plants specifically held quality control inspectors responsible for product quality. "If anything goes wrong," one young inspector stated, "there is a tracking number as well as the inspector's name on the certification. There is absolutely no way [we] can avoid responsibility. If the product fails, the inspector is fined 100 *yuan*."[28]

At other plants, poor product quality drew collective punishment, with all members of the assembly line fined, forced to fix the defective items (without additional compensation), or both. At Jupiter's audio speaker plant, for example, a customer once returned a large shipment of defective speakers and demanded that the products be redone. All line workers and workshop directors were fined 50 *yuan* and forced to work overtime for two weeks to redo the products to the original and correct specifications. Even factory managers were held responsible for such deficiencies. One division administrator told me that it was common in such instances for the manager to be fined 200 *yuan*.[29]

---

*Managers thus wanted to eliminate any possibility of the "indulgency pattern," a state of affairs in which leniency dominated and workers retained the upper hand in determining when and how work was to be executed; see Gouldner, *Patterns of Industrial Bureaucracy*, chap. 2.

To make matters even worse, some managers posted the names of violators, their offense, and the amount of the fine on a blackboard. One vice-manager at Phoenix emphasized that the fine itself was not important. Through the public posting of violations, "everyone can see and learn from them. It's embarrassing to have your name on the blackboard for everyone to see; so workers will try to avoid another violation. A five *yuan* fine is not too heavy, but it will remind them to be careful."[30] The sting of "losing face" (*meiyou mianzi*) would thus ensure a level of compliance that fines alone could not. This policy was the direct opposite of the informal and less public reprimands managers handed out in the past.

Astonishingly, enterprise management was not satisfied with its control over workers in the factory and sought to shape and regulate workers' personal habits and lifestyles as well. In an analysis of managerial structures in American industry, Richard Edwards points out that through the effective use of sanctions workers were forced to exhibit the traits of the "good worker," qualities that did not have an immediate bearing on worker productivity.[31] This is precisely what managers in rural factories sought to accomplish. Punctuality, for example, was rewarded with a monthly bonus if the worker punched in on time every day of the month. One "tardy" during the month, however, disqualified the worker from receiving the bonus. In other cases, the employee was fined one *yuan* for each minute he was late.

Even more important to management were proper attitudes and clean living. Unbecoming conduct such as crass speech and vulgar behavior routinely resulted in fines of ten *yuan* and higher. At another firm in Wenzhou I call Sparta, efforts to transform the workforce literally took on the feel of boot camp:

When new recruits first arrive, everyone must undergo intensive military training during the first month. This sounds harsh but it is useful in many ways. Workers not only build up physical strength but also develop discipline and will power. *Even if they don't stay on [at Sparta], the training helps them become useful and productive citizens. Our company is interested in training people to be upright and useful in society, not just in our workshops.*[32] (Italics added)

Although enterprise leaders at Phoenix and Jupiter never went so far as to institute boot camps, they nevertheless shared the belief that virtue was the basis of solid work and good citizenship; it was a foundation they were determined to instill in their workforce. At Jupiter, for example, managers indirectly promoted "family values" by penalizing cohabitation among unwed employees with a 200-*yuan* fine. In their opinion, tolerating such unwholesome arrangements would lead only to even greater decadence and eventually the un-raveling of the company's moral and social fabric. To their dismay, growing labor instability indicated major disagreement with and op-position to this vision.

In spite of management's earnest attempts to make the new sys-tem work, the institutional structure did not yield the kind of lever-age and control leaders had envisioned. Rather, actual production and social considerations once again determined the effectiveness of the new *modus operandi*. In contrast to upper-level management, the factory-level managerial staff at both Jupiter and Phoenix remained ambivalent about the new strategy and never reached a consensus on the formal, rules-oriented approach. The influence of collective norms and values lingered in the workshops, and factory manage-ment styles consequently varied considerably, running the gamut from lax to stringent.*

In numerous plants, especially those where assembly line methods had yet to take a solid hold, managerial nonchalance regarding rules reflected a pragmatism and concern with potential social friction. Factory-level managerial staff wanted to maintain as much flexibility as possible in tackling production demands and avoiding social con-flict. Rules, it seemed to them, were an unnecessary constraint on such efforts. One vice-manager at a Phoenix plant charged that up-per management "just pass down regulations to us from above and don't know if they are helpful. They should come work here for a while before going back [to their offices], and then they'll know something about managing."[33]

Although work rules were not entirely ignored in even the most relaxed factories, they certainly were not the primary or even a

---

*What was supposed to be a tightly knit organizational system soon turned into a "loosely coupled" one, blunting the thrust of management's grand strategy; this idea was formulated in Weick, "Educational Organizations as Loosely Coupled Systems."

major concern. In most cases, the staff simply read the work rules to workers; very few plant managers issued handbooks to incoming employees or demanded that they become familiar with the contents as a condition of continued employment. In fact, they were quite content with simply presenting them orally and posting them whenever and wherever they found it convenient or, more commonly, whenever they remembered to do so. On one of my early visits to a smaller plant at Phoenix, an official from the central office emphasized the appeal of eliminating the handbooks:

We used to give workers a handbook but we stopped last year. What we do now is tell them orally. We give them a brief introduction to the guidelines when they arrive. If they make a mistake, we correct them and explain to them what the proper method is. The old method seems so rule oriented and impersonal: it lacked "human feeling" (*renqing*). We like this way of doing things better.[34]

Workers in these factories were also nonplussed when I asked about work regulations. "We're not fined here, and it's pretty loose," related one female assembler at Phoenix. "When I first came here, they didn't give us a handbook or explain the rules. . . . If we do something wrong, they just tell us not to do it again."[35] A young male quality control inspector at another Phoenix plant echoed similar views: "We don't have a lot of rules here. . . . They only want us to be clean and on time. We can't spit and must make sure our workspace is tidy."[36]

To factory-level managers, work rules often embodied unrealistic expectations or standards. On the issue of worker recruitment, a female workshop director made some telling points:

If new people want to work here, management will always say it wants people with at least a high school degree. But this kind of work is not really complicated. It just takes some time to get used to things . . . so you don't need a fancy education to do well, just some common sense. Anyway, we usually waive these requirements if you've been recommended by a friend or relative who works here. All you need then is to have finished middle school.[37]

Another male workshop director confided that his position was due entirely to "distant kinship ties with the [enterprise] chairman. My older brother is married to his younger sister." At the same time, he understood that he would "never move to a higher position. What can I do when all I've got is an elementary school education?"[38] To be sure, standards were necessary, but they also needed to be reasonable. Overly strict guidelines would cut off job opportunities for friends and relatives and even disqualify a large portion of current employees. The resulting social fallout would be too much for even the most united enterprise to bear. So long as production was not adversely affected, lower-level management saw no harm in accommodating social concerns as well.

The impact of social considerations was even more manifest when managers actually attempted to enforce rules. Managerial staff, many of whom had themselves been production workers, were extremely reluctant to fine workers. In fact, many staff members sympathized with the workers since many still remembered the demanding conditions under which they had labored. One workshop director expressed strong reservations about her duty to punish:

We hardly ever fine workers now. Although I have the authority to fine them, I usually don't dock their pay when pay day arrives. . . . I just don't feel good about fining them. I used to be an assembler myself, and I still remember how bad it felt to be fined. Everyone works hard for their pay, and I'm reluctant to take it away from them. I guess I'm just not ruthless enough.[39]

In contrast, the head of quality control at one of Phoenix's plants worried about the long-term impact of punishment on the worker. For him, "the real problem with discipline is deciding how much is enough. . . . Our goal should be to discipline and teach, not to destroy them [workers]. With a salary of only 800 *yuan* per month, a 15- to 30-*yuan* fine would really make them take notice."[40] Others were less philosophical and more concerned about their personal relationships with workers. Another workshop director emphasized to me that "I don't like to fine them because we're still friends after all. I see them often after work, and I feel awkward saying they violated such and such a rule. Most of the time I just tell them to be careful about the rules."[41] In these plants, management's fear of damaging personal relations with workers obstructed the full implementation and enforcement of a formal, rules-based orientation.

In plants where work rules were strictly enforced, the "factory regime," as Michael Burawoy calls it, appeared almost tyrannical in comparison.[42] With assembly line techniques in operation, managerial staff felt that only tough rules could prevent potential customer complaints. Despite worker protests to the contrary, managers remained steadfast and less affected by the social considerations that were central in the more relaxed factories. In these cases, the managerial ideology undergirding factory policies garnered much wider agreement and support. One of the toughest managers at Phoenix offered this justification:

Some people have criticized me for my strict approach to management. I impose stiff fines, and some people say I should also give out rewards for good work. But my rules should be seen in the same light as traffic rules. Do you reward each person individually for stopping when the light is red? How much would you give him? The reward comes on a broader level. When everyone follows rules, everyone arrives at their destinations quickly and easily. It's the same in the workshops.[43]

For him, the only way benefits could be reaped was to divorce production demands from social values whenever possible. Any time these concerns came into direct conflict, production unquestionably won out. He argued that social harmony was irrelevant if the enterprise went bankrupt.

In strict workshops, the managers constantly monitored all aspects of the operation, making sure workers were putting forth their best efforts at every moment. In the Phoenix plant overseen by the respondent just cited, an "enforcer" inspected each workshop twice a day, at approximately 10:00 in the morning and 3:00 in the afternoon, and fined workers for any infraction of the plant's rules. Other plants adopted variations on this theme of strict enforcement. Another plant at Phoenix created a chief of human resources who not only checked on workers at 10:00 and 3:00 but also inspected their work stations before they returned home. The plant vice-manager saw this final inspection as a necessity:

They [the workers] must clean up their work station when they leave. It used to be hard because they had no place to put tools and parts. But a short while ago we put in push carts at each station so they can better organize their materials. It just saves a lot of time because when workers come the next morning, they can start work right away. If there are any violations, they are marked by station and we can easily see who is at fault. That person's name and infraction will then be posted. The worker will know he must pay a fine, and so will everyone else.[44]

These Taylorist expectations spawned a great number of complaints. One young female supervisor in the supply department angrily protested:

The only thing I don't like here are the fines. They absolutely love to fine you for every little thing. If you even drop a piece of paper on the floor, you'll be fined five *yuan*. Everyone is fined at least once a month. I've already been fined a few times for dropping paper on the ground, and so has everyone else who works on this floor. The manager takes a small issue and makes a big deal out of it. He's only interested in hitting us with these petty fines. Sometimes they just fine people too much. We don't make a lot to begin with so if we're fined heavily, we can barely survive. A lot of workers will leave because they think the system is unfair.[45]

For workers, these fines represented not only an utter disregard for their financial welfare but, more important, an assault on their dignity. Public shaming in particular was a sore point, leading one shop director to conclude that "you have to give workers some 'face' [*mianzi*]. If they think they've been humiliated, they won't listen to you next time."[46] Workers indeed recognized the importance of complying with factory rules but rejected the social stigma factory management tried to attach to noncompliance. That the number of violations never decreased significantly indicated that workers cared little for the views of their superiors and even less about internalizing them.

Despite their dissatisfaction, workers rarely engaged in any overt or organized acts of resistance. In both enterprises, workers generally eschewed direct confrontation in favor of more subtle tactics. For instance, in factories where workers shared a stronger rapport with their superiors, workers aired their grievances directly with the manager in hopes of resolving their differences through the informal processes of dialogue and persuasion. Workers in stricter factories could not even consider this as a viable option. Instead, workers expressed their frustrations by using what James Scott vividly describes as "weapons of the weak."[47] In such cases, worker responses upended prevailing authority relationships in ways that reaffirmed the worker's dignity without threatening his employment. This was achieved through the use of social sanctions that could be inflicted either inside or outside the factory with little or no financial cost to the worker. Employees, for example, often gossiped about the managers and the supervisors, snubbed them, or excluded them from social activities. These tactics were often used to devastating effect, as evidenced by the response of this female workshop director at Phoenix:

When you correct female workers, they accept it, and you think everything is just fine. But then they begin to gossip behind your back and say how I'm unfair and other terrible things. . . . If I didn't do something right, they should tell me and I'll try to change, but if they say things behind my back, there's nothing I can do. . . . So I just make a few comments and leave it at that. It's not worth it because everyone just ends up angry. . . . What's the point anyway if I win? It's harder to get along with them later on.[48]

In other instances, workers spread vicious rumors, sometimes with sexual overtones, about their targets. For example, one female supervisor at a Phoenix plant was said to be intimate with a higher-ranking male manager and to have gained her promotion because of her "looseness" rather than her ability or hard work. At other times, rumors and personal putdowns were used to irritate and snub managers who had violated informal norms and made work especially difficult for workers. At a different Phoenix plant where electrical switches were produced, I saw how a group of female assemblers harassed a male supervisor each time he conducted an inspection. One worker would begin by asking, "What's the matter with you today? The inspection is taking too much time!" Another would then join in with "He's probably tired. I bet it's because he was up all night having sex!" At this point, the entire group would break out in uproarious laughter, much to the embarrassment of the supervisor, who then stormed out of the room.

When I asked them why they engaged in what seemed to me a risky venture, they were rather nonchalant. They declared that it was all in good fun and, more important, that these periodic putdowns prevented the supervisors from becoming overbearing and smug. Furthermore, they seemed totally unconcerned that this might affect their job situation because they could hide behind a screen of relative anonymity. If they encountered any problems, they simply blamed someone else for telling them the supervisor was engaged in such activity and deflected any accusation that they intended to malign his character. In short, they were merely repeating what *someone else* had said. What is perhaps most interesting about this example is that the workers involved seemed to understand how far they could go without triggering a serious backlash.

At other times, workers disrupted the flow of work by turning work rules against managers. Workers commonly refused to assemble products unless all the components met the enterprise's standards for quality. Others stuck carefully to their "job descriptions" and would not help with other tasks when deadlines were pressing or the factory was understaffed. Under established work rules, they were not obligated to perform such assignments nor could they be fined for refusing. It was an important reminder that workers would not sit by passively and acquiesce to management's every demand.

Over time, however, these strategies did little to ameliorate the enormous physical and mental strain workers experienced. Feeling that management was unfairly squeezing them at every turn, workers developed a deep sense of deprivation and resentment. Increasingly, enterprise members, especially younger employees, grew bitter about their tenure at these rural companies. Workers were "beginning to feel that their time here is a waste. Some people say they wasted the best years of their lives working in the factory."[49] Perceiving few benefits in staying at the job, workers exercised the only option that remained—quitting. According to a member of Phoenix's Human Resources Department, annual turnover rates usually hovered around 20 percent for production workers.*[50] However, in some factories the turnover rate regularly exceeded 30 percent. A key difference during this stage as compared to the earlier stage of survival is that exit was almost always permanent: few workers ever sought employment again with either enterprise once they left. Even area natives who could have returned at a future date chose to pursue other options

---

*The 20 percent turnover rate was nearly double previous rates and represented a major loss in the sense that managers were constantly seeking new replacement workers and familiarizing them with enterprise procedures and practices.

rather than go back. The bonds that had once linked relatives and friends together in harmony had deteriorated to previously unimaginable lows.

The Fragmented Enterprise

Thus far I have analyzed the challenges and consequences of instituting a new production orientation and a new system of centralized authority at Jupiter and Phoenix. As enterprise leaders moved to implement their strategies, they unwittingly undermined labor stability within the workplace by contradicting the principles on which their companies were originally founded. Rationalized production routines destroyed the impulse for "heroic storming"; strict managerial control over the workforce gutted informal cooperation and collective well-being as the operational norms of work. Although these fissures were initially caused by social tensions within both companies, pressures from the outside widened them still more.

The logic of expansion allowed, even called for, the influx of unprecedented numbers of outsiders (*waidiren*), nonlocals distinctly different in personal background, experience, and understanding of work. Just as New York in the nineteenth century and Shanghai in the early twentieth were transformed by wave after wave of new immigrants, so, too, were Wenzhou and Jinhua. During expansion, two distinct waves of migrants altered the social and political terrain at Phoenix and Jupiter. The first wave consisted predominantly of better-educated, highly skilled, and generally middle-aged personnel; the second wave, mostly of less educated, less skilled, and generally younger workers. Although the increasing diversity of the workforce strengthened production capabilities, it also accelerated the fragmentation of the enterprise community by altering status distinctions and frames of identity within the enterprise. Consequently, it raised new questions about how cohesion and a sense of common purpose could be maintained.

The first wave began as a response to glaring skill deficiencies in both enterprises. Expansion called for people who could immediately assume critical positions and tackle the technical and organizational challenges that baffled current employees. The search for such personnel initially induced managers to do exactly what they had done during the previous stage of survival: turn to their networks of kin and close acquaintances for help. This time, however, their personal networks could not provide the type or number of people desired by both Phoenix and Jupiter, for expansion demanded more advanced technical skills, not just an ability for imitation. Such needs spurred enterprise leaders to reach the momentous decision to seek assistance from sources *outside* their networks.

This was not an easy decision by any measure, but the timing could not have been more propitious. National reform policies, especially regarding state-owned enterprises (SOEs), created new conditions from which rural enterprises ultimately benefited. As the Chinese government sought to make these firms more competitive, many highly skilled employees in numerous SOEs, including engineers, were laid off or forced into early retirement throughout the 1980s. Still in their early forties and fifties, these former state employees possessed the skills rural enterprises coveted and were open to the possibility of working a few more years in the now-flourishing countryside. In addition, Jupiter and Phoenix enjoyed an advantage over other areas: their close proximity to advanced industrial areas like Shanghai and Jiangsu's Su'nan region, where state and collective enterprises were numerous, gave them relatively easy access to potential recruits whom they could woo intensively. For the potential employee, the prospect of a job not that far from his current home was appealing. It appeared to be a win-win situation for all.

Nevertheless, Jupiter and Phoenix still needed to convince job candidates to sign on, and they did so through attractive contract offers. Typical packages included a monthly base salary of nearly 1,000 *yuan* in addition to fringe benefits that other enterprise members did not enjoy, including subsidies for food, housing, medical care, and travel expenses, especially those incurred during *chunjie* (the Lunar New Year) when travel costs were high. More important, these personnel qualified for year-end bonuses that could add thousands, even tens of thousands, of *yuan* to their annual earnings. In some ways, these efforts paralleled the pursuit of free agents in professional sports: both firms engaged in major bidding wars and often included special options other firms could not match. One case at Jupiter dramatically illustrates this turn. A respondent recounted to me the shock he felt over some of the terms of his initial employment offer. During a dinner with Jupiter representatives, a senior executive pressed him:

If it's not about money, then what is it? Is it your family? If you're worried about them, I can assure you that we'll take care of them. By the way, do you find local women attractive? Do you have a son? If not, you can always try to have one here. We can set you up so that you can have a family in two places, and no one will know.[51]

Although he accepted the job, the respondent politely declined the offer of a mistress. Clearly, the terms strayed beyond those of more conventional offers, veering into a shady area of immorality and even criminality. Although such offers are no longer openly made to prospective employees, they symbolized the desperation and even recklessness of enterprise management.

This approach to personnel recruitment in general and these of-fers in particular proved to be highly problematic for several reasons. The first problem was one of authentication. Simply put, company executives found it exceedingly difficult to distinguish a con artist from the "real deal." Some candidates presented phenomenal cre-dentials on paper but were considerably less impressive in person. At Phoenix, for example, company executives hired a management consultant to facilitate the implementation of their new strategy only to find that he was a fraud. Not only had the company wasted a "signing bonus" on him, but they were even forced to buy out his contract and pay him to leave town. Initially, they were so afraid of offending this supposed expert that they even ignored obvious signs of incompetence. Although this is an extreme case, it shows that the single-minded pursuit of expansion objectives could sometimes cloud the judgment of company leaders. Their growing distance from other members of their own networks isolated them from the diverse perspectives and collective wisdom that might have saved them from these costly mistakes. Second, and perhaps more signifi-cant, these aggressive recruitment efforts widened the chasm be-tween the privileged and the rank and file and underscored to many locals (*bendiren*) their declining status in the enterprise. As employ-ees perceived a major disconnect between their work and their re-muneration and rank, more and more of them lost heart and began viewing their positions as they would any other job—as solely a means of putting food on the table.

Although these compensation packages precipitated intense jealousies and social friction, even more dissension arose when outsiders actually arrived at the company. Their presence directly upset the established company hierarchy by simultaneously displacing locals from technical positions and carving out a new occupational niche for outsiders.[52] Outsider dominance in these areas soon became overwhelming. At Phoenix, for instance, outsiders filled nearly 70 percent of all technical and design positions.[53] At Jupiter's newer plants, where advanced machinery was in use, the number of outsiders in technically skilled positions rose to similar proportions. By taking high-ranking positions once entirely staffed by locals, outsiders had now become serious competitors and threats to the interests and positions of locals.

Despite the general observation expressed by one Jupiter administrator that "whether we like it or not, we need outsiders because they have skills we don't have,"[54] locals were slow to accept outsiders as equal members of the enterprise. Initially, locals questioned the wisdom of hiring people who possessed more "book knowledge" than everyday practical experience. They challenged the very definition of skill that management used in selecting and hiring new staff members. When these attacks failed to change company policy, locals questioned the outsiders' commitment to the firm. Outsiders, they insinuated, had not gone through the crucible of enterprise survival and would never demonstrate the kind or level of commitment and dedication to the firm that locals displayed. In their eyes, outsiders were taking advantage of a grand opportunity, receiving much more in compensation than they offered in skills or knowledge. The outsiders, on the other hand, were perplexed by this response. They saw themselves as professionals, fully devoted to completing the tasks assigned them. They believed they were highly sophisticated and above the clannish and provincial sensibilities that seemed to drive the behavior of locals.

To a large degree, these views were reinforced by deeply ingrained stereotypes of specific regions and peoples across China. Regional stereotyping is hardly a new phenomenon, but it is important here because, for the first time at Phoenix and Jupiter, native-place origin became a salient albeit divisive marker within the enterprise community.[55] During the survival era, advanced skills were tightly intertwined with local identity: locals were able to handle all technical issues on their own. Now, under expansion, advanced skills were increasingly identified with people who were not area natives. They were not only an unfamiliar presence but, what is more significant, an alien and threatening menace. In tandem with legacies of isolation and self-reliance, these suspicions created enormous barriers to interaction and cooperation between locals and outsiders.

Most company meetings, for example, were conducted in local dialect, not the *putonghua* (Mandarin) that most Chinese understand. The outsiders, according to a senior level advisor at Phoenix (himself an outsider), were those "with looks of incomprehension on their faces. . . . We all just sat silently and waited for them to speak *putonghua* again."[56] Although many locals, especially those in their fifties and sixties, spoke little if any Mandarin and could not communicate without lapsing into dialect, the larger problem was that those who *could* speak Mandarin would almost instantly switch to dialect whenever an important decision was to be made. This sense of secrecy reinforced perceptions among outsiders that locals were trying to set themselves off as "charismatic groups that see themselves as differing from others in character, not simply role" and created an environment that was increasingly neotraditional.[57] All critical decisions thus remained under the purview of locals; outsiders as a rule were excluded from this process.

Even worse than being ignored in meetings was being overruled on issues of production. Nonlocal technical staff felt continually frustrated by the refusal of local managers to heed their recommendations on product quality. One nonlocal working in Phoenix's quality control office was depressed about his situation: "When I gave managers some recommendations for improving products, they told me to mind my own business. After that I became indifferent. I was trying to help them, but they wouldn't let me do anything."[58] Despite the outsiders' proven expertise in technical matters, ultimate authority still rested in the hands of locals. In fact, locals dominated all positions from factory manager to division head to enterprise president (with two exceptions at Phoenix and none at Jupiter). Outsiders resigned themselves to making recommendations and hoping rather than expecting them to be enacted. The problem with this behavior, of course, was that it defeated the purpose of hiring outsiders in the first place. By failing to interact with the outsiders whom they had worked so hard to recruit, neither company could take advantage of the expertise or wisdom of these people. Instead of broadening their horizons, they were narrowing them; rather than becoming more flexible, they were becoming more rigid. In so doing, they rejected the openness and frankness that had distinguished them from rival firms and, consequently, alienated many of the people they initially welcomed into their companies.

The second wave of migrants spread these antagonisms from administrative offices and conference rooms to every corner of the enterprise, especially the production workshops. Compared with the first wave of outsiders, these nonlocals possessed no special skills or knowledge, were generally less cosmopolitan, and came from extremely impoverished areas such as Jiangxi, Anhui, Hunan, and Sichuan provinces.[59] What they offered was raw, physical labor, a resource increasingly in short supply at both firms. These laborers held the same status that Irish immigrants did when they first migrated to Lowell, Massachusetts, New York City, and Jersey City in the 1800s, and they evoked a similar nativist response.[60] They could fill niches only on the lower rungs of the occupational ladder and, consequently, enjoyed few benefits or privileges within the enterprise.[61]

Despite their modest profiles, these nonlocal laborers managed to divide the enterprise further. Many factory managers, for example, appreciated their willingness to work long hours and take on dangerous tasks. One Phoenix factory manager expressed these views in the following manner:

Eighty percent [of the 140 workers] are *waidiren*. To be honest, this factory would not be what it is without them. They do most of the dirtier and more dangerous work. Locals won't do that anymore because they can now leave that work to outsiders. It's not uncommon for outsiders to lose fingers or get hurt in some other way while operating the machines.[62]

Although this manager was himself a local, he found the outsiders employed at his plant to be more reliable and more cooperative than locals. He suggested that locals were spoiled by their own success and no longer willing to expend the effort necessary to sustain the factories they so painstakingly built. Some managers liked outsiders so much they even made use of outsider networks to recruit additional workers for their plants. In their factories, outsiders commonly constituted 50 percent or more of all production workers. These rather enlightened attitudes were exceptions to the rule, however; most managers clung to prevailing stereotypes, concluding that outsiders, especially those from the most poverty-stricken areas like Jiangxi, were no more than thieves and thugs and thus unwelcome in their community.[63] In these plants, locals typically outnumbered outsiders by a ratio of two to one. These conflicting sentiments signaled a new confusion in managerial ranks regarding the treatment of locals and sharpened already hard-edged contradictions within the workplace.

These splits were also mirrored in the dynamics among production workers. Although local workers were not threatened in the same way that locals in technical positions were, they nevertheless felt outsiders pressured them to work harder than they wanted. Many locals simply concluded that "outsiders are different from us. They'll do anything to make extra money. We work hard too, but they're always looking for more work. I bet they wouldn't sleep if they had the chance to work twenty-four hours a day."[64] At Jupiter, the contempt locals felt took on more personal overtones: "Outsiders have different habits than we do. . . . Most outsiders are dirtier. They won't pick up any garbage even if it's in front of their rooms. A local would remove that trash."[65] Interestingly, this was the same conclusion local managers had drawn of local workers in the not too distant past. Locals conveniently forgot this fact once outsiders became targets of their scorn. Outsiders were not afraid to respond and often retorted that "locals don't care about the quality of their work or whether they stay employed."[66] These exchanges rarely developed into more serious confrontations, but they remained sore points in relations between locals and outsiders.

Together, these waves of outsiders left an enduring imprint on both enterprises. Although locals initially unleashed a torrent of complaints and resentment against outsiders, seeing them occupy the most exalted and the lowliest positions in the company raised new concerns. Locals eventually came to question whether it was the outsiders or the enterprise leaders who were most responsible for the inequities of their situation. After all, outsiders were only responding to opportunities that local management had created. Locals began to wonder if native-place solidarity meant anything to company executives and whether perhaps they had more in common with outsiders working alongside them than they first imagined. Slowly, as their tenure at the enterprises lengthened, the outsiders reached similar conclusions. These sentiments were, however, still relatively undeveloped and only bewildered members, leaving them wondering how the enterprise had reached such a strange state. Although they undoubtedly disliked the predicament they were in, they were at a loss as to how to escape it.

Concluding Remarks

The process of expansion proved to be a sobering experience for both firms. Despite a number of constraints that hampered the full implementation of the new systems, Phoenix and Jupiter still managed to achieve significant growth. By the end of this stage, Phoenix had established a total of forty-three plants, and Jupiter had over a hundred. In comparison to many of their rural competitors, they appeared far more advanced and stable. Still, even the best-intentioned plans foster unintended consequences.

As this stage of expansion progressed, disturbing trends emerged within the enterprise. Most notably, a swelling undercurrent of discontent surfaced as enterprise members increasingly opposed management's new demands and conditions of work. Enterprise leaders initially failed to understand this evolving state of affairs, but some developments were startlingly clear: the strategy behind expansion operated on a logic that was almost completely contrary to the norms of social trust, mutual reciprocity, and collective well-being that were an integral part of the firm's early struggles to survive. In addition, the arrival of outsiders to fill slots previously occupied by locals confused and outraged a large portion of the enterprise community. This was seen as the ultimate betrayal and led to an eroded sense of purpose and community.

The rancor and dissension within the enterprise reached a point that could no longer be ignored. As driven as company executives were by their organizational vision, they were nevertheless aware and chastened by the social chaos their policies had unleashed. Leaders at both firms realized that without social stability in the enterprise community, the process of enterprise building would be pointless. There would be no one to work in the factories, and no one with whom to share the profits they had so painstakingly worked for. The enterprise had reached a state of major internal crisis, and it was clear to management what they had to do next. Company leaders felt compelled to rebuild the social bonds that were the bedrock of their strength and reintegrate marginalized members back into the community. How Phoenix and Jupiter went about this new mission is the subject of the next chapter.

FIVE

Enterprise Reintegration
Reconsidering Growth
and Community

We must try to take care of the needs of our workers, not all their needs, but enough so that they feel they are valued here. It helps lower their stress levels, and it's something we care deeply about.

—Respondent #102, personal interview, June 16, 1998

THE TENOR AND INTENSITY of the conflicts that afflicted Jupiter and Phoenix shocked leaders at both firms. Taking the trust and reciprocity that emerged during the survival era for granted, enterprise management assumed that the new, performance-based financial incentives would improve output and efficiency without undermining workplace stability. To their surprise, employee discontent with this new regimen produced disruptive behavior, even flight from the enterprise, and reminded leaders that profitability and organizational stability remained tenuous unless both the material and the social concerns of the rank and file were acknowledged and satisfied. Enterprise management realized that it faced a major quandary. On one hand, the desire for increased efficiency dictated that they preserve and even deepen the gains made through rationalization, especially those derived from the contributions of skilled outsiders. On the other hand, greater cooperation and more peaceful labor relations could not be guaranteed without eliminating disputes and turmoil among employees. The goal of reconciling these seemingly unbridgeable rifts changed the logic of organizational dynamics and moved both firms beyond the stage of expansion and into a new phase of enterprise reintegration. The core task of reintegration is to *simultaneously* consolidate improvements in production capabilities made during the expansion stage and restore the tight-knit, trust-filled relationships of the survival era. In short, both companies want to attain what appears to be a contradiction in terms: they are seeking to fuse a bureaucratic organizational structure with a regenerated, collectively oriented, and egalitarian ethos. To date, Phoenix and Jupiter have achieved moderate success in this endeavor but continue to search for new ways of enhancing social harmony and cooperation within the enterprise.

This chapter analyzes the major shifts in policy that began at both firms from the mid- to late 1990s through 2004. For this current stage, I explain how the challenge of rebuilding the enterprise community remains complicated and demanding because of strong market pressures and continuing internal dissension. Outside the enterprise, new rivals are seeking to displace Jupiter and Phoenix, largely through lower pricing, a strategy that both firms once used so effectively themselves; inside the enterprise, the unending stream of work orders, the swelling ranks of new personnel, and a fortified bureaucracy are generating greater jealousy and resentment. These developments have prompted enterprise leaders to restructure their organizations in order to balance contradictions within the workplace.

In tackling these challenges, Phoenix and Jupiter have moved to reshape their authority structures and reduce the wide formal status distinctions that appeared during expansion. However, despite the best intentions of senior executives, the antagonisms and conflicts that were especially acute during expansion have not been fully resolved by the new system but only masked by it. Although leaders have tried to return to a less rule-bound managerial approach by devolving decision-making power to lower levels of management and concentrating more on overall direction and strategy, the status and authority of company bureaucrats continue to be a source of frustration and friction. To defuse these and other tensions, enterprise leaders have created an "enterprise family" orientation based on fictive kinship. Through a surprising partnership with the Chinese Communist Party and other party-affiliated groups, company executives are organizing and coordinating efforts that attempt to blur and submerge distinctions of official rank, kinship, and native place under this broader company identity.

In addition, management now provides more collective benefits to employees to reinforce the impression that membership in their "family" offers privileges unavailable elsewhere. This development is particularly striking not simply because it demonstrates the leadership's willingness to use "slack resources" to enhance institutional stability, but because it highlights the continuing appeal of practices more commonly associated with *danwei* socialism.* This program also works at a symbolic level—activities such as speech and singing contests and sporting events are designed to reinforce the notion that the enterprise is the critical, new locus of identity and interaction where the perspectives and behavior of enterprise members can and will be reshaped.† These new policies are intended to serve as the foundation for enterprise development at Jupiter and Phoenix for the foreseeable future. However, their implementation is one of the most formidable tasks enterprise leaders have confronted so far. They must persuade all members of the enterprise family that their new gestures are serious commitments rather than symbolic rituals. This is the most critical test for what has so far been one of the most successful experiments in local-level development in the Chinese countryside.

---

*"*Danwei* socialism" refers to the system established under Mao where a "hierarchy of state-owned [urban] workplace units" offered its employees "secure jobs, affordable housing, inexpensive medical care" and other benefits as part of a larger effort to foster and maintain the workers' political allegiance; see Lü and Perry, *Danwei*, 3.

†What Lynn Hunt (*Politics, Culture, and Class*, 72) noted about new revolutionary practices in the French Revolution is equally applicable here: "These ordinary activities became invested with extraordinary significance."

Flexible Management: A Better
Path to Organizational Stability?

In many ways, the rules-oriented, hierarchical pattern of authority that characterized the expansion stage served both enterprises well. In the production arena, standardized work procedures improved the organization and management of the workshops, leading to increased output, improved efficiency, and, in some cases, higher wages. Yet this rationalized orientation also had a darker side: the imposition of rules often eroded worker initiative and control over the work process while increasing the obligations imposed on workers. The result was resentment and a sense of alienation among the workforce.[1] Company executives realized that to resolve these problems, they would have to relax their control over some enterprise activities and entrust lower-level management with greater authority over factory-level affairs.

Enterprise leaders thus began to envision and implement a more decentralized, flatter authority pyramid that would be more responsive to the particular circumstances and challenges of the shop floor. Whereas Jupiter's central offices had previously attempted to monitor all aspects of factory activity, they now focus on researching and developing new product lines, finding new investment opportunities, and laying out the company's long-term strategy. As a result, day-to-day management of production is once again left almost entirely in the hands of plant-level managers. According to a senior official at Jupiter, under the changes that began in the early 1990s:

We set the overall direction of the enterprise, and we respond to changes in the market and make adjustments to stay competitive, . . . but we are also flexible. Each of our subsidiaries has its own management system. This should not be surprising because all the products are different: there are different technical and capital requirements, productivity rates, and levels of efficiency.[2]

This restructuring has allowed Jupiter's central offices to focus on critical tasks that plant-level management has neither the resources nor the time to execute. For example, Jupiter has created a special department devoted to providing essential information about product specifications and government regulations to smaller firms in its area. By establishing closer links with these producers, not only is Jupiter trying to create a network of reliable subcontractors to provide it with quality components, but, in so doing, it is helping to diffuse important knowledge and skills not readily available through local vocational programs. Enterprise leaders hope that such outreach programs will eventually spread prosperity throughout the local community.[3]

Phoenix's initial restructuring efforts followed a similar, if not steeper trajectory. Started in 1997, these policies were finalized by 2000, creating a system of ten *gufen gongsi* (shareholding companies) under the control of the *jituan* (conglomerate offices).[4] Like Jupiter, Phoenix's central offices now perform only what company leaders consider to be the most essential functions: sales, investment, finance, and technical development.[5] This reorganization eliminated several departments and over four hundred employees or nearly 40 percent of central office personnel between September 1997 and May 1998. However, this initial effort was diluted and then reversed by surging growth. Since the cuts were made, new departments have sprung up to oversee the needs of a workforce that in 2004 exceeded 13,000 people, a nearly fivefold increase in the total number of personnel since 1998. As a result, the ratio of managerial staff to shop floor workers has not changed appreciably. Company records show a total of 1,220 employees in management positions in 2003, for example, or approximately 11 percent of all employees, an outcome that slightly exceeds the company's goal of limiting staff to 10 percent of the total workforce.

Still, this growth in management personnel has not undercut other aspects of the two firms' restructuring drives, such as decentralization. At both Phoenix and Jupiter, decentralization is formally defined by the contract (*hetong*) the central office signs with each of the divisions and plants within the enterprise. At the beginning of each fiscal year, the parameters of the relationship are laid out in substantial detail. Although the central office is usually in charge of drafting the initial document, lower-level management, especially plant managers, are encouraged to "write out a list of goals and a plan of action regarding their fulfillment."[6] The contract typically specifies production and profit targets as well as the division of revenues.

Each factory can either pay a set amount to the central office or a percentage of its total income: how much additional revenue each factory is allowed to retain simply depends on its performance. If profits meet or exceed pre-set targets, plant management, and even workers, earn bonuses; if not, their discretionary funds for the following fiscal year are reduced. In a way, these contracts represent an unusual blend of bureaucratic control and initiative. Although the retreat from the leadership's previous drive toward standardization and domination of work processes is notable, it is nevertheless only a partial one at best. Plant managers do indeed enjoy greater decision-making power, but there is no mistaking that their somewhat beefed-up authority has only been granted in hopes of realizing broader organizational priorities.

Despite these constraints, however, most factory managers at both firms have launched earnest attempts to improve productivity and restore solidarity within their workshops. Following the lead of their superiors in the central offices, plant managers have minimized staff numbers to contain overhead and bureaucratic red tape. In some of Phoenix's plants, these efforts have resulted in the reduction of managerial staff from 10 percent of the workforce to 5–6 percent. In addition, in 1998 the differences in official salaries between the highest and lowest paid employees in the factory were not, in principle, to exceed a 3 : 1 ratio. In many plants, workshop directors and those of similar rank earned on average 200 *yuan* more than workers (900 *yuan*), and higher-level staff including the factory manager earned a few hundred more than their subordinates, reducing the ratio further to roughly 2 : 1. Why company leaders chose these particular weightings is unclear, but the parallels with wage scales in state-owned enterprises are remarkable. What is clear, however, is the desire to recreate a sense of rough egalitarianism without entirely jettisoning the material incentives and managerial structure vital to the company's earlier success.

Still, in spite of these efforts to reduce the compensation gap, neither company has retreated from continued rationalization of production. In fact, enterprise leaders were more committed than ever to refining the assembly line orientation and dominating their respective sectors through the development of a "more complete product line and a massive increase in the scale of production."[7] Phoenix achieved this end by simply sticking to the manufacture of low-voltage electrical products and staying away from high-risk ventures such as real estate development, where the allure of spectacular and immediate returns proved irresistible to many other enterprises, to their misfortune. In fact, several former and current Phoenix employees told me that a few rival companies in the area nearly went bankrupt because of their inability to pass up "get rich quick" development schemes in Wenzhou and even outside Zhejiang province, most of which eventually soured. The opportunity costs were apparent only in hindsight: the capital they could have otherwise invested in expanding their own operations was lost, forcing some firms to lay off workers or, worse, close their doors altogether.

At Phoenix, this commitment to rationalization led to such developments as the adoption of sophisticated semiautomated machines to replace humans in the performance of such tasks as wire-coiling. Although the imported machines were extremely expensive (they were often top-of-the-line Italian imports), managers state that they are faster and more consistent and free workers for other jobs on the line. Similar logic has been applied to inventory control. During my 2004 visit to Phoenix, I was stunned to see a completely automated system in one of the warehouses: a robot would retrieve a selected item from among hundreds of products after a human operator entered a request into a computer. Evidently, foreign business people expressed similar reactions about Phoenix's operations, according to a top executive:

When representatives from foreign companies visit, they are astounded by our production setup. They never imagined that our facilities would be so clean and advanced. In fact, our chairman visited some [competitors'] factories in Europe, and our operations were superior to theirs. Because of our reputation, foreign competitors are now seeking us out for joint production projects. We're now working with GE and European companies as well.[8]

Increased automation not only improved production output and efficiency but, more important, burnished Phoenix's image as a leading enterprise in its sector. Its growing reputation as a leading manufacturer had led to queries from more established, foreign companies about cooperative ventures, a development that Phoenix's leaders delighted in but had not expected. In workshops where product assembly is not automated but still largely completed by one individual, each workstation has been expanded and reorganized with all necessary parts neatly stashed in small bins in front of the worker. As the worker puts together the product, she simply goes down her line of bins for the needed components, simulating an assembly line in miniature. Although this setup heightens output, it does so by stripping away the worker's ability to arrange her workspace and replacing it with management's vision of efficient production.

This vision is reinforced by formal work requirements and informal expectations that carry over from the previous stage of expansion. Most, if not all, of the plants have retained the system of fines that workers detested; however, management has become more restrained in meting out punishments, preferring to issue fines only as a last resort. As an assistant manager confided:

Yes, we still have fines, but we try not to use them too much. We encourage workers to be more aware of what they are doing (*zijue*) so that they can avoid repeating the same mistakes. But when we do fine someone, we explain to them very clearly why they are being fined. At that point, they have nothing to say and accept it. For example, if components have been dropped around the workstation or the area is sloppy, we fine them 10 *yuan*. For quality problems, we fine 30–50 *yuan*. Whenever a fine is handed out, I have a meeting with the worker in my office. I let him explain the situation, and then I explain our rationale. There is a lot more communication than in the past, when managers punished workers and just walked away. No wonder workers were furious. We are now more like Western companies in this regard. And here we try to operate with *renqing* [human feeling]. We usually give workers a number of chances. The first violation results in a verbal warning, the second violation is recorded in their dossier, and it's not until the third time that we fine them. As a result, no more than ten workers are fined per month.[9]

This quote underscores management's desire not only to communicate its goals to workers more effectively but, more important, to give them a chance to improve their performance. It is a recognition that although standards must be maintained, the desired results cannot be achieved without patience and the clear articulation of goals and procedures. At the same time, workers deserve some credit for the decrease in fines as well. Although many are clumsy when first starting out in the workshops, most, if not all, improve their skills quickly and become focused more on doing their jobs well than on "complaining and confronting their supervisors." In contrast to the previous stage of expansion when workers were often "very emotional" and would not "listen to reason,"[10] workers are now more inclined to accept a fine if it is warranted and will work hard to avoid repeating the same mistake. To them, it is better to move on rather than confront a supervisor in a battle they feel they ultimately cannot win. This is not to say that workers no longer disagree with or protest against managerial decisions: they most definitely do. However, they are picking their fights more carefully and engaging their superiors when the likelihood of success is considerably greater. This change in attitude suggests a subtle but significant shift in strategy, one that focuses on enhancing the workers' ability to maximize financial rewards with the least amount of social friction. This approach has also helped to gradually defuse tensions on the shop floor, allowing managers to devote their energies to other aspects of reintegration.

Further organizational learning is reflected in a program in which managerial staff, especially recently hired college graduates, spend a minimum of two months working on the production line next to ordinary workers.* Whereas some employees clearly felt the experience was eye-opening and worthwhile, other new hires complained that being on the line is "good training but [a waste] of time if I'm here too long."[11] Such attitudes sometimes precipitated reactions from others on the shop floor. Amused by a new hire's inexperience, production workers would often tease the new employee mercilessly about his or her inexperience and constant fumbling on the production line. Although such harassment occasionally led to heated arguments on the floor, it was, for the most part, conducted in the spirit of good fun and became a ritual of initiation into the world of

---

*On the surface, this policy loosely resembles the old Maoist policy of sending people to the countryside (*xiafang*) to learn from the masses. In fact, some of the staff members occasionally joked that they were continuing the revolution. For a detailed discussion of the experiences of urban youth sent to the countryside, see Chan et al., *Chen Village Under Mao and Deng*.

the line worker. The first time I worked in one of Phoenix's switch plants, for instance, all the other workers stopped momentarily to watch me put a switch together. I needed three times the normal amount of time to complete the job, prompting the whole room to break out in uproarious laughter. "Not bad," was the response from my counterparts, but said one worker, "you'll need more practice if you want to assemble a switch that actually works."

By the end of the training period, these new staff members had become intimately familiar with every aspect of the product, and more important, they had arrived at a new understanding of workers and themselves. The experience taught college graduates (myself included) a sense of humility and a new respect for the difficult demands of production. In fact, by the time their stints on the line ended, many staff members had developed strong friendships that proved especially useful once they assumed their managerial duties. Rather than resorting first to more coercive tactics like fines to elicit worker compliance, staff members try persuasion and consultation to secure a desired outcome or behavior, precisely the same approach enterprise founders employed in the earliest days of the enterprise. In this way, many hoped flexible management would lead to greater openness and harmony and restore some semblance of the rough egalitarianism of the past.

What is perhaps more significant in making the organizational structure "leaner and meaner" were the first cautious steps company leaders took toward reducing some of the status distinctions that had emerged during the expansion phase and toward creating new opportunities for disgruntled employees. According to one of the high-ranking officials overseeing Phoenix's restructuring, these changes "are meant to give the younger, better-educated employees a chance to maximize their potential. Many have talent but feel blocked by older employees. By moving them down [from the central office to the factory], they have the chance to really accomplish something."[12] In fact, underscoring management's commitment to the new policy, some of the founder's closest relatives were dislodged from their high-ranking positions. By 2004, the makeup of Phoenix's upper echelon of management, especially its board of directors, had been dramatically transformed to include individuals who were not part of the original kinship and social networks on which the company was built. Individual accomplishment, not personal connections, was now supposed to determine compensation and rank within the enterprise.

Imperfect Results: The Unanticipated Challenges of Explosive Growth

Even though some of the most resented aspects of rationalized authority were eliminated, the results of the restructuring process have nevertheless been mixed. Competitive pressures, the demands of a fast-growing customer base, and the desire to launch new products have contributed to a growth, rather than a reduction, in company bureaucracy. This should not be surprising, for success typically leads to the hiring of more personnel and a desire for enhanced control and coordination of enterprise affairs. At Jupiter, for instance, the creation of new divisions centered on cutting-edge products like pharmaceuticals, items clearly outside the firm's original sphere of competence, necessitated the accelerated incorporation of outside experts. At both firms, sustained growth precipitated the emergence and entrenchment of vital, although sometimes unpopular, departments. Accounting and human resources are just two examples of departments that have come to the forefront during reintegration to manage key functions, but whose missions often conflict with the goal of resuscitating a more personal, community spirit.

Although the routinization of critical functions has improved the company's overall efficiency, many members at Phoenix expressed frustration with the effects of an increasingly fine division of labor. Responsibility for specific job tasks, they note, is either so bounded or so unclear that memoranda and directives are commonly kicked from one department to another "like a ball" (*ti piqiu*), resulting in shirking and poor coordination.[13] Similarly, a high-ranking staff member in the Office of Administration complained that some divisions and offices had minds of their own and often took to "changing [higher-level directives]. Sometimes their situation prohibits them from implementing the directive or it's something else. Sometimes personnel at the lower levels don't understand the directive, and so we have to hold additional meetings to discuss it."[14] In other instances, his time was taken up in unproductive meetings in which "we just sit and listen to our superiors talk. There isn't any time limit on each agenda item either. They keep talking and talking—it's a waste of our time. It's very much like a state-owned enterprise."[15]

This reference to being like a state-owned enterprise, a sentiment echoed throughout the company, represents dissatisfaction not only with bureaucratization but also with the individuals seen as responsible for it. In fact, many respondents expressed antipathy toward the outsiders who had left SOEs for positions at Phoenix, as well as former local government cadres who have recently joined the company, deriding the new "white collars" (*bailing*) as parasitic opportunists. "They're just trying to meet goals [production and financial] on paper. They have it easy: they always want us to attend training sessions, but if goals aren't met, they blame us. If things go well, they receive more dividends. They basically split all the profits we're required to send to corporate headquarters. This isn't a fair and just environment."[16] He added that the sense of unfairness among employees also stemmed from promotions that were perceived as unjustified: "There is so much redundancy—what do these mid-level administrators do anyway? . . . Because they [upper management] are afraid to hurt anyone's feelings, everyone is made an assistant director. Everyone wants to be a general, but not a soldier."[17] For one respondent who eventually left Phoenix, these new personnel epitomized a dramatic shift in organizational ethos:

I left for a number of reasons but one of the major ones was that the culture of the company was changing. As the company hired more former employees of SOEs, these new people brought with them both good qualities and bad. They brought a lot of expertise, but they also brought a different kind of attitude toward work. These people don't ever do more than they are supposed to. . . . No one wants to take responsibility for anything because they are afraid it will hurt their position in the company.[18]

Additional resentment stems from management's efforts not only to recruit a more skilled workforce but also to reward more on the basis of *what* employees supposedly know rather than *whom* they know. In years past, the formal educational requirements were more modest for production line applicants, most of whom, for example, held only an elementary school or a middle school diploma and secured their positions in part through helpful kin and friends. The director of Phoenix's Human Resources Department stated that "we now require production workers to have a high school diploma; lower-level managerial staff, a *dazhuan* [vocational school] degree; and technical staff, a college degree or higher."[19] Although the policy was effective in bringing in new talent, it also allows and justifies wider differences in remuneration. Indeed, when looking at the 22 official classifications that exist for Phoenix employees, the compensation ratio between the highest- and lowest-paid employee far exceeds the 3:1 target, hitting 17:1 now that the company president's monthly salary is 20,000 *yuan* compared to an average of 1,200–1,500 *yuan* for line workers. Although the ratio between the highest and lowest monthly salary in some plants remains 3:1 or 4:1, in others it can be as high as 90:1.[20]

If we consider year-end bonuses, the differences between top and bottom are staggering. Although the most productive workers could often earn an additional 30 to 50 *yuan* per month (360–600 *yuan* per year) in the late 1990s, these bonuses were dwarfed by the 1,000-*yuan* bonuses garnered by junior management and the "one-time" bonuses of 80,000–100,000 *yuan* for senior personnel who "have made significant contributions to the company."[21] Perhaps more disturbing to the workers is the secrecy surrounding bonus determinations. As one Phoenix manager told me: "I take these forms home and fill them out there—no one must see them. So I don't work on them at the office. After I'm done, I send them back to the central office for final approval."[22] By 2004, the gap between top and bottom increased still further: plant managers can receive 500,000–600,000 *yuan*, and those of higher rank, 700,000–800,000 *yuan*.[23] Year-end bonuses for other employees vary according to sales but fall in the range of 3,000–4,000 *yuan* for workers and 7,000–10,000 *yuan* for workshop directors and other lower-ranking managerial staff.[24] It is not surprising that such results do not diminish, but instead reinforce, suspicions that some workplace groups enjoy undeserved benefits at the expense of others.

To be sure, defenders of company policy point out that the vast majority of workers' salaries have risen considerably in absolute terms, allowing many, for example, to replace bicycles with scooters. In fact, the workers' parking areas, especially those in the busier

plants, were marked by seemingly endless rows of scooters and no bicycles at all, a striking contrast to the late 1990s when nearly all
workers walked, rode bicycles, or took the bus to work. However,
two additional points must be made. First, in some plants, wage increases have been offset by reductions in bonuses, as one respondent
points out:

Because there are a lot of ventures with foreigners, they [management]
changed the wage scale to put themselves in the most favorable light. Before, monthly salaries were 700–800 *yuan* per month, but now they are
2,000 *yuan* per month. Foreign companies are impressed by the growth, and
they can feel good about working with Phoenix—no one feels that he is
exploiting workers here. It's good public relations. Phoenix can say how
well they treat the workforce by stating, "look at how much salaries have
increased over the last few years." Actually, the company just cuts back on
yearend bonuses, which have been reduced to almost nothing, whereas before everyone received something.[25]

Thus, the absolute increase is sometimes smaller than it appears. In
other instances, a worker may not receive his full monthly salary despite exceptional work performance, as was the situation in one of
Phoenix's busiest factories:

In one plant, business was really booming, and some workers actually received 3,000–4,000 for the month, even on piece rates. Another worker hit
5,000, but the company didn't pay him the full amount. It held on to 30
percent and added that amount to the worker's wages the following month
because managers were worried that other workers would be angry or resentful.[26]

When performance exceeded expectations, management felt compelled to violate its own rules in order to forestall potential social
tensions in the workshop, even though it was unclear that such action was warranted. Second, when the scooters are juxtaposed with
the black Audis and BMWs lined up in the managerial parking lots,
it is clear that the managerial staff enjoys a substantially greater
share of the profits. Such comparably lavish lifestyles could not be
sustained otherwise. Although many managers shoulder great responsibilities and spend what often feels like countless hours in
their offices, numerous employees find it difficult to accept current

arrangements and wonder whether the new policies are truly intended to strengthen solidarity or to camouflage divisions and privileges.

Of greater concern to some are the signals the company is sending to employees. Although the vast majority accept the notion that compensation should be linked to performance, many do not see the principle being applied consistently and fairly and blame managerial staff for taking more from Phoenix than they contribute. To them, the message is that rewards are based on arbitrary determinations of worth rather than observable and measurable contributions. This has generated disenchantment in many sectors of the enterprise and spurred an unusual ruthlessness among some to secure greater compensation. One plant manager, a member of the enterprise since its earliest days, was exasperated by these developments:

Enterprise restructuring has created instability within the workforce. In order to staff some of the new divisions, management offered stock to personnel who were willing to move. One young woman received 20,000 *yuan* in shares at the Shanghai company and was absolutely thrilled. But what about those employees who worked with devotion for years? They didn't receive any shares—is that fair? My company was affected as well—one of my former employees admitted that he deliberately created a ruckus with me so that he could have an excuse to leave for another company where the overall compensation would be higher. They finally stopped this practice this year, but it's created a very unhealthy environment. Everyone is looking for an opportunity to make more money, and it's taken away people's focus on work. It's not right for someone who's put in so little time here to reap such large rewards.[27]

Others, hoping to secure a low-level position, have utilized less confrontational and more deceptive tactics. For example,

Some applicants will supply a fake diploma or use their connections in the company to get around [official requirements]; so most production workers are in reality still middle school graduates. Before they are allowed to begin work, we interview them, but it's often hard to tell the difference between a middle school and high school graduate. If their responses are reasonable and they look like good people, we will usually hire them.[28]

Hence, beyond the official pronouncements about merit, qualifications, and contributions, there is an ongoing struggle to match up all three in a way that employees consider acceptable and fair.

What makes the realization of relative equity even more challenging is that restructuring and decentralization have given rise to small fiefdoms within both enterprises, institutionalizing rather than synthesizing sometimes clashing managerial approaches. In many ways, this acceptance of diverse practices creates confusion at the plant level. One of the senior leaders in charge of overseeing Phoenix's ongoing reorganization process observed that

the biggest problem we face is that our management approach is still very individual based. We can't seem to get away from a dependency on certain people to get important things done. We need to establish a more systematic approach to management that utilizes rules more effectively. We need to be more professional. . . . If we are going to solve these problems, strong leadership is going to be most critical.[29]

In other instances, looser control has reignited sometimes intensely personal rivalries between enterprise subunits, leading to competitive, sometimes spiteful, behavior among enterprise executives. At Jupiter, for example, one general manager, jealous of a distant relation's success as general manager of another subsidiary, began producing the same products at a lower price in a blatant challenge to his relation's position within the company hierarchy. This duel ended only when the company founder intervened and forced the two into an uneasy truce. When I revisited one of the toughest plant managers at Phoenix, a member of the enterprise's founding generation, to discuss the results of the reintegration drive, he, too, expressed similar sentiments, arguing that current policies

hurt the cohesiveness of the company in many ways. . . . The leaders of some of the divisions refuse to merge their operations with others, even though this would improve efficiency dramatically. They have resisted for years, because that factory is their "territory." By maintaining control over their operations, they can take advantage of their positions to enrich themselves and their relatives. Each year their reports indicate that the costs of components have increased. This is because their suppliers are their relatives—their uncles, their cousins! They also write off expensive dinners as business expenses, whereas we can't even charge a beer when entertaining guests. The corruption has gotten worse in some places since you were last here.[30]

In addition to uneven prospects for advancement, the loosely coupled enterprise also subjects employees to inconsistent demands and treatment. The relaxed, paternalistic factory regimes continue to be lax in rules enforcement, and the strict, "tyrannical" regimes remain unyielding. Central management's indifference to, even toleration of, this state of affairs has allowed plant managers to continue many of their previous policies. For example, according to the strictest factory manager at Phoenix, rebuilding the enterprise community was pointless if high standards and superior performance were not maintained. "All the other managers," he noted, "are afraid they'll offend someone. . . . They're only thinking of themselves and their reputations. No one wants to be the bad guy, but I don't care much about that. I'm interested in keeping costs down and having everyone work efficiently."[31] At Jupiter, the mismatch between work performance and compensation sometimes resulted in employee frustration. A workshop director explained:

Usually I don't receive many complaints but occasionally a worker will complain that she does the same work as another worker but received 50 *yuan* less for the month. Of course, we're making observations and keeping records, so there's not a whole lot they can do if they're not happy. We sometimes will make adjustments for the next month's wages, but if they complain too much, we'll fine them. They can sometimes be too much trouble.[32]

Yet in other instances, the results have been more positive. Aside from workers leaving work to return to their native places or to start families, better communication and reduced social friction has dropped turnover rates in some Phoenix plants to 3–5 percent in contrast to the nearly 20 percent turnover that still exists in other factories.[33] Even some former workers seeking to return to their previous positions have been welcomed back with no questions asked or ill will. As pragmatic as this policy is (former workers are almost always more skilled and familiar with work routines than new entrants), it also represents a significant change in managerial attitude. Many managers have become more understanding and forgiving and now recognize that workers often cannot avoid other pressing matters in their lives. Employer-employee relationships do not have to come to a permanent end; in fact, they can be restarted to the benefit of both parties.

Phoenix's emphasis on improved communication has led some of its plants to establish small groups (*banqian hui*), which meet for five–ten minutes prior to the official start of the workday, much like quality control circles in Japan. Under this system, managers expect workers to shoulder more responsibility and meet ever higher expectations for output and quality. A male assistant manager in his mid- to late twenties remarked that these groups were only moderately successful in identifying and solving production problems because "some workers are just not as capable or aware of problems as others."[34] There seemed to be little acknowledgment of other burdens borne by employees. There was no mention of spouses, children, families, let alone some private time for oneself: it was almost as if the worker existed solely to produce for the factory. If tackling work problems were not enough, these groups are also expected to discuss larger social issues like HIV/AIDS once a month in hopes that awareness will be heightened and long-term personal pitfalls will be avoided. However, given that the groups meet for only ten minutes prior to starting work, it is difficult to imagine how employees can meet the high expectations management has set for them. Still, they put up with the situation, often grateful to have a job when many of their friends are out of luck. While waiting for a basketball game to begin, one male worker explained to me that over 170 workers had been laid off at his plant and had not found new positions at other Phoenix plants yet or received their severance pay. He was simply relieved that he was not one of them.[35] For him and many others, unemployment is a fate much worse than being saddled with additional morning meetings.

Although the decentralized structure reduced official status distinctions and increased opportunities for individual advancement, it did little to mitigate informal status differences. Despite declarations that job assignments would be determined overwhelmingly, if not exclusively, on the basis of merit, membership in kinship and native- place networks continues to affect hiring decisions and rank. Managers are still inclined to select candidates whom they know and consider more trustworthy. As one outsider technical specialist at Phoenix suggested, "Management is scared that if we are given more authority and responsibility, we'll learn all the company's strategies and secrets. They're afraid this information will fall into the hands of competitors if we leave."[36] Although some employees are bound by formal nondisclosure clauses in their contracts, no effective legal mechanism exists to ensure compliance. Such suspicions appear to have affected the composition of the managerial staff. In 1998, few outsiders served as plant vice-managers at Phoenix; moreover, only one outsider made it to the position of factory manager, and this was only by virtue of his longstanding personal friendship with the enterprise founder. In the central offices, only one nonlocal occupies the position of department head; all other positions are staffed by locals. Although a 1998 "purge" of factory-level managers removed a significant number of distant relatives and locals from the managerial ranks, closer relations like the founder's brother and brother-in-law remain firmly ensconced in high-ranking positions. As president and vice-president of Phoenix, they wield enormous authority and remain well placed to guide the implementation of the founder's decisions and initiatives.

Even as local-outsider friction has declined in the past five years, employees disagree on how much progress has actually been made. Younger staff tend to be more positive and hopeful. A twenty-something local female member of Phoenix's Central Accounting Office stated flatly that

the company has gotten better about trusting nonlocals with important jobs—it wasn't always this way. In my accounting department, for example, almost one-third of the staff are nonlocals. When I first arrived in 1996, all the positions were exclusively reserved for locals. Enterprise leaders thought access to our financial data had to be restricted because this was critical and confidential information that only the most trusted people could see. But now they've changed their views and can accept these staffing changes.[37]

Similarly, an outsider in his early thirties who rose to assistant manager of a division from quality control inspector in 1998 expressed positive sentiments: "Locals don't discriminate against outsiders as much as before. In fact, most of our workers and mid-ranking personnel are outsiders. The leaders have more respect for workers and pay more attention to their needs. There is still some friction on occasion, but it's not as bad as in the past."[38] In contrast, an older, male mid-ranking outsider who works in Phoenix's Public Relations Department expressed resignation: "I've accepted the fact that I'm not going to move up to a high-ranking executive position. There are only so many positions—president, division general manager, etc.—and they will be staffed by locals. I don't complain about this because there's no point in doing so."[39] For him, the new company policies were well intentioned but only disguised power dynamics that would always favor locals over outsiders. His response to these circumstances was to simply invest the minimum amount of energy necessary to fulfill his official responsibilities; he devoted his remaining time and energy to his own pursuits, including the publication of literary essays that explored the pleasures of the scholarly life. By the summer of 2004, he had already started to craft a second set of essays that picked up and extended some of the themes he had explored in his first volume. What these contrasting perspectives suggest is that although senior executives can tolerate outsiders in the enterprise's lower levels, they still find it difficult to accept outsiders into the company's elite positions. This situation reflects in large measure the continued influence of what Mark Granovetter calls "strong ties,"[40] which in this case are the relationships nested in the kinship and social networks anchoring the enterprise's personnel core. As long as this group remains on the scene, their domination of decision-making processes is not likely to wane, despite their somewhat diminished numbers.

The persistence of informal status distinctions was even more pronounced at Jupiter. The managers of each of the enterprise's most profitable subsidiaries were led by a member of the president's inner circle:

At this enterprise, many of the key positions are staffed by [the president's] relatives and people who once helped him. At A, his niece's husband is the general manager. At B, his son is the GM. At C, it's a close relation who once saved him from major trouble. At D, his son-in-law is the GM. There's really nothing we can do about this. It's very hard to trust outsiders with large amounts of capital. The management system isn't strong enough yet to prevent abuse, and so the president must use people he can rely on.[41]

Even at lower levels, similar patterns of domination by locals are evident. At the factory manager rank, 142 of 158 managers hailed from the local prefecture; of the remaining sixteen, nine were from other prefectures in Zhejiang province, and seven were from outside the province. Moreover, 390 out of 404 workshop directors were locals; of the remaining fourteen, ten were from other parts of the province, and four claimed a native-place outside the province.[42] It is also worth noting that among the groups just mentioned, 79.7 percent of the managers and 87.9 percent of the workshop directors did not hold a vocational school or college degree, contrary to the enterprise's own requirements. These breakdowns reveal just how daunting it is for even skilled outsiders to gain entry to what must appear to them to be a closed community. It also underscores the difficulties of balancing the professed desires of enterprise leaders to build a more inclusive enterprise community while maintaining loyalty to the members of their personal networks.

The existence of different managerial approaches and treatment within the same enterprise gives workers a sense that their work experience is really a matter of luck rather than a reflection of their individual performance. If they find themselves employed at a more relaxed and paternalistic factory, they are fortunate; if they work at a strict plant, they are star-crossed. Hence, even as the flexibility that both firms introduced into their managerial practices gave managers more space to maneuver, it also produced more cracks through which workers could fall. The degree to which both firms filled these gaps depended on the leadership's commitment to making employees full-fledged members of the "enterprise family."

Recasting and Rebuilding Enterprise Solidarity

Despite the expenditure of significant resources on higher compensation and bonuses, senior enterprise leaders did not fully achieve the results they longed for. Trust and social harmony among employees remained fragile, presenting company executives with a major dilemma: either risk further deterioration in worker morale or find a new strategy for dealing with these serious threats to enterprise stability. Unable to eliminate competing allegiances altogether, managers have tried instead to limit their divisive impact and to promote cooperation and unity in their firms. Above all else, this new approach emphasizes expanding boundaries of identification to the new enterprise family. Through fictive kinship, all members of the enterprise are bound together in common cause as personal status is subordinated to the broader concerns and well-being of the enterprise.

Now, employees are "brothers and sisters" in the Phoenix and Jupiter families first and natives of Wenzhou, Jinhua, Shanghai, and Beijing second. This new undertaking delineates the contours and symbolic terrain of the new "enterprise culture" (*qiye wenhua*).

Compared with IBM's and Toyota's near-legendary efforts at building corporate culture, these attempts do not appear particularly striking. On closer examination, however, these efforts are innovative for two reasons. First, leaders at both firms are attempting to distill the most critical attributes of their early success and adapt them to fit their new circumstances. They have taken membership in kinship and native-place networks, both exclusive modes of association, and redefined them to be more inclusive without fundamentally distorting the principles that govern them. This shift tacitly acknowledges the unifying power of kinship ties as well as their corrosive effects. If these ties bind only specific segments within the enterprise together and exclude others, division, not solidarity, results. In order to avoid this outcome, company leaders have thus enlarged the definition of membership in their "clubs" but kept intact the requirements and responsibilities of membership.

Second, this new policy is notable because of the entity that management is enlisting to implement this vision: the Chinese Communist Party. The party, long considered a major obstacle to the effective functioning of Chinese factories, is now serving as management's junior partner in rebuilding trust and social harmony at Jupiter and Phoenix. This development strikes against the conventional wisdom in most scholarly debates regarding the party's intrusion into enterprise affairs. Victor Nee, for example, once argued that party involvement in economic activities at both the micro- and macro-levels would severely impair the long-term development of healthy market institutions.[43] Although Nee suggests that cadre involvement in the short term may indeed boost enterprise performance, long-term meddling will produce inefficiency. A young party member at Phoenix cast the company's desire to work with the party in a slightly different light:

Phoenix is not like other companies. By inviting the CCP into the enterprise, the company is doing precisely the opposite of what other companies are doing. A lot of enterprises fear the party's presence in the enterprise.

They think it's bothersome, or they think party activities will hurt operations. It's true that in the past we would stop work to carry out party activities, but we can't do that anymore.[44]

However, as David Wank has pointed out in his study of clientelist relationships between entrepreneurs and local officials in Xiamen, these bonds are not necessarily detrimental to either side and can in fact be beneficial because of the enhanced security each provides the other.[45]

Thus, contrary to concerns that the partnership between party and enterprise will hurt production, I suggest here, like Wank, that the relationship between the party and managers is not necessarily detrimental to the enterprise's long-term profitability or its organizational stability. Reconnecting with the party was a logical move because a stronger party presence in the enterprise helped deflect potential criticisms from officials that both firms were taking the "capitalist road." This was especially critical during the 1980s when the direction and the permanence of reform policies were unclear. Jupiter's founder and president, a former local party secretary, clearly understood that his enterprise's unexpected success would trigger major political problems if he failed to use at least some enterprise assets to advance a socialist vision.

For Phoenix's leadership, working with the party made even better sense. The crackdown on private enterprises following the Tiananmen Square demonstrations in 1989 reminded business leaders throughout Wenzhou of their political vulnerability. By providing the party with a greater stake in maintaining the success of private firms, they hoped to forestall future political attacks as well as open new opportunities for the all-important *guanxi*, or connections, between enterprise and party to deepen. Although political pressures have eased considerably since then, especially after Deng Xiaoping's "Southern Tour" reaffirmed the CCP's commitment to deepening market-oriented policies, some at Phoenix believe linkages with party cadres provide the enterprise with more than political protection. The head of enterprise administration gave this description:

Although they [former cadres] aren't always familiar with the micro-level details of the company, they see the macro-level issues very clearly. They are familiar with government laws, especially on taxes, and they are very good at coordinating the work of different departments. For them, it's like coordinating the work of different government agencies. This has helped us improve our overall efficiency; we didn't have this kind of knowledge or experience before.[46]

A former technical chief who worked at Phoenix for five years echoed this sentiment, arguing that "by bringing them in and placing them in [important] positions throughout the company, they are keeping them in reserve for when they might need them to resolve a bigger problem. Just think how easy it would be to get things done when ex-cadres tap their old connections."[47] Even in 1998, the nature of this relationship was on full display when I attended a special banquet held in honor of foreign technical experts who had helped Phoenix upgrade critical aspects of its production. As I rode with the founder in his Cadillac to our destination, the local head of the Public Security Bureau cleared a path for us, his sirens blaring as a declaration of our importance. If that were not enough, he also forced other cars to the side of the road by threatening to ticket them and impound their cars over his loudspeaker. Few other firms, if any, in the area commanded such privilege and prestige.

However, this relationship is more than a simple nod to political expediency or utilitarianism. Senior executives at both firms truly believe that the party formally stands above kinship and native-place loyalties and want to use this reputation and the party's specific competence in organization and persuasion to legitimize their new enterprise family orientation. Working in tandem with the party, enterprise management is consciously attempting to break the conflation of privilege and social identity. For them, the enterprise family embodies a broader, general commitment to all segments of the organization over the particular interests of specific groups within the firm.

Through the Communist Youth League, the Women's Federation, and the trade union, the party seeks to bolster enterprise stability over the advancement of its own political agenda. Through these three organizations especially, the party maintains a lattice-like presence that affords it multiple opportunities to reduce, even prevent, labor conflict within the workplace. However, the enterprise-party relationship is not an equal one: the enterprise's needs clearly remain the top priority. One administrator at a Jupiter division characterized the situation as follows:

In the past, the party secretary and the factory director were two different individuals, and this often led to conflict. One would want to do something one way, and the other would want to do it another way. This situation often created a deadlock because each person wanted to be "top dog" (*zuo laoda*). Now what we do is vest party authority in the highest managerial position. The most powerful person in our division, the general manager, also serves as the division's party secretary. This way there are no conflicts between these positions, and the entire operation runs smoothly.[48]

Party officials accept this situation, not only because approval of the party's proposed initiatives rests with enterprise management, but also because their own salaries do as well. These financial constraints serve as an implicit check on party authority and have restricted the party's ability to re-establish clientelist ties through what Andrew Walder calls "principled particularism."[49] In fact, it appears that the reverse has come to pass: the party has become the enterprise's client, performing whatever task the enterprise leadership designates for it. One of the highest-ranking party representatives at Phoenix acknowledged that the party is now indeed in a supporting role:

Party members play a leadership role here . . . but we must also be realistic. This is not a state-owned enterprise or a government organization. No one here is going to read Lenin or Marx and think about their works deeply. People don't have the time for that. As for economic production, all we can do is advise because economics is not our main specialty. We try to help workers be more productive and stable but we can only do so by example. . . . We can work with management as a partner, and management should see us as a friend and supporter.[50]

Still, for party representatives in Wenzhou and Jinhua, becoming an integral part of rural enterprises in any capacity has become a badge of honor, given the rather negligible role party cadres previously played in companies. In both enterprises, the party continues to champion its standards of membership and behavior, but it cares less about pursuing its own formal objectives and more about maintaining its new status as a mediator and respected authority within the enterprise.

Even so, the limited duties the party now assumes are hardly insignificant. It serves as the eyes and ears of management, bringing critical employee concerns and possible solutions to their attention. For a young party activist at Phoenix, this is a serious mission:

[We] focus on what enterprise leaders don't have the time or the skills to do: communicate with the rank and file of the company. Sometimes the leaders are so busy running the business that they don't know how workers feel, what concerns them. Upper management has already ceded this task of communication to us. Our goal is to serve as a bridge between the top and the bottom.[51]

To achieve this end, party officials at Phoenix periodically hold special drop-in sessions with enterprise management, during which employees can voice their concerns. For workers who fear their criticisms will affect their job prospects, Phoenix has even installed suggestion boxes at numerous locations to allow workers to express their views anonymously. The company offers a small cash payment as a reward for an especially useful suggestion, should the individual sign his or her name. Although several individuals have been lauded and rewarded for their recommendations, they are rather unusual and rare cases. Furthermore, Phoenix set up an electronic message board through the company website in 2002. While I sat in his office, the trade union chairman proudly showed me the various employee postings. He proclaimed that the electronic posting system "is actually very democratic (*hen minzhu*) because employees can express any grievance they have and everyone can read their post. We read them each day and try to resolve reasonable requests as quickly as possible."[52] For leaders, these channels of dialogue are more than cornerstones of a new openness: they serve as a means of heading off discontent before it potentially disrupts the social harmony they aim to achieve.

Moreover, each of the CCP-affiliated organizations devotes itself to reducing work-related alienation among specific segments of the workforce and to increasing opportunities for individual fulfillment and social interaction. Phoenix's Communist Youth League (CYL), for example, was established in the mid-1990s as a key link in building enterprise culture (*qiye wenhua*). By working with employees under twenty-five who had not yet attained party membership, the

CYL sought to enlist their energies and ideas into broader efforts to make the workplace more caring and responsive to the needs of employees. This remains, however, a formidable task. In 1997, the CYL secretary, a woman in her late twenties, noted that the long hours her colleagues worked made it nearly impossible for her to recruit new members, let alone carry out her mission. Fatigue discouraged all but the most stalwart from attending meetings and events. Despite these early problems, conditions had improved markedly by 2004: an ever-expanding workforce meant the pool from which to draw potential recruits had grown considerably. According to the new secretary, a quick and cheerful woman in her mid-twenties, there were already over 3,900 members throughout the enterprise, and they accounted for the vast majority of CYL members in the county, a development that delighted local party officials. To her,

the reason why we organize events is so that employees don't feel like there is no life beyond work. Of course, their main reason for being here is to earn money—I understand that. But their time here should be more than going to work in the morning and returning home at night—what's the point of that? . . . I always tell members that should they leave the company, they can take these experiences and memories with them. It will remind them of good times.[53]

Despite their long work days, many members remain enthusiastic about organizing and participating in CYL events. One male in his mid-twenties commented that organizing events was "a kind of training (*duanlian*) and a great way to meet people. It's an opportunity for us to develop our talents."[54]

Similarly, Phoenix's Women's Federation (Fulian) branch has experienced considerable growth, expanding from twelve members in 1998 to a few hundred in 2004. The group's goal has been and continues to be advancing the economic and social well-being of women at the enterprise. In the late 1990s, Fulian representatives concentrated on improving promotion opportunities for female employees; in fact, their efforts produced a noticeable increase in the proportion of women reaching the rank of workshop director or higher. In the past few years, their focus has expanded to work-related stress and personal relationships. Many female employees complain that increased workloads have strained their relationships with their husbands and families and, in the case of single women, hurt their prospects for marriage. The Fulian head, a woman in her early thirties, noted that just listening to women's concerns is an important service because

the employee is sometimes embarrassed, reluctant to talk, especially if the representative is male. So often they call me directly, and we talk on the phone. What we do is listen carefully to them. After the worker is done describing her complaint, we analyze the situation, then lay out the consequences of taking a certain action. We try to help them find the best solution to their problem, but it's very difficult. There is only so much we can do.[55]

Phoenix's trade union was first set up in 1993 and remains the most important of the three party-affiliated groups, given its all-encompassing mission.* As the official advocate of worker interests, the union is involved in a wider range of work-related issues than the other two organizations, including compensation, labor disputes, job security, work conditions, collective benefits, and enterprise-wide social events. Given their mission, union representatives focus mostly on expanding work opportunities and equalizing benefits. As the union chairman put it, "Workers need to have their financial concerns taken care of if their productivity is to stay high. Without improvement in this area, workers cannot concentrate on doing a good job. After all, they are here because they want to improve their material situation."[56] At the same time, management expects union representatives to assist it in keeping workplace dynamics peaceful and harmonious and profits high. Although such expectations are similar to those faced by the leaders of Japanese unions, Chinese union officials are further constrained by competing and sometimes contradictory objectives. They are expected to help control the very workers whose interests they are supposed to represent and defend.

Because of the union's supporting role within the enterprise and the formidable slate of topics it faces, it is not surprising that its representatives have adopted a gradual, issue-specific approach to improving the lot of workers. Although some of the initiatives such as

---

*Although Phoenix's union was established prior to the company's more concerted reintegration efforts, it did not become actively engaged in tackling work-related issues until the late 1990s.

the recently enacted pension system originated with management and local government officials, others, for example, the proposed worker's compensation and medical insurance programs, appear to spring from the union itself. Still others come from the workers, as was the case with Phoenix's termination policy. Indeed, the chairman stated that this remains one of the more difficult challenges of his tenure:

Terminations are a sensitive issue. At the end of each year, workers are evaluated, and the poorest performers are fired. The problem is that workers feel they are not being treated fairly because they think current standards are unreasonable. What happens is that workers with the lowest score on the evaluation are fired. A score of 91 or 92 may seem low compared to a 97, but if the minimum for a passing grade is 90, why should the worker be terminated? They should be if they score a 60, but not a 91. We thought the workers had a valid point, and so we're now pushing management to establish clearer and fairer evaluation criteria.[57]

For workers, the termination policy embodies management's obsessive fascination with rationalization. Most felt that each worker should be given the opportunity to make up for sub-par work, but dismissal despite officially acceptable work is viewed as a betrayal and a violation of the pact between worker and employer.

Although communication and concern for worker welfare has undoubtedly increased, perhaps the more significant result of this new enterprise-party partnership is the broader program to make membership in the enterprise family more tangible, beneficial, and attractive. To rebuild reciprocity and trust throughout the entire enterprise community, management and the party moved to demonstrate their concern and commitment to the well-being of enterprise members in more concrete, material terms—that is, through the provision of collective benefits. Phoenix's management, for instance, has worked to ensure that every employee enjoys a minimum level of benefits, thus restoring some balance to the scales of moral economy underlying the worker-management relationship. At Jupiter, factories periodically handed out a range of daily necessities such as packets of detergent, bars of soap, towels, and cooking oil. At Phoenix, sodas and bottled water were distributed, especially during the summer months when cool drinks (*lengyin*) were in high demand to beat the sweltering heat. In 2004, this practice continued in the form of a 35-*yuan* monthly bonus given to each employee to buy ice-cold Coke.[58] On special holidays like the Lunar New Year (*chunjie*), gifts of fruit baskets, clothing, and even red envelopes (*hongbao*) stuffed with small amounts of cash were distributed. Even so, "we can't increase the number of gifts or buy more expensive ones; otherwise, the costs are too high. Each year it costs the company approximately 3,500–4,000 *yuan* [per employee] to provide these things. . . . We have to keep costs under control."[59]

Shortly before my first visit to Phoenix in 1997, the labor union successfully lobbied for the extension of subsidized meals to workers in addition to managerial staff. By 2004, the tiny canteen had been transformed into a massive cafeteria serving breakfast, lunch, and dinner. When eating at the cafeteria, each employee swipes a meal card and the cost of the meal is deducted from the credit in a pre-paid account, much as American college students do when they eat in their dining halls. What is striking, however, is that despite the official goal of community and egalitarianism, the quality and assortment of food vary according to rank, with senior staff receiving the best selections (including fresh fruit!), all of which are enjoyed in private rooms separated from those of the rank and file. In contrast, the majority of employees can select more modest "value meals," which consist of a simple soup, rice, and a few main dishes for a total cost of 3.0–4.5 *yuan*. Although the dining area is filled with smaller tables to promote a more intimate feel, employees nevertheless found it difficult to have a conversation when several hundred people were all trying to do the same thing. To be sure, the mad rush at mealtime was unavoidable, but it had become so overwhelming and impersonal that many simply chose to eat elsewhere, even if it meant paying more. More important, the need to feed a vast multitude of employees efficiently had eclipsed the sense of togetherness and personal connection that in the late 1990s had pervaded what was then the company canteen.

In addition, some factories have recently implemented more far-ranging plans to provide housing and even pensions to workers whose tenure at the factory has exceeded fifteen years. By 2004, Phoenix constructed new dormitories that house most of its mid-level and higher-ranking managerial staff, special consultants to the company, and several thousand workers. Staff lived two to a room in comparatively luxurious quarters, outfitted with a private bath, television, phone service, internet connection, and air-conditioning. In contrast, workers lived four to a room and enjoyed most of the same amenities, although their floors were not fully tiled nor did they enjoy air-conditioning (instead, ceiling fans were installed in their rooms). In contrast to strictly financial rewards, these efforts focus on combating longer-term worker concerns and go beyond basic efforts to share the wealth: they symbolize obligations managers must fulfill (*yinggai zuode*) not only as members of their community but as its leaders. It is a way to show that they value people more than profits.

In this light, Phoenix's pension program represents a major source of pride among management in part because no other enterprise in the immediate area offers a comparable benefit. Although I was unable to secure hard data on the other firms in the county, anecdotal evidence suggests that they simply do not have the money to match and sustain a similar effort. According to respondents, the pension system requires contributions from both employees and the enterprise, with employees contributing 8 percent of their average monthly wages and the enterprise providing 18 percent of that amount. Of this, 16 percent is forwarded to the government, and the other 2 percent remains in the bank. "This portion [2 percent] is given to the employee when he leaves the company. . . . In order for a worker to receive a full pension, she must contribute to the program for fifteen consecutive years."[60] The assistant director of Phoenix's Human Resources Department boasted that "there is no law that requires us to do this. This program was started on the initiative of our chairman. He believed that this was something we should do as a service to our employees. It represents an investment in them."*[61] Although it remains unclear whether the program was launched because of the founder's vision and magnanimity or national regulations, the convergence with Maoist-era *danwei* practices is striking, although explicit calls for political allegiance are no longer made.[62] Enterprise

---

*Some respondents have disputed this depiction, pointing out that national laws require large enterprises to implement such programs.

leaders now see employee welfare as a sound investment in the company, one that "promotes a 'virtuous cycle' (*liangxing xunhuan*) rather than a vicious one (*exing xunhuan*)."[63]

All these initiatives have been followed by an assorted array of events and contests that are loosely known as *biwu* ("matches of skill," a term evoking martial arts competitions). These events run the gamut from bicycle races, Chinese chess, and tugs-of-war to cooking and typing competitions, karaoke sing-offs, and speech contests.[64] Under the direction of the party, these activities are not only contests of individual prowess but also a combination of mass campaign and large-scale "party." Party officials encourage employees to participate as much as possible and try to imbue these activities with the electricity and high purpose of party-backed rallies. One singing contest at Phoenix generated more excitement than anticipated:

Most recently we held a *karaoke* competition. Over ninety people originally registered for the contest, and so we held tryouts and cut the number of contestants down to thirty. Each contestant sang two songs, and the competition lasted from 7:30 P.M. to 1 A.M.! Almost everyone stayed until the end to lend moral support to the representative from their factory. People bought so many flowers that local flower shops were completely sold out. Some participants couldn't even hold all the bouquets given. It was fantastic because of the festive atmosphere and the goodwill of everyone involved.[65]

For management, these seemingly ordinary events are not mere diversions or entertainment: they are opportunities to reinforce identification with the enterprise over other social allegiances. Although these affairs often contain a competitive strain, they are friendly in nature and emphasize enterprise unity over individual rivalry. During my first research stint at Phoenix, I was also drawn into this process, playing on Phoenix's basketball team against the teams of other local firms. My Phoenix teammates often boasted that of all the firms in the area, only Phoenix was worthy enough to catch my attention as a research site. Because I hailed from America, "land of the NBA," they were convinced that I could single-handedly guarantee them victory. Luckily, we won the two games in which I played, and I promptly retired before they realized I was not a true franchise player. More important, though, the games revealed how hard-nosed competition could be channeled toward building a tighter-knit enterprise community. The basketball court became a venue where all employees of differing status and rank could temporarily forget their disagreements and join together to cheer for their team.

The union's current agenda focuses on deepening efforts to improve the workers' material situation and "[their] lifestyle, the non-work activities of company employees."[66] In 1998, the union established a small reading room with the hope that workers would have an outlet for reducing work-related stress and a more effective means of resisting the temptations of late-night card playing and *mahjong*.[67] Union officials recognized that quiet time spent in reading and self-reflection might also benefit workers. Unfortunately, the initial effort was unsuccessful: workers rarely frequented the library, and when they did, they were interested only in reading martial arts novels (*wuxia xiaoshuo*) and other "trashy materials." Many employees did not respect the rules and often returned borrowed materials well after the due date and in damaged condition.

By 2002, the situation had changed dramatically. Phoenix moved its small library/reading room to the cafeteria/meeting complex and expanded its holdings to include more "serious" works. In addition to martial arts novels and popular magazines, the library was stacked with classics of Chinese literature, philosophy, and history. There were also books on the latest computer software, business management, and current affairs in China and the world. In talking with a CYL member who volunteers at the library, I discovered that despite heavy workloads, employees were not only eager to read for self-improvement but simply curious about the world around them. There were often numerous requests for the most popular books, and workers were given ten days to complete a book before it had to be returned. The volunteer explained that it was a joy to see so much excitement among fellow employees: it showed there was considerably more depth to them than most people assumed.

Just up the street, outside the confines of Phoenix's industrial park, there is now an internet café, a surprising development since the adjoining village is one of the poorest in the county. Perhaps even more astonishing is the role Phoenix played in its establishment. Although the café is privately owned and independent of

Phoenix, its owner initially lacked the startup capital to purchase the computers he needed. A top executive suggested that Phoenix could sell him a batch of their old castoffs at a very low price. This deal resulted in a win-win situation: the café owner now has a thriving business and a steadily growing clientele drawn from Phoenix's workers; Phoenix has a nearby space where its employees can surf the internet, keep up with friends at a relatively low cost, and stay out of trouble. In fact, at 8 *yuan* per hour, employees often raced to the second-floor cafe immediately after work to grab one of the 40 stations available. Some would stay for an hour, and others for three or more, sharing time at the station with other friends who had got off work. As I typed my own e-mails, I could clearly see that the workers were enjoying themselves and took great pride in their growing facility with computers. Some were even communicating with faraway pals through real-time video connections: one young fellow even went so far as to serenade his girlfriend through this hookup, winning admiration from some for his romantic gesture and consternation from others for his off-key singing. Still, that he could do such things testified to the new, technologically driven opportunities for social engagement that have helped ease loneliness and frustration among employees.

By enhancing long-term financial security and recasting and consolidating social bonds, management is attempting to reduce labor discontent in the workplace, a goal undoubtedly shared by government and party officials. Nevertheless, it is important to remember that the program is made possible by the company's success. Without high demand for its products, Phoenix would not have the "slack resources" necessary to fund the program. Over the long haul, executives believe these activities can buttress the new enterprise family orientation and lead to greater stability at both the individual and the collective level. Singing and speech contests especially have become a didactic means of molding the "political thought" of the employee. Most participants sing songs with socialist or revolutionary themes and give inspiring talks about their experiences at the enterprise. At Jupiter, "the most important thing about such events is that it's an opportunity to teach, [an opportunity] to talk about the company and personal goals, and what we should try to achieve."[68]

Here, the symbolism is ironic and unmistakable: party slogans are being used to persuade workers not to resist but to accept the work demands management is imposing on them.

In addition to promoting the subtle reshaping of the individual, the party often adopts a more active stance in resolving social problems, especially if inaction might heighten discontent and instability. One of the most astonishing examples at Jupiter focused on personal relationships or, more precisely, the lack of them. A party official considered prolonged bachelorhood a potentially destructive social condition: "There are many single people here of all ages. As they get older, they become lonely, less stable, and more likely to be involved in bad activities [drinking, prostitution, dance halls]. That eventually affects their work and even public safety. . . . We try to arrange opportunities for single people to meet [a partner]."[69] At Jupiter, matchmaking has become one of the party's highest priorities. In contrast, party representatives at Phoenix sometimes assume the role of marriage counselor, attempting to reduce marital strife by calling together enterprise executives and their spouses to dispel doubts and suspicions. To them, social turbulence at a more personal level requires just as much attention as social conflict at the collective level. A Women's Federation representative commented that "many wives, not knowing how hard their husbands work, often call us and wonder why their executive husbands stay so late at the office. We brought them together to clear the air. We don't want them to think their husbands stay out late and fool around. At this company, we're one big family, and we want stable and happy relationships."[70]

Imperfection Redux: The Party's Limited Impact

Like the efforts to restructure the enterprise, the results from plans spearheaded by party-affiliated organizations varied considerably. On one hand, overall communication between management and the rank and file has improved considerably. In both enterprises, meetings—ranging from those focused on small groups within a plant to enterprise-wide gatherings—are regularly scheduled, and postings through the internet have helped management better understand employee needs and create more effective responses to employee problems and concerns. On the other hand, the trade union chairman noted that some employees take advantage of these channels to vent their frustrations:

Take our recent water shortage for example. Here's a message complaining about how inconvenient it is to have water for only an hour each day in the evening. This is a problem caused by nature. There just hasn't been enough rainfall this year. We know it's hard on everyone, so we've tried to pipe in extra water from another town, but there just isn't enough to go around. Sometimes there isn't much we can do, but the employees feel better when they have an opportunity to "get things off their chests."[71]

Other enterprise members remain indifferent to these efforts, choosing instead to concentrate on work, individual fulfillment, and family needs independent of party and management plans. They see little possibility of improvement and have thus decided to use their time in other ways.

Despite the party's continued push for meetings to be held at least once a month, its representatives are resigned to the fact that production demands still take precedence over their objectives. In the plants where turnover rates still hover around 20 percent and shortages of shop floor personnel are common, workers have been especially hard-pressed to meet delivery deadlines and rarely focus on party-related issues. Phoenix's CYL secretary noted that workers in one plant could not even meet to select new leaders after their previous representatives left Phoenix for jobs elsewhere:

They kept putting it off, saying the workload at their factory had been unusually heavy. I kept pestering them and they kept delaying until I said I would relay this [their continual postponement] to their manager. They didn't want this to happen, and even though I eventually discussed this with the manager, he was supportive and encouraged them to move forward as quickly as possible. Not all managers are so understanding. They are usually very focused on production and profits until they see how participation in our events benefits workers. Support for our activities and our organization does not extend throughout the entire enterprise.[72]

Even when employees participated in party-led meetings, they often seemed distracted or indifferent. While researching Jupiter in July 1998, senior management granted me special permission to attend an enterprise-wide meeting that was exclusively for CCP members. As party leaders rose to address the audience, I was astounded by the seriousness of the speakers on stage and the relative indifference of the rank and file seated below. Many of the young workers were bored with the proceedings and saw the gathering as a reprieve from the drudgery and grind of their daily work, an opportunity to watch a spectacle. In fact, a group of young men seated in front of me were delighted more by the verbal gaffes of the speakers and the shenanigans of those around them than by the message of dedication and unity that was being conveyed.

In contrast, Phoenix employees maintained a more respectful demeanor, at least on the surface. At a plant-wide meeting held in July 1997, all employees listened attentively to the manager as he admonished and pleaded with them to take more pride in their work and dedicate themselves to becoming more productive members of the enterprise and society. Some confided to me afterward that although they were not sure they could realize the goals the manager had outlined, they would give it their best out of sympathy and admiration for him. By 2004, the behavior of Phoenix's employees began to mirror that of Jupiter's. That summer, all party members attended a two-day affair commemorating the centennial of Deng Xiaoping's birth and celebrating his vision for a modern, secure, and prosperous China. During the proceedings, however, employees chatted on their cell phones, attending to work demands and personal business when they were supposed to be paying close attention to the speakers. In fact, a few of my respondents, including the CYL secretary, answered my calls, much to my surprise since they were supposed to be listening intently to a seemingly endless series of lectures on Deng.

Although party meetings could be irritating, they did not infuriate employees as much as did swings in collective benefits. Under the *hetong* system, managers are subject to intense formal pressure to achieve profit targets; failure often means a reduction in their individual bonuses or even the loss of their jobs. Although many of them believe that workers do indeed deserve collective benefits, they feel such items can be considered only after their primary goals have been reached. They are always quick to point out that fulfilling the terms of the contract is their paramount consideration and that reaching this objective does not require profit-sharing with employees. The problem is that in factories where the distribution of goods (especially cool drinks) has become an established practice, sudden cutbacks spawn feelings of relative deprivation and injustice. One worker at Jupiter described the situation in this way: "Recently, we were given new uniforms . . . [and] because the uniforms cost 70 *yuan* per worker, management decided not to give us a cool drink bonus this year. How are we supposed to endure the heat? It's really hot, but they don't care."[73] A workshop director at the same plant echoed similar sentiments, feelings which suggest that a strong sense of moral economy persists among the enterprise workforce: [74]

We worked overtime again tonight. . . . It's really difficult now because it's hotter and all we have are fans. . . . The managers sit in their offices all day, and they feel fine but they ignore our work conditions. . . . The company is getting cheap this year. They're so cheap they won't even give us detergent to wash our clothes. Damn, it only costs 5 *yuan* a bag at most! They won't even give us any shampoo or soap either.[75]

Even under the best of circumstances, managers are hard-pressed to keep workers satisfied. Many workers, especially those belonging to the same native-place network, often discuss and compare the benefits offered by the different factories that employ them. Gifts like porcelain tea sets were perceived by some workers at Phoenix as not "cost[ing] a whole lot" and generated views that "our manager is really stingy."[76] These perceptions could be allayed only by better gifts like the small suitcases handed out by the same factory the following year. These rising expectations were nearly impossible to overcome, a fact that led some managers to shirk such responsibilities whenever possible.

Although some managers sympathize with the workers who are shortchanged in the process, one Jupiter administrator conceded that there is little they can do:

This year hasn't been good—I'm not even sure we'll break even. We can't even give out cool drinks this year because we can't afford it. I feel badly for the workers because there's nothing we can do. The [central office] doesn't have any guidelines or requirements on subsidies or other benefits; this is determined by each subsidiary. I guess it's just bad luck for workers who work here instead of another factory where they give out more things.[77]

What is more discouraging, however, is a lingering sense of dissatisfaction and unease among a growing number of employees and even party representatives regarding prospects for change within the enterprise. Although numerous respondents lauded the improvements precipitated by the party, they also noted that there was still much progress to be made. The director of Phoenix's Fulian branch, for example, told me that her group still suffers from weak organization as well as an approach designed to simply "avoid the worst possible scenarios" (i.e., disruptive worker behavior, especially on the shop floor). She further stated that

we have to be practical and implement programs that accomplish many things. We have to deal with major priorities first before turning to other concerns. Even as we try to meet women's needs, production comes first. There's only so much that can be done. But our workers want us to think differently and go in a new direction (*chuangxin*). The problem is that it takes time and energy for people to change their thinking—it doesn't happen very quickly.[78]

Furthermore, she pointed out, the decline in the number of excursions organized by the enterprise represented a missed opportunity for employees to develop camaraderie and rapport with one another. These developments gave many members of the enterprise the impression that although the state of affairs at Phoenix is not likely to get worse, the chances of dramatic improvement are slim.

Others expressed similar sentiments in relation to the union. This is rather surprising since the union oversees and continues to push for more and better benefits for all. Some employee dissatisfaction appears to be driven by the perception that despite numerous achievements, the union is co-opted by enterprise management and cannot truly act on behalf of workers. The assistant director of Phoenix's Computer Department, whose father serves as a union representative in a state-owned enterprise in Hunan province, was critical of the union's efforts:

I don't think our union is very effective or does very much. The leaders are passive—they do not initiate any programs that improve the lives of workers. Sure, they organize activities but even when they do, they wait for others to come up with ideas. Take the recent basketball tournament. Even though it was officially sponsored by the union, the idea came from an employee at the grassroots, not from the top. It was my friend in [X] office who wanted to do this because he really loves basketball and thought it would be fun to have a major competition.

Despite this, he expressed high expectations for the union, ones that the union or any other organization would be hard-pressed to meet:

To me, a union should try to improve employee wages first and then work and living conditions. Organizing events doesn't help with any of these things—I personally don't feel they've had much of an impact. Perhaps they have a problem with the staffing because I never see them around— they certainly aren't in my office. What they should do is come up with an agenda, a list of things they want done. Then they should approach management and push for things to get done. They should be more active and not wait around for management to take the lead because they won't. I don't think company leaders—except for a few—really respect or think highly of the union.[79]

Even plant managers were skeptical of the union. In fact, one specifically pointed to the union's lack of autonomy as the reason for its impotence:

Our trade union isn't very effective. They are supposed to represent the worker's voice, but the union doesn't empower them. They don't have the capability because they are not independent. It's probably different in foreign or joint ventures—there they are supposed to protect Chinese workers from foreign exploitation. But here they haven't resolved problems that the company leaders aren't already aware of.[80]

Such observations underscore the difficult circumstances the union faces as it tries to aggregate and advance worker interests.[81] Its partnership with management sometimes undercuts its credibility, generating suspicion among workers. The pension program is a good example of this. Although the program enhances the long-term economic security of employees, at first most workers perceived the additional deduction from their monthly wages as further exploitation. Without fully comprehending the benefits of the program, they complained that this was an unjustified subtraction from their already meager earnings. Not until program details were more thoroughly explained, and not until workers leaving the company actually received their contributions back, did the furor subside.

The union chairman admitted that accommodating so many disparate interests is virtually impossible. Nevertheless, he believed that the union can still play a positive role in transforming Phoenix into one of the most progressive enterprises in the country. He was particularly open to new ideas and practices, especially those outside China:

Our system is not very good but we're trying to improve it. Our government is paying much closer attention to the needs and rights of workers, and we are studying the laws and regulations in advanced industrial nations. We're trying to create a similar framework. We would like to meet with the International Labor Organization (ILO) and learn from foreign trade unions, but it's a sensitive issue. It's like talking about human rights, and so our government restricts open discussions and exchanges with foreign unions, although we've met some delegations from the World Bank regarding these issues. We post all the new laws regarding work on the company's web site and hold competitions to see which workers have the best grasp of these laws.[82]

He hopes that by helping workers become more aware of their rights, they will eventually develop a greater sense of empowerment and participate more actively in shaping the enterprise's future.

For better or worse, the flexible, enterprise family structure I have described now serves as the bedrock on which the fates of Jupiter and Phoenix rest. This new approach is designed to fulfill lofty aims, goals considerably more complicated and challenging than previous core tasks. In the survival era, enterprise leaders focused on channeling the trust and solidarity contained in their private kinship and personal networks to their enterprises. During the expansion stage, they attempted to improve production through rationalization. But now, during the reintegration phase, leaders must advance production while actively forging and sustaining enterprise solidarity. The goodwill of employees can no longer be tapped: it must be produced through the combined efforts of executives and employees alike.

Whether this process succeeds or fails will depend in large measure on the depth of leadership's commitment. Memories of unfairness and native-place discrimination remain fresh in the minds of most employees; both enterprises will have to replace those images with new ones of social harmony and inclusion. If the new policies are to endure, they will require constant attention and renewal, a difficult proposition given management's preoccupations with production. As a member of Phoenix's planning department noted, "The problem is everyone is more concerned about production. No one wants to spend time to work on party activities. It's also hard because we can't hold any activities during work hours. After work, everyone is either tired or uninterested. It's really very discouraging."[83] Without a consistent and firm commitment to building the enterprise family, all these efforts will appear to be nothing more than empty ritual.

Still, in shifting the locus of identity from exclusive kinship and native-place groups to the enterprise, the barriers dividing individuals have been punctured and made more porous. In fact, there are some faint signs that the dynamics of interaction are slowly changing. One nonlocal worker explained the situation in this way:

I live in a house with others from my hometown because I didn't know anyone else when I first arrived. It's fun being with them, but that doesn't mean I don't hang out with locals. Lots of them live near me, and some are even from my plant. I like to be around all types of people. I mean it gets really boring if your friends are all the same.[84]

Such thoughts were unheard of just years before, but they perhaps signal a new wave of social change poised to sweep through and transform the Chinese countryside.

Concluding Remarks

In the current stage of reintegration, the leaders of Phoenix and Jupiter have again shown their knack for adaptation and innovation. In trying to restore the sense of common purpose and solidarity that was previously the fount of their success, they took direct action to recreate crucial qualities of their glorious past. They leveled status distinctions, extended collective benefits to all enterprise members, and projected a new sense of inclusion and belonging through the use of fictive kinship. Both firms even invited the Chinese Communist Party back into the enterprise to increase the like-lihood of success.

To a great extent, these efforts have succeeded, but ultimate suc-cess remains uncertain. As these policies take root, managers and workers alike will have to negotiate an acceptable balance between the demands of the "technical" and the needs of the "human."[85] Jupiter and Phoenix now possess considerable resources that can be deployed to solve these problems, and yet throwing as much money at the problem as possible is most certainly not the answer. Enter-prise stability will depend heavily on the degree to which a sense of mutual commitment, trust, and inclusion can be restored. Phoenix and Jupiter are truly at a critical juncture. If the new tolerance and generosity of the enterprise family can fire the imaginations of all employees and spread to all corners of the enterprise, both firms' prospects of achieving the goal of reintegration will become consid-erably brighter.

SIX

Conclusion
What Lies Ahead?

SCHOLARS HAVE LONG NOTED that industrialization poses major challenges for communities that embark on or, in some instances, are forced to march through this tortuous course. Observers have also contended that the process necessitates a major transformation on several fronts, not only in the realm of production but also in the social and political spheres. In communities blessed with abundant resources and strong institutions, the argument runs that the chances of industrialization taking root are considerably greater than in areas lacking them. For communities undergoing this process with few assets at their disposal, the effects are often more devastating: industrialization can increase inequality and rip apart the social sinews that bind citizens together, fragmenting groups and places along new fault lines. Even worse, such efforts may generate a backlash effect, locking in a vicious cycle of "arrested development."

Set against these more conventional perspectives, the histories and recent experiences of Wenzhou and Jinhua stand out as nothing less than extraordinary. Despite environments seemingly unfavorable to development, Jupiter and Phoenix became the triggers for industrialization in their respective communities, bringing factory work to places long considered "backward" and impervious to such dramatic change. New economic opportunities generated by the post-1978 reforms, coupled with effective institution-building, laid the foundation for a massive shift from an agrarian to an industrial way of life. With the establishment of these firms and others like them, numerous areas throughout rural China reached what Malcolm Gladwell calls a "tipping point," a threshold beyond which momentous change takes place very quickly.[1] The results of this process are well known: China has become one of the world's leading industrial workshops and is poised to overtake many of the most formidable industrial powers in the global economy. The burden of leading this charge, however, has increasingly fallen on the shoulders of the men and women who labor in the factories of the Chinese countryside. It is a weight that is becoming heavier with each passing day.

It has often been said that hindsight is always 20/20. When tracing how a specific outcome came to be, it is easy to point out how decisions made at "critical junctures" generated seemingly unstoppable momentum toward the consolidation of particular policies or results. To be sure, self-reinforcing feedback effects were critical in setting Jupiter and Phoenix on their particular developmental paths. During the survival stage especially, the negative impact of historical circumstances initially drove enterprise founders to look inward rather than outward for potential solutions to their dilemmas. The negligible presence of the local state and the relative isolation of these communities forced would-be entrepreneurs to mine their kinship and social networks for capital, expertise, information, and labor to a degree rarely matched elsewhere. In so doing, they gradually displaced the negative feedback effects of isolation and state incapacity with the positive feedback derived from their kinship and social networks.

Still, although these networks remained the organizational cornerstones of Phoenix and Jupiter, a reliance on them alone could not ensure profitability and institutional stability. At each developmental stage, leaders at both companies faced critical decisions on how to respond to market demands as well as to the changing needs and interests of a growing workforce. Like business executives elsewhere, they often stumbled by taking for granted the trust and goodwill of their employees, in the belief that their companies' long-term viability depended overwhelmingly on efficiency and scale of production rather than on equity and a sense of community among their workers. To their credit, they recognized their mistakes and implemented new practices designed to restore the camaraderie and cooperation that were the hallmarks of their firms at the time of their founding. Although neither company can claim unqualified success, the results thus far do suggest some modest gains in morale and workplace harmony. The challenge facing them now is to deepen this progress while continuing the advances in their productive capabilities.

Few scholars would have predicted that such massive change could occur in these neglected and forgotten communities in such a short time. In addition to possessing few natural advantages, Jinhua and Wenzhou residents proceeded to build their factories in what to outside observers appears to be the wrong manner. Contrary to the local state corporatism perspective, enterprise leaders rarely relied on the knowledge or authority of local cadres. In both areas, local officials never assumed a leading role in enterprise-building simply because they commanded neither the resources nor the skills for such a mission. And contrary to modernization theory, enterprise members did not totally jettison their group-oriented, preindustrial values for individually based, "modern" values. Instead, they continued to follow well-established social norms and worked for the welfare of the group as a whole to a much greater degree than was the case at other Chinese firms. Despite "getting it wrong," Phoenix and Jupiter have succeeded spectacularly. And because they did, their experiences provide us with a much fuller and richer view of industrialization, expanding our conceptions of what is possible and altering our understandings and approaches to the process of organizing and harnessing labor for factory work.

In this final chapter, I briefly recap the argument presented in this book. I also review what we can learn through micro-level studies and how they inform the current debates about China's market transition and larger processes of economic and social change. Finally, I end my discussion with an evaluation of the challenges that lie ahead for China's rural enterprises. The course they are treading remains treacherous in many ways, but there is still good reason to be optimistic about their prospects for achieving lasting success, for they continue to be some of the most dynamic organizations in reform-era China.

The Argument Revisited

This book explores how industrial transformation occurred in two unlikely areas, the prefectures of Jinhua and Wenzhou in China's Zhejiang province. Although Zhejiang has historically been considered an area of exceptional refinement and prosperity, these two places remained, for most of the twentieth century, on the fringes of mainstream economic and social life in the province. Neither region achieved the levels of comfort or luxury enjoyed by the northern Zhejiang areas of Hangzhou and Ningbo. In fact, both areas suffered under difficult ecological constraints, a situation that left area natives with a narrow range of options for economic survival. Despite some increase in output during the early reform period, agricultural production offered such limited growth opportunities that many were forced to turn to sideline activities such as small-scale handicraft production and trading. Others, frustrated by the precariousness of this existence, migrated to other areas in search of more permanent employment and relief from financial duress. The historical weakness of Jinhua's and Wenzhou's economies thus boded ill for broader community development. It obstructed the wider provision of critical social services, especially in education, and stymied many individuals who aspired to something grander than a life on the margins. With at best rudimentary educations, students soon discovered that breaking out of subsistence-level jobs and into steady, lucrative, and more professional occupations was a formidable, if not seemingly impossible, goal. For these communities, the stunted nature of public services and institutions constricted their ability to push the local economy in new directions.

This perpetual state of economic underdevelopment persisted even after the founding of the People's Republic. Several factors reinforced this outcome. First, contrary to scholarly assessments that characterize the Chinese state as monolithic and totalitarian, the Chinese state possessed neither the resources nor the organizational capacity to extend its control over every corner of Chinese society. This forced leaders in Beijing to be highly strategic in deploying state resources. Because the parts of Wenzhou and Jinhua prefectures I visited were extremely remote, barricaded in almost every direction by rugged, mountainous terrain, state officials were reluctant to invest significant capital in infrastructure to connect these areas with the rest of the province. Wenzhou was especially problematic because its proximity to the Taiwan Strait placed it on the front lines of any potential military conflict with the rival Nationalists on Taiwan. As a result, the Chinese leadership chose to deploy China's limited resources elsewhere and left the residents of Wenzhou and Jinhua to fend for themselves. In fact, such considerations, at least in part, delayed the opening of an airport in Wenzhou until 1990 and the completion of rail links to the provincial capital of Hangzhou until 1998. Even more astounding is the fact that the airport was built largely with private, not public, funds. Today, there are new plans to once again use private money to replace this airport with one that can handle much greater traffic, one befitting the area's growing economic clout. Thus, although the post-Mao reforms created opportunities for new economic activity, the local state's relatively minor role in Wenzhou's and Jinhua's post-1978 growth underscores the degree to which entrepreneurs were compelled to rely on kin and friends for support in their quest to build their factories.

Although the enormity of these structural forces is clear, they alone did not determine the fates of Jinhua and Wenzhou. Recognizing their impact on these communities is an essential part of my analysis, but of greater importance is understanding how they shaped the formation and evolution of the strategies and actions of the actors themselves. That is to say, it was not just context that mattered, but what people did (and when and how) under those circumstances that was central to determining the outcomes examined here. Indeed, in any study of China's rural enterprises, the people who actually work in the factories day in and day out must take center stage, especially because the success or failure of the enterprise depended on these relatively neglected members of these firms. At the same time, in turning the spotlight back on them, I am certainly not suggesting that the members of Jupiter and Phoenix were all-powerful or all-knowing individuals who easily overcame every obstacle in their path, for they, too, suffered from personal faults, weaknesses, and mistakes in judgment. Rather, in describing how they adjusted to and eventually overcame the challenges they faced, I have tried to show how their perceptions of the world profoundly influenced the way in which they ultimately sought to reshape it.

In my view, the eventual success of Phoenix and Jupiter rested precisely on the ability of enterprise leaders to combine a collectively oriented, trust-based, and reciprocal social ethos with an individual performance-based, profit-driven, industrial production regimen. This sometimes unwieldy and often contradictory organizational amalgam successfully channeled the energies of all enterprise members toward the relatively unfamiliar task of industrial production and served as the pivot on which enterprise operations turned. In short, the founders of both companies took "social capital" and used it to generate high levels of material wealth and effect unprecedented social change. Today, they are excelling in the very spheres in which the local Chinese state, at least in these communities, failed.

Although a tall order, maintaining a balance between competing and often conflicting work and social demands was a central and arguably the most critical concern in each of the three stages that I suggest define the developmental paths of these enterprises. In the first stage, enterprise survival, enterprise leaders successfully maintained this equilibrium because they relied overwhelmingly on their kinship networks and native-place ties for assistance. Indeed, the scale of this dependence was enormous: relatives and close acquaintances provided everything from start-up capital to vital information on market trends to technical expertise and, even, physical labor. More important, they infused the firm with a rough sense of egalitarianism and a feeling of common purpose; this, in turn, inspired them to pursue their goals with the determination and grit of "heroic cadres." Together, they supplied competence, camaraderie, and community, thus assuring high levels of labor and social stability to counteract the severe demands of industrial work.

Once the threat of firm failure subsided, Jupiter and Phoenix entered the next stage of their evolution, expansion. Seeking to increase profits and fend off new competitors, enterprise leaders moved to rationalize and expand factory operations. This new enterprise objective or core task was highly ambitious because it entailed a dramatically new approach to production, one that stressed specialization, adherence to impersonal rules, and greater managerial control over the work process. This strategy was designed to transform these firms into great, multidivisional enterprises. Although these plans fueled impressive increases in production output, they also instigated enormous social turmoil within the workplace community. The heavy emphasis on skills, defined roles, and hierarchy struck directly at the social norms and values that had guided the enterprise through the previous stage of survival. These tensions were further exacerbated by the arrival of "outsiders," new personnel who were not members of the same kinship or native-place networks that, up to that point, had anchored these enterprises. New social gulfs surfaced, ones that could not easily be bridged by the promise of higher salaries alone. Enterprise leaders were greatly surprised by these developments and were forced to reconsider their long-term goals and strategies.

The tensions that emerged during expansion resulted from the increasingly contradictory pull between the demands of production and the needs of the community. In seeking to preserve the gains of expansion and restore the social bonds crucial to success during the survival era, enterprise leaders propelled their firms into the next stage, reintegration. In this new phase, enterprise managers have enacted new policies that, to a large degree, restore decentralized decision-making and managerial flexibility, recalling in some ways the *modus operandi* of the survival era. The result has been a flatter authority structure and a reduction in *official* status distinctions. More important, both enterprises have moved to reshape the foundations of their organizational identity. Whereas Phoenix and Jupiter were highly dependent on family members in their earlier history, both firms have now created a new "enterprise family" orientation in which every member of the enterprise is seen as a valuable component of the community.

This newly emerging identity is rooted in practices that seem contradictory. Although both firms remain committed to the rationalization of production, they have also added paternalistic practices that run counter to the logic of hard, cold efficiency, in particular, a range of collective benefits to demonstrate their concern for employee well-being. But perhaps the most intriguing development has been the return of the Chinese Communist Party to these firms. Defying conventional prescriptions that enterprise and party remain separate (*zhengqi fenkai*), Phoenix and Jupiter have instead asked the party to join them in defining the boundaries of the new company identity. Although the party does not interfere in the sphere of production, it does take a leading role in organizing activities designed to reinforce a sense of cohesion and solidarity and, hence, decrease social tensions and labor conflicts. Attempting to blur differences based on kinship, organizational status, and native-place through singing contests, basketball games, excursions to scenic sites, and other nonwork activities, enterprise leaders are clearly hoping that the party can help them rebuild the tight social bonds that once knit the enterprise together. This emerging partnership marks a major reconfiguration of state-society relations at the local level. In contrast to the leading role played by the local state in counties studied by other observers, the local state in Jinhua and Wenzhou prefectures plays only a complementary, albeit an important, part in enterprise development. The party is again relevant, although not all-powerful. Put another way, without the party as "Robin," enterprise management would find it exceedingly difficult to continue as "Batman" and achieve the twin goals of enhancing economic prosperity and social stability.

To date, these programs have produced mixed results. Although some employees remain frustrated by slow progress on compensation and job security, the vast majority of the workforce now enjoys substantially better benefits on a number of fronts. Shop floor work conditions have been upgraded with the addition of improved climate control and work safety systems, and new pension and disability programs have been implemented. On the nonwork front, both companies now provide tastier, more nourishing meals at heavily subsidized prices and regularly schedule a broader array of social events. Since 2000, for example, Phoenix has increased the number of such activities on its calendar to roughly one every two to three weeks; this compares favorably with the previous rate of one every six to eight weeks. These affairs range from, among many others, athletic contests to singing competitions to movie screenings, all designed to provide some relief from the pressures of the shop floor and the office.

It remains to be seen whether these programs will be successful in the long term, but their emergence is significant in the sense that they represent management's willingness to tackle persisting questions about how the demands of work and community can best be reconciled and fulfilled. Contrary to popular stereotypes of high-ranking enterprise executives as rapacious, coldhearted, and soulless, the senior managers at both companies seem genuinely concerned about the futures and well-being of their employees. For a time, however, they were engrossed in other developmental and institutional issues, ones that, although important to the survival of their companies, prevented them from devoting their full attention and energy to stabilizing shop floor relationships that had become tense and bitter. In putting these paternalistic practices in place, enterprise leaders have revealed both their nostalgia for the values of an earlier era and a strategy for promoting internal cohesion and social harmony in an institutional environment in which both are becoming much harder to sustain.

The implementation of these programs also signals an important transformation in the mindsets of production-line workers. Instead of simply tolerating workplace inequities or lashing out in anger and frustration, they have learned to use organizational mechanisms not only to air their views but, more important, to push for substantive change. Although they still lose more battles than they win, they are once again exercising initiative and forcing enterprise management to be more accountable for its actions. In a way, the members and especially the leaders of Phoenix and Jupiter have come full circle in terms of their search for a recipe for long-term industrial success. Even as they continue to seek out new technologies and more effective production and management approaches, they have been reminded that how they manage workplace relationships will ultimately determine whether or not these enterprises will endure.

A Grassroots Understanding of Rural Enterprises

By using a micro-level approach, this book attempts to offer a nuanced and dynamic picture of the events and processes in China's rural enterprises. It also describes and analyzes the inner workings of such enterprises and the motive forces and critical decisions behind their emergence and success. To be sure, this approach is highly sensitive to access restrictions and questions about the reliability of respondents' testimony (see Chapter 1). Nevertheless, such in-depth studies can nevertheless yield important insights unobtainable by other means. Aggregate data and simplifying assumptions about human motivation can provide preliminary directions for further research regarding enterprise dynamics and behavior; however, they cannot replace sustained attention to the thoughts, decisions, and actions of enterprise members, from the founders at the pinnacle of the company hierarchy to the production workers at its base. Although these details are often considered "noise" that needs to be eliminated by analytical "filters," they often reveal much about the shape and direction of specific patterns of employee behavior. By focusing on these factors, we can learn how difficult decisions are reached and why some outcomes "stick" and others do not, and when and why goals and institutional practices diverge. To be sure, the larger ecological, political, and social legacies in both locales were significant, but their primary impact was to set the broader parameters within which the practices and identity of the firm were forged. By folding these concerns into one framework, we create a much stronger basis for understanding how rural development proceeds and how it affects the well-being of the men and women who are pivotal parts of the process.*

Although my study highlights the common challenges of production and community and the unique ways in which Phoenix and Jupiter overcame them, I am by no means arguing that their particular experiences are representative of all rural enterprises in China. In a nation as vast as China, significant variation should be expected, for every community is endowed with different levels of resources and particular historical legacies that shape their experiences and

---

*Here, I agree with Philip Selznick's (*TVA and the Grassroots*, 250) conclusion that only through a "reconstruction . . . of the conditions and forces which appear to have shaped the behavior of key participants" can we make sense of organizational dynamics.

prospects for transformation in distinct and momentous ways. Nevertheless, in trying to understand the process and consequences of industrialization in the Chinese countryside, we can distinguish the common challenges of production and community and the particular solutions created to overcome them without exaggerating the universality of these experiences.

In this sense, my work is modest in its claims about the course of rural development in China. My study does not dismiss outright the findings of other scholars who have studied the emergence of rural factories in the post-Mao reform era; rather, it complements them. Jean Oi's insightful assessment of rural enterprises and their connections to local cadre-entrepreneurs may indeed be an accurate one, but only for the areas she studied, not all of China. Similarly, I believe my analysis explains the path and trajectory of rural industrialization in the resource-poor communities of rural Zhejiang, as well as perhaps other communities that share similar legacies and profiles, but much more research needs to be conducted in order to confirm the wider validity of these findings. It is especially important that greater efforts be made to evaluate the developmental prospects of communities in China's vast interior. Undoubtedly, this is one of the most daunting tasks facing students of China today. From Guangdong province in the south to Heilongjiang in the north; from Zhejiang in the east to Xinjiang in the far northwest; the number of communities requiring additional study is staggering. As research opportunities in China increase, our research agenda should and must make room for more micro-level studies. Certainly, conducting such research is no easy task, for it is highly labor-intensive and requires a major commitment of resources, time, and energy even before any notable findings might be made. This study offers one way of fulfilling this objective—through an examination of the factory from the inside out and from the ground up; it provides a way for us to see how the people who are central to this process—the executives, the managers, the administrative staff, and the workers—understand and react to the factory environment in which they live and act.

Research of this kind has important implications for larger theoretical debates in a number of areas. In China studies, we can begin testing hypotheses about enterprise formation and institutional change in the Chinese countryside. By using a developmental stages framework, it becomes evident that enterprise success is not simply the outcome of oppressive labor practices, but the result of a complex set of responses to market demands, advanced technologies, and new personnel. What Kathleen Thelen concludes in regard to the evolution of skill formation and labor institutions in Germany is equally applicable to understanding the transformations analyzed in this study:

> Formal institutions do not survive long stretches of time by standing still. The language of stasis and inertia is particularly unhappy because as the world around institutions is changing their survival will not necessarily rest on the faithful reproduction of those institutions as originally constituted, but rather on their ongoing active adaptation to changes in the political and economic environment in which they are embedded.[2]

Put in the context of this study, the success of Jupiter and Phoenix is due largely to their willingness and ability to adjust to new economic and social developments without completely jettisoning the elements at the very core of their success. Furthermore, their experiences underscore how change does not need to be radical in order to be significant. Sometimes, small changes can make a big difference.

In addition, such work lays the groundwork for potentially fruitful comparisons not only of different rural enterprises but also of rural and urban enterprises as they tackle common organizational challenges in the post-1978 reform period. In fact, current discussions are beginning to take up issues other than the "red" versus "expert" concerns that shaped the earliest debates on Chinese enterprise management.[3] These efforts nudge China studies closer to developments in other fields such as American labor studies, in which examinations of industrialization patterns in the United States incorporated the diverse experiences of Paterson, New Jersey; Philadelphia; and New England.[4] In addition, they lay the foundation for comparisons of labor processes in different national and even historical contexts.[5]

For political scientists, understanding China's rural industrialization process offers new insights into old questions, especially in the realm of labor politics.[6] Contrary to the predictions of modernization theory, for example, my analysis indicates that alternative organizational forms combining collectively oriented social norms with profit-driven, demanding, individual performance–oriented, industrial production structures can effectively harness the energies of peasants—people who theoretically make poor workers—to achieve production breakthroughs. Thus, preindustrial values need not be completely abandoned before industrialization can proceed. In fact, this study suggests that social identities based on common kinship and native-place allegiances can play crucial roles in stabilizing the firm against potentially debilitating social conflict, especially in its earliest stages of development.

At the same time, the experiences of both firms reveal that enterprise members continually contest and negotiate the boundaries of social identity as well as notions of work equity. Sometimes, workers support company policies; at other times, they express frustration and resist the directives of their superiors, even though such actions may undermine their futures at the enterprise. For them, an optimal outcome is defined not solely in terms of financial gain but along personal and social dimensions as well. Knowing when and why specific norms and values resonate with enterprise members tells us much about the possibilities of transforming a disparate group of individuals into a cohesive and effective workforce. Moreover, it also shows that enterprise members are more apt to support new policies when the pace and sequence of institutional change do not force them to reach impossibly beyond their grasp. In this sense, such dynamism suggests that the search for a "one size fits all" approach to industrial success is futile. What these developments tell us is that once common organizational challenges are identified, each enterprise community can and should draw on its own resources and experiences to devise a strategy of action that both heightens its competitiveness in the marketplace and preserves the essence of who it is. For Jupiter and Phoenix, the dexterity with which this task was handled explains the course of their development over the past few decades as well as their prospects for positive transformation in the future.

Future Challenges

The meteoric rise and continued success of China's rural enterprises constitute a stunning and unexpected accomplishment. Many observers, especially advocates of a full-scale transition to a market-based, capitalist economy, have lauded rural factories for responding to consumer demands and operating under "hard-budget constraints." Even so, such views raise new questions about rural enterprises: How long can they continue to play vital roles in the rural economy? Will they eventually die out, and if they do, what will be their legacy in China's rural communities? In this final section, I try to provide some preliminary answers to these queries by looking at what lies ahead for companies like Phoenix and Jupiter.

The challenges that have loomed on the horizon since the late 1990s are formidable and will tax rural firms to the extreme, but they are not unfamiliar. One of the most daunting is staying competitive in China's marketizing economy. Although unceasing demand for Phoenix's and Jupiter's products catapulted these firms into leading positions in their respective sectors, in a way their very success also made them more vulnerable. Any significant shift in consumer preferences could lead to unmovable inventories and major financial losses at both firms, forcing them to cut back their large-scale operations and their massive labor forces. In fact, heightened customer demand for low-cost, high-quality goods was just beginning to affect Phoenix's production strategies in 1998. Inconsistent quality often led to irate customers storming the company's customer service desk, shouting obscenities and demanding refunds for shoddy goods.

Concerns about quality rippled through the company and forced some factory managers to rethink the actual organization of work. One manager who had previously been enthusiastic about the possibilities of assembly line production eventually reverted to "batch-oriented" production, or what Michael Piore and Charles Sabel call "flexible specialization."[7] Although this reversal meant that each worker was responsible for making smaller quantities of a vast range of switches and indicator lights rather than large numbers of a few products, he was surprised to find that his workers were generally much happier with the batch orientation than they had been with the assembly line system, under which they were assigned fewer work tasks and responsibilities. Although he bemoaned their lack of teamwork and his failure to implement a more rationalized production system, he nevertheless acknowledged that product quality and morale had improved markedly. For a short time at least, such policy shifts have allowed some of Phoenix's divisions to retain a competitive edge over domestic rivals. Even so, most members of the company feared that even these changes would not be enough to hold off the anticipated entry of foreign competitors into the low-voltage electrical product industry.

Top-level managers at Phoenix considered these actions to be only a temporary retreat from their long-term goal of becoming the most efficient, most innovative producer of low-voltage electrical products in China and a true competitor in the global market. If Phoenix is to compete successfully against the likes of Siemens and General Electric, its strategists believed that it needed to accelerate, not slow down, investments in productive capacity and personnel training. By 2004, it had become clear that, despite the appeal of batch-oriented production, Phoenix had staked its future on building and maintaining economies of scale in its myriad product lines. In fact, not only had the company begun replacing its outdated equipment with more current, often automated imported models, but it had also started establishing new operations in other areas, most notably the city of Wenzhou itself, the provincial capital of Hangzhou, and Shanghai. Although the recent completion of a new industrial park in a nearby village brought together many of Phoenix's previously far-flung operations, the company's overall growth far outstripped its ability to house its plants under "one roof." Given the economic and political difficulties Phoenix had encountered in expanding the industrial park in Wenzhou prefecture, company leaders saw no alternative to establishing newer divisions elsewhere.

Interestingly, several company representatives saw this move as not only inevitable but also beneficial to the company's long-term development. When I pressed them further on this point, they first explained that the respective local governments offered very favorable terms for establishing new operations within their jurisdictions.

It also facilitated the hiring of new, skilled personnel, of the sort that previously had been reluctant to work for Phoenix because of its "backwater" location. This new willingness to accept job offers from Phoenix allowed the company to accelerate its drive toward professionalization throughout its ranks and to deflect accusations of cronyism.[8] Indeed, for many recent college graduates, Hangzhou was seen as a wonderful place to work, a medium-sized city with all the benefits of a major metropolis and few of its drawbacks. Many of the managerial staff with whom I had become close friends during my first research stints at Phoenix confided that they hoped one day to transfer to the new divisions. In the meantime, some had purchased flats and moved their families to Hangzhou while they remained behind at their posts in Wenzhou prefecture. Like many other young couples, my friends were concerned about quality of life issues, especially educational opportunities for their children and access to medical and social services. They preferred to keep their families together, but nevertheless they were willing to endure what they hoped to be a temporary separation in exchange for access to these highly sought-after services.

Individual gains aside, launching operations near major urban areas offered the added benefit of putting the enterprise in closer touch with its customers, allowing it to keep up more easily with the latest product developments and trends. But what is perhaps more significant is the company's highest-ranking leaders concluding that this exposure would aid Phoenix's transformation from a family-operated shop into a truly global producer of low-voltage electrical products. To become a top company, it would have to resemble one in organization, capabilities, and reputation, and that could come only through more, not less, engagement with the market. Ultimately, Phoenix's founder chose to embrace this development rather than avoid it. While we rode in his sleek, new, black 7-series BMW, he told me that although his company would never forget its roots in Wenzhou prefecture, it now faced competitive pressures that required it to reconfigure, expand, and deepen its regional networks. Reminiscent of the experiences of companies in Silicon Valley and along Route 128, Phoenix appears determined to take advantage of the potential synergy among capital, education, local government, and manufacturing that is coalescing outside its original home base.[9] And like the dynamic firms of Silicon Valley, Phoenix recognizes that increased collaboration could potentially enhance its competitive advantage. Back in 1998, both Phoenix and Jupiter were eager to sponsor university research in hopes that such efforts would lead to infusions of both new knowledge and personnel for the companies. Some researchers welcomed this new partnership, for it allowed them to carry on with their research projects while also helping their students secure jobs upon graduation.

Still, the uncertainties of the market, the desire to stay one step ahead of the competition, and government pressure to phase out outdated products have together spawned even more radical policies at both firms. Both Phoenix and Jupiter have attempted to move away from labor-intensive products to more "high tech" (*gaokeji*) or, perhaps more accurately, high value-added goods. Enterprise leaders believe that a continual shift toward the most profitable market niches is a necessity, even if it leads to the eventual dissolution of its original production base. As a result, Jupiter has decided not to expand or upgrade its extant textile operations and will, instead, allow them to wind down according to the dictates of the market. Once profits dwindle to zero, these operations will be shut down.* To make up for this lost revenue, enterprise leaders plan to invest millions of dollars in production technology to manufacture cellular phone and notebook computer batteries, even though they have neither the research nor the production infrastructure in place to fully support this venture. Phoenix has also followed a similar strategy of refusing to make new, significant investments in "old" technology. After years of planning and discussions, the company finally established a computer software division to create business management programs for Chinese companies. Top leaders at both firms hope these new divisions will anchor their entry into the "new" economy.

These moves are bold strokes, but they are also risky ventures, in some ways more perilous than the initial decisions to create these

---

*In 1998, Jupiter was selling high-quality sweatshirts embroidered with sports emblems for approximately US$5.00; their net profit per sweatshirt was one dollar. These products easily sold for over $50.00 once they reached American retail stores.

enterprises. First, these new projects require massive capital outlays of millions of dollars with no guarantee of quick returns. Prospects for success rely on the *potential* sales of these products rather than established and proven demand. There is little evidence to suggest that these plans were launched as a result of market research by members of the firm's personal networks or even outside consultants. At Jupiter, perhaps more ominous are the widespread rumors that a number of these projects were chosen by the founder himself. If true, it suggests that a more arbitrary, even whimsical, approach to strategic planning and development has become ingrained in the company's decision-making process.

If leaping into newer sectors with fierce, often better-known competitors becomes a more common practice, Phoenix and Jupiter will be playing not to their strengths, but to their weaknesses. They will be turning their backs on the formulas that made them the successes they are today. Despite their surprising transformation from small-scale imitators to leading manufacturers, the items they hope will anchor their continued charge into the future require, among other things, a highly skilled workforce, one that neither firm can currently field, at least in numbers that would generate a return commensurate with the sizable investments they have made in planning, capital, land, and labor. In Jupiter's case, the shortage of qualified personnel has already severely curtailed production of one of their most highly touted new products, advanced capacitors. Although managers have been justifiably careful in personnel selection, their inability to assemble a large enough team led to two straight years of red ink and little promise of profits in the foreseeable future. When I was given a tour of the plant in 1998, the equipment was in nearly pristine condition. It had undergone some initial testing but otherwise remained idle as the managerial team tried to decide whether it was safe to proceed with a limited production run. Their fears about possibly damaging their newly acquired and expensive machinery led to costly delays and essentially shut down the manufacturing process.

Their plans for producing advanced batteries are likely to suffer a similar fate. The managers of this new division have quickly discovered that setting up these new operations properly is more challenging than they had anticipated. Even periodic visits from foreign consultants have not helped to significantly alleviate deficiencies in technical expertise, staffing, and communication that continue to plague the new plant. One American consultant I met was skeptical about the chances of pulling this project off. Almost none of the Chinese personnel at the new operation could read the technical manuals for the equipment imported from Germany, nor could they communicate effectively with the German representative who visited once every six months. Although the current status of this project remains unknown, these were inauspicious beginnings.

Phoenix's path appears equally filled with potential hazards. Designing computer software for a Chinese market in which Microsoft and Sun Microsystems are establishing a presence is a tall order. Software and other intellectual property endeavors require qualitatively different talents as well as a managerial approach radically different from the one employed in running Phoenix's factories. When I inquired about the division in 2004, company representatives informed me that—reluctantly—the project had been abandoned. Faced with seemingly insurmountable staffing challenges (most of the top Chinese computer programming graduates were being hired away by the likes of Microsoft), management chose to end this project and rededicate itself to its bread-and-butter products. Moreover, as Phoenix's chief rival became financially overextended through numerous speculative real estate deals, the company finally realized that although it may have been fashionable to branch out into new ventures, these did not necessarily augment core operations and might instead undermine a company's financial underpinnings.

Hence, the massive investments necessary to start and then to make these new production lines viable, coupled with the possibility of sharp and even prolonged financial losses, will only intensify the financial burdens borne by both firms. Such pressures have already forced leaders at both companies to re-evaluate, modify, and even abandon their previous plans to improve their firms' competitiveness. Neither the funds that could otherwise be devoted to improving the collective benefits of enterprise members nor those slated for party-led efforts to build company identity are likely to increase unless profits continue to grow. So far, slack resources have not been in short supply, and considerable amounts have been devoted to improving employee welfare. Even so, with the new, decentralized organizational structure in place and reduced emphasis on the implementation of uniform policy throughout enterprise subdivisions, a heightened sense of deprivation may once again materialize among employees. Employees constantly discuss differences in remuneration packages and work conditions with their friends and relatives: indeed, that news often sparks discontent and even a drop in work performance.

A source of additional disaffection is likely to be the contradictions that first emerged during the phase of expansion and still persist. If and when new, high-technology products are introduced, new employees with advanced skills will be hired to assemble them. Most of these workers are likely to be outsiders simply because few locals possess the requisite technical skills to keep such production lines running smoothly. Despite the emphasis on reducing status differences and privileges within the enterprise and the professed commitment to rebuilding mutual respect and egalitarianism throughout the enterprise community, the better treatment these workers will command will perpetuate and even accentuate the gap opened by the demands of production. In short, both companies will undermine their own objectives and reinforce skill and status differentials even as they attempt to recapture a collective spirit of cooperation and trust.

To date, these contradictions have not precipitated the debilitating bickering or conflict that senior leaders at both firms feared. In fact, in some plants, the number of disputes between workers and managerial staff has declined. Nevertheless, personnel at every level of the company hierarchy do perceive inequities in treatment, and this has produced lower morale in many cases. Status and native-place distinctions persist and remain central in the ongoing debates over what constitutes fair compensation and respect. At times, they even solidify misperceptions and stereotypes and deepen suspicions that employees have of their superiors and, sometimes, of their co-workers. Although some complain and hope that company leaders will work to enact new policies to ameliorate these problems, those impatient for change often end up quitting and heading elsewhere.

And for many who remain, a sense of sluggishness sets in, making a day at work a rather unfulfilling and unhappy experience.

Such challenges will intensify and further complicate efforts to redefine the parameters of the "enterprise family" identity. In both firms, the workforce, from production workers to managerial and administrative staff, now numbers in the thousands, a staggering figure even in comparison to the most successful firms in advanced industrial economies. Jupiter's and Phoenix's achievements have spawned heightened expectations for better compensation and work conditions among their employees, expectations that diverge from the vision of their bosses. To their credit, both companies have invested considerable resources and energy into rebuilding a sense of familiarity and closeness throughout the ranks. They have even gone so far as to buck conventional wisdom by inviting the Chinese Communist Party to help them in this endeavor. Nevertheless, the hard reality is that the increased numbers of employees at both enterprises make the realization of close relationships nearly impossible. Even when managers attempt to reorganize workers into smaller, more personal clusters like quality control circles, these groupings remain qualitatively different in structure and spirit than comparable units at Gore Associates, the manufacturer of Gore-Tex.

In *The Tipping Point*, Malcolm Gladwell describes how small groups at Gore maximize the benefits of "institutional transactive memory" not only to establish clear roles for each member but, more important, to spur improved performance through a heightened sense of collective commitment.[10] Here, bureaucratic structures and regulations are minimized because informal norms and expectations serve *de facto* as an incentive structure and enforcement mechanism. In contrast, Phoenix and Jupiter have kept their larger bureaucratic structures intact, even if they are less visible and intrusive than they once were. Although this helps ensure a higher level of coordination among the various divisions, it nevertheless reinforces a sense of "us" versus "them," line workers versus managers and executives. The result is a hardening rather than a softening or breakdown of the formal status distinctions throughout both enterprises.

Under such circumstances, the claims of "family" may hold little sway over employees when the vast majority of them do not know their coworkers by name or cannot engage one another in sustained and meaningful social interaction outside work. In fact, the newest dormitories at Phoenix's new industrial park complex discourage rather than facilitate informal exchange. The location and occupants of the five buildings clearly reflect the segmented nature of the organization itself, with consultants and specialists in one, managerial staff in the second, and production workers in the remaining three. Little mingling between these groups occurs outside the company cafeteria and the common recreation areas between the buildings. Although the company is now able to house over two thousand employees (more than a fivefold increase over 1998), amenities such as in-room telephone and internet connections allow enterprise members to retreat from the hurly-burly of life at Phoenix and disengage from coworkers, at least temporarily. In one sense, this development provides employees with a private, quiet space they did not previously enjoy, a space that can be used for individual relaxation and renewal. At the same time, the cost of this increasing insulation from the outside may be a slow attenuation of the social bonds that once served to bind the organization closely together.

If this drift continues, singing contests, dances, and sporting events will seem like empty rituals to many, but I would suggest that they can still fulfill an important function. For many enterprise members, these events remain the only forums in which they can temporarily set aside differences of rank and background and interact on more personal, informal terms. These are opportunities for individuals to see one another not as line workers, workshop directors, or managers but as people who share similar hopes and dreams. They can create moments of both revelation and inspiration. Not surprisingly, participants in these events tended to feel more connected, more alive, especially those who came from more modest backgrounds. For example, at a speech contest tryout at Phoenix in August 2004, a middle-aged woman who had worked as a custodian for two years elicited the loudest cheers of the night when she told the audience that she had finally learned to respect herself because everyone at Phoenix did so. Even she, a custodian who cleaned the bathrooms each day, a person who had not even finished middle school, could be appreciated, at least for one brief moment, for who she was and not just what she did.

Still, in highlighting the difficulties ahead, I do not want to leave the grim impression that these companies are on the verge of collapse nor suggest that their success was solely the result of good timing or luck. It would be foolish to underestimate their resolve and ability to overcome adversity, for they have already proven skeptics wrong. These companies have unequivocally demonstrated that they were and remain resourceful and innovative in ways that many of their competitors could never be. The recognition by the leaders of Jupiter and Phoenix of the importance of the issues now facing them and the continual search for better solutions are at the very least reasons for cautious optimism. Indeed, some of their community-building policies are slowly bearing fruit. Communication has become more open, and enterprise members are at least listening more intently and trying harder to understand and work with fellow employees. From the nonlocal worker wooing the attractive, local Wenzhou girl living a few houses down the road to the new friendships emerging between local managers and outsider staff members, old barriers are breaking down and changing the long-held stereotypical perceptions people have of one another.

Even if rural enterprises do not survive current pressures, they will nonetheless have a profound impact not only on the companies that succeed them but, more important, on the rural communities that sheltered and even embraced them. Although rural enterprises may assume very different organizational forms in the future, these early experiences will continue to be instructive and valuable references as leaders press forward with new plans. Rural enterprises faced the formidable trials of erecting effective organizations and maintaining social solidarity and sparked a wave of unprecedented industrial advance in the Chinese countryside. These cases thus embody a spirit of hope and transformation for communities that previously struggled mightily with such tasks. At a critical historical moment, they ushered in an industrialization that not only brought new prosperity and positive change to previously impoverished areas but also altered how people in rural areas understood themselves and the world in which they live. Citizens of the Chinese countryside finally realized that they, too, could shape their destinies in accord with their own visions and goals. Like citizens in other periods and places, they achieved a sense of personal efficacy that few had thought possible. Whatever the future course of industrialization, this legacy will forever be etched into the historical landscape of rural China.

Reference Matter

Notes

For complete author names, titles, and publication data for works cited here by short forms, see the Bibliography, pp. 207–19.

Chapter 1

1. See the Organisation of Economic Co-operation and Development, *Economic Survey of China*; or http://www.oecd.org/document/15/0,2340,en_2649_201185_35363023_1_1_1_1,00.html (accessed Sept. 30, 2005).

2. *Zhongguo xiangzhen qiye nianjian*, 7.

3. National Bureau of Statistics of China, comp., *China Statistical Yearbook*, 2004, 122–23.

4. Deng Xiaoping, cited in Zhou and White, "Quiet Politics and Rural Enterprise in Reform China," 461.

5. This position is most clearly articulated in Sabel, *Work and Politics*, 101–12. See also Thompson, *The Making of the English Working Class*.

6. See Thelen, *How Institutions Evolve*, 32–33. The classic statement of firms as shifting political coalitions remains Cyert and March, *A Behavioral Theory of the Firm*.

7. See Putnam, *Bowling Alone*.

8. Selznick, *Leadership in Administration*, 17. Italics in the original.

9. For a succinct overview, see Stark and Nee, "Toward an Institutional Analysis of State Socialism."

10. Kornai, "The Hungarian Reform Process"; for his policy recommendations, see 86–94. On China, see Guthrie, *Dragon in a Three-Piece Suit*.

11. On transaction costs, see Williamson, *The Economic Institutions of Capitalism*; Coase, "The Nature of the Firm"; and Demsetz, "Towards a Theory of Property Rights."

12. Steinfeld, *Forging Reform in China*, 27–38.

13. For an overview of the main issues of contention, see Putterman, "The Role of Ownership and Property Rights in China's Economic Transition"; and Walder, "Corporate Organization and Local Government Property Rights in China."

14. Weitzman and Xu, "Chinese Township-Village Enterprises as Vaguely Defined Cooperatives." Weitzman and Xu also argue that informal mechanisms of trust and exchange ("the *gemen* spirit") allowed China to implement a gradual approach to reform rather than the "big bang" path adopted by Eastern Europe and Russia.

15. See Nee, "Organizational Dynamics of Market Transition."

16. For an analysis of how capitalist behavior is upending socialist practices, see Guthrie, *Dragon in a Three-Piece Suit*.

17. Oi, "Fiscal Reform." See also idem, *Rural China Takes Off*.

18. Walder, "Local Governments as Industrial Firms," 269.

19. Oi, "Fiscal Reform," 119–21.

20. Stark and Bruszt, *Postsocialist Pathways*.

21. Pierson, *Politics in Time*, 153.

22. See W. Richard Scott, *Organizations*.

23. See, e.g., Hershatter, *The Workers of Tianjin*; and Perry, *Shanghai on Strike*.

24. Ching Kwan Lee, *Gender and the South China Miracle*, 160.

25. Jowitt, "Inclusion," in idem, *New World Disorder*, 88. The framework is further explained in Calvin Chen, "Leninism, Developmental Stages, and Transformation."

26. Burawoy, *The Politics of Production*, esp. chap. 3. See also Ching Kwan Lee, *Gender and the South China Miracle*.

27. Frazier, *The Making of the Chinese Industrial Workplace*.

28. My understanding of this process has been influenced by the work of Richard Madsen, esp. *Morality and Power in a Chinese Village*. However, his analysis of "moral discourse" in a Chinese village focuses more on how these discussions impact political legitimacy within a local community, whereas I concentrate on the rural factory.

29. See Gerschenkron, "Economic Backwardness in Historical Perspective," in idem, *Economic Backwardness in Historical Perspective*.

30. For an analysis of how employees defy managerial practices through strikes and other resistance tactics, see Scullion and Edwards, *The Social Organization of Industrial Conflict*.

31. For an excellent discussion of "multiple conjunctural causation," see Ragin, *The Comparative Method*, esp. 23–25.

32. Gold, "Guerrilla Interviewing Among the *Getihu*."

33. See Geertz, "Thick Description," in idem, *The Interpretation of Cultures*.

34. See Ragin, *The Comparative Method*.

35. Many scholars see ethnographically oriented studies as less "amenable to replication" and theory validation; see, e.g., Friedman and McDaniel, "In the Eye of the Beholder."

36. Many of the problems I encountered and the techniques I employed to overcome them parallel those discussed in Walder, *Communist Neo-Traditionalism*, 255–69; and Chan et al., *Chen Village Under Mao and Deng*, 2–9.

37. For an explanation of how the cautious approach of Zhejiang's provincial leaders affected the pace and nature of economic reform in the province, see Forster, "The Political Economy of Post-Mao Zhejiang." For a comprehensive overview of neighboring Jiangsu's developmental experience in the post-Mao reform period, see Samuel Ho, *Rural China in Transition*, esp. chap. 3.

Chapter 2

1. National Bureau of Statistics of China, comp., *China Statistical Yearbook, 2005*, 62.

2. See Chen Weixin, ed., *Su, Zhe, Yue*.

3. Perry, *Rebels and Revolutionaries in North China*, 7.

4. See, e.g., Gereffi and Wyman, eds., *Manufacturing Miracles*; and Deyo, *The Political Economy of the New Asian Industrialism*.

5. Alan Liu, "The 'Wenzhou Model' of Development," 697.

6. For other perspectives, see Yia-Ling Liu, "Reform From Below"; and Whiting, *Power and Wealth in Rural China*.

7. Forster, *Zhejiang Province in Reform*, 61.

8. Schoppa, *Chinese Elites and Political Change*, 13.

9. *Zhejiang nianjian*, 32.

10. Ping-ti Ho, *Studies on the Population of China*, 10.

11. Although I agree with Keith Schoppa that Wenzhou lagged far behind Ningbo, I disagree with his conclusion that Wenzhou was a part of the "outer core" of Zhejiang and thus more developed than other regions within the province simply because of its close location to waterways. It is more accurate to consider Wenzhou a peripheral area.

12. For a historical overview, see Rankin, *Elite Activism and Political Transformation in China*.

13. Wenzhoushi difangzhi bianzuan weiyuanhui, *Wenzhou shizhi*, 31, 259, and 1431.

14. Bramall, "The Wenzhou 'Miracle,'" 48–49.

15. Parris, "Local Initiative and National Reform," 243.

16. Bramall, "The Wenzhou 'Miracle,'" 53; Whiting, *Power and Wealth in Rural China*, 68.

17. Dong Fang, "Wenzhouren fujia yifang de aomiao," 31.

18. Ibid., 31.

19. Ibid., 39.

20. Pan, "Politics of Marketization in Rural China," 199–200.

21. Wenzhoushi difangzhi bianzuan weiyuanhui, *Wenzhou shizhi*, 345. Unfortunately, the gazetteer does not disaggregate this data or clearly distinguish the differences between illiterate and semi-illiterate.

22. Ibid., 346.

23. Ibid., 345–46.

24. See Saxenian, *Regional Advantage*, esp. chap. 1.

25. Wenzhoushi difangzhi bianzuan weiyuanhui, *Wenzhou shizhi*, 344.

26. Ibid., 1047.

27. Ibid.

28. Ibid., 1032.

29. For a full discussion of "inward orientation," see Migdal, *Peasants, Politics, and Revolution*.

30. Parris, "Local Initiative and National Reform," 243.

31. For a contrasting view on peasant perspectives on the market, see Popkin, *The Rational Peasant*, esp. 63–72.

32. X *shizhi*, 245. I have not given the full citation here in order to maintain the confidentiality of Jupiter's identity. The full citation can be obtained by contacting the author.

33. Ibid., 111.

34. See Yeh, *Provincial Passages*, esp. 31–46.

35. X *shizhi*, 118.

36. Ibid.

37. The term "economic take-off" comes from Rostow, *The Stages of Economic Growth*.

38. The experiences in Jinhua and Wenzhou contrast sharply with the findings of Andrew Walder (*Communist Neo-traditionalism*), who suggests that the Chinese Communists created a formidable network of clientelist ties, especially in factories.

39. See Vivienne Shue's essay "Peasant Localism and the Chinese State," in idem, *The Reach of the State*, 33–71.

40. Yia-Ling Liu, "Reform from Below," 309. My evaluation of Wenzhou in this section draws heavily from her account; see esp. 309–13.

41. Ibid., 311.

42. For the strategies villagers and local cadres used to hide their harvests from excessive state appropriation, see Oi, *State and Peasant in Contemporary China*, 124–28.

43. Parris, "Local Initiative and National Reform," 243.

44. Ma Jinlong, "Wenzhou moshi yu Wenzhouren de gexing," 28.

45. Whiting, *Power and Wealth in Rural China*, 69.

46. Ibid., 63–66.

47. Ibid., 68.

48. Bramall, "The Wenzhou 'Miracle,'" 54.

49. *X shizhi*, 533.

50. Ibid., 332.

51. Ibid.

52. Cf., e.g., Huaxi village in Zhejiang's neighboring province of Jiangsu, which is more akin to the villages Jean Oi writes about in her analysis. For a fuller discussion, see Pan, "Politics of Marketization in Rural China," 235–38.

53. *X shizhi*, 532.

54. In *Institutions, Institutional Change, and Economic Performance*, Douglass North argues that specific institutional arrangements will lead to suboptimal, path-dependent outcomes. David Landes (*Wealth and Poverty of Nations*, 17–28) contends that institutional and cultural limitations prevented the Chinese from developing a spirit of scientific inquiry and innovation.

55. Saxenian, *Regional Advantage*, 38–39.

56. *[Jupiter] jingsheng, [X] ren*, 70. I have not given the full citation here in order to maintain the confidentiality of Jupiter's identity. The full citation can be obtained by contacting the author.

57. Weber, *Theory of Social and Economic Organization*, 358–63.

58. Gerschenkron, *Economic Backwardness in Historical Perspective*, 24.

59. Gerschenkron (ibid., 16–21) refers specifically to the experience of Russia in the nineteenth century. See also Oi, *Rural China Takes Off*.

60. See Putnam, *Making Democracy Work*.

61. Gladwell, *The Tipping Point*, 35–38.

62. Surowiecki, *The Wisdom of Crowds*, 29–31.

Chapter 3

1. See Putnam, *Making Democracy Work*, chap. 6; and Coleman, *Foundations of Social Theory*.

2. For a clear picture of factional divisions and conflict in factories, see Walder, "The Chinese Cultural Revolution in the Factories." Also see Perry and Li, *Proletarian Power.*

3. *[Jupiter] jingsheng, [X] ren,* 82.

4. Respondent #35, personal interview, Aug. 9, 1997.

5. The debate regarding public and private interests in China harkens back to long-standing debates about the virtues of the public good and the selfishness of private gain; see Parris, "The Rise of Private Business Interests."

6. Respondent #18, personal interview, July 24, 1997. For an overview of how innovation and entrepreneurship have been portrayed in the broader scholarship, see Martinelli, "Entrepreneurship and Management."

7. Respondent #90, personal interview, May 12, 1998.

8. Respondent #4, personal interview, July 8, 1997.

9. For a review of the role these ties play in the economic development of East Asia, see Hamilton, ed., *Asian Business Networks.*

10. See Granovetter, "Economic Action and Social Structure."

11. Fei Xiaotong, "Jiadishi chuangxinye," 215.

12. Respondent #35, Aug. 9, 1997. On the different forms of financing in Wenzhou, see Tsai, *Back-Alley Banking,* 127–30.

13. Respondent #91, personal interview, May 20, 1998.

14. Granovetter, "The Strength of Weak Ties."

15. Saxenian, *Regional Advantage,* 32–33.

16. Respondent #4, personal interview, July 8, 1997.

17. See Simon, *Administrative Behavior.*

18. See Zhu, "Fishing Gear Enterprise," 52–76; and R. Ma, "Plastic Medical Products Factory."

19. Respondent #95, personal interview, May 28, 1998.

20. *[Jupiter] jingsheng, [X] ren,* 88.

21. See Walder, *Communist Neo-traditionalism.*

22. See Naughton, "China's Transition in Economic Perspective," 36.

23. *[Jupiter] jingsheng, [X] ren,* 28.

24. Zhongguo shehui kexueyuan, Jingji yanjiusuo, ed., *Zhongguo xiangzhen qiye,* 49.

25. For a discussion of the impact of industrialization in America, see Gutman, *Work, Culture, and Society in Industrializing America.* For a comparison of this process in Russia, see Glickman, *Russian Factory Women.*

26. Respondent #102, personal interview, June 16, 1998.

27. For an analysis of the impact of specialization in tobacco factories that emerged in urban China during the early twentieth century, see Perry, *Shanghai on Strike*, 136–41.

28. *[Jupiter] jingsheng, [X] ren*, 93.

29. The ideal of the "jack-of-all-trades" emerged during the disastrous Great Leap Forward; see Schurmann, *Ideology and Organization*, 233.

30. For a discussion of the Soviet impact on Chinese factory management, see Kaple, *Dream of a Red Factory*.

31. Selznick, *The Organizational Weapon*.

32. These efforts share strong similarities with the activities of party cadres in the stage of transformation; see Jowitt, *New World Disorder*, 88–120.

33. For a comprehensive analysis of Stahkanovism, see Siegelbaum, *Stakhanovism and the Politics of Productivity*.

34. Sabel, *Work and Politics*, 104.

35. Respondent #27, personal interview, Aug. 2, 1997.

36. Respondent #53, personal interview, Aug. 24, 1997.

37. Thompson, "Time, Work-Discipline, and Industrial Capitalism," 61.

38. Ibid., 73.

39. Respondent #105, personal interview, June 22, 1998.

40. Ching Kwan Lee, *Gender and the South China Miracle*, 76.

41. Stephen Hymer, cited in Edwards, *Contested Terrain*, 25.

42. Respondent #6, personal interview, July 9, 1997.

43. Respondent #105, personal interview, July 13, 1998.

44. Respondent #32, personal interview, Aug. 8, 1997.

45. On worker commitment, see Sil, *Managing "Modernity."*

46. See Nelson, *Managers and Workers*.

47. Ibid., 45–56.

48. Bendix, *Work and Authority in Industry*, 37.

49. Ibid., 51.

50. See Hirschmann, *Exit, Voice, and Loyalty*.

51. For an overview of this process, see Hong Yung Lee, *From Revolutionary Cadres to Bureaucratic Technocrats in Socialist China*.

52. Chan et al., *Chen Village Under Mao and Deng*, 170.

53. Shue, *The Reach of the State*, 113.

54. Oi, *State and Peasant in Contemporary China*.

55. Respondent #102, personal interview, June 16, 1998.

56. Latham, "The Implications of Rural Reforms for Grass-Roots Cadres," 157.

57. For a more detailed discussion, see Whiting, *Power and Wealth in Rural China*.

Chapter 4

1. In chapter 2 of *Strategy and Structure*, a case study of DuPont, Alfred Chandler highlights the importance of effective control and coordination of enterprise activities.

2. See Chen Huixiang, *Zhongguo qiye de pipan*.

3. This is clearly a case of institutional mimicry; see Meyer and Rowan, "Institutionalized Organizations."

4. Edwards, *Contested Terrain*, 111–62.

5. For an analysis of the social implications of such arrangements, see Rofel, "Rethinking Modernity."

6. Respondent #20, personal interview, July 28, 1997.

7. Respondent #72, personal interview, Sept. 2, 1997.

8. Respondent #12, personal interview, July 17, 1997.

9. Ibid.

10. Respondent #82, personal interview, Apr. 22, 1998.

11. Respondent #22, personal interview, July 30, 1997.

12. Respondent #6, personal interview, Sept. 5, 1997.

13. Respondent #6, personal interview, Apr. 23, 1998.

14. Respondent #70, personal interview, Sept. 3, 1997.

15. Here, the parallel with the efforts of late nineteenth-century American enterprises is particularly striking; see Chandler, *Strategy and Structure*, 19–51.

16. Respondent #30, personal interview, Aug. 4, 1997.

17. Respondent #95, personal interview, May 28, 1998.

18. Respondent #50, personal interview, Aug. 23, 1997.

19. Respondent #95, personal interview, May 28, 1998. This view is a striking contrast to the conclusions on East Asian industrialization drawn by Frederic Deyo in *Beneath the Miracle*.

20. Respondent #30, personal interview, Aug. 4, 1997.

21. Respondent #93, personal interview, May 25, 1998.

22. Respondent #86, personal interview, Apr. 29, 1998.

23. Respondent #54, personal interview, Aug. 25, 1997.

24. Respondent #21, personal interview, July 28, 1997.

25. Respondent #94, personal interview, May 27, 1998.

26. For an argument that the entrepreneur's break with traditional values in England during the Industrial Revolution was a major factor in the ultimate shape of factory organization, see Bendix, *Work and Authority in Industry*, 73–116. Sidney Pollard also draws a similar conclusion in *The Genesis of Modern Management*.

27. Respondent #92, personal interview, May 26, 1998.

28. Respondent #50, personal interview, Aug. 23, 1997.

29. Respondent #96, personal interview, June 1, 1998.

30. Respondent #26, personal interview, Aug. 1, 1997.

31. See Edwards, *Contested Terrain*, esp. 147–52.

32. Respondent #32, personal interview, Aug. 8, 1997.

33. Respondent #5, personal interview, Aug. 12, 1997.

34. Respondent #2, personal interview, July 7, 1997.

35. Respondent #51, personal interview, Aug. 24, 1997.

36. Respondent #39, personal interview, Aug. 14, 1997.

37. Respondent #68, personal interview, Sept. 5, 1997.

38. Respondent #41, personal interview, Aug. 14, 1997.

39. Respondent #86, personal interview, Apr. 28, 1998.

40. Respondent #29, personal interview, May 7, 1997.

41. Respondent #30, personal interview, Aug. 4, 1997.

42. Burawoy, *The Politics of Production*.

43. Respondent #10, personal interview, May 8, 1998.

44. Respondent #54, personal interview, Aug. 25, 1997.

45. Respondent #79, personal interview, Sept. 7, 1997.

46. Respondent #43, personal interview, Aug. 16, 1997.

47. James Scott, *Weapons of the Weak*.

48. Respondent #68, personal interview, Sept. 5, 1997.

49. Respondent #19, personal interview, Aug. 14, 1997.

50. Respondent #18, personal interview, Aug. 6, 1997.

51. Respondent #115, personal interview, July 10, 1998.

52. These developments follow Elizabeth Perry's observations in *Shanghai on Strike* (32–64) regarding the structure of labor markets in Shanghai, although the distinction between "northerner" and "southerner" was not as crucial in my cases.

53. Respondent #18, personal interview, July 24, 1997.

54. Respondent #103, personal interview, June 18, 1998.

55. On regional stereotyping, see Shih, *China Enters the Machine Age*; and Eberhard, "Chinese Regional Stereotypes."

56. Respondent #15, personal interview, July 22, 1997.

57. Jowitt, *New World Disorder*, 135.

58. Respondent #55, personal interview, Aug. 25, 1997.

59. On the plight of migrant workers, or the "floating population," see Solinger, *Contesting Citizenship in China*. Although Solinger focuses on the urban setting, the dynamics carry over to the rural environments as well.

60. See Milton Cantor, "Introduction," in idem, ed., *American Working-class Culture*, esp. 16–21.

61. A particularly good parallel was the nineteenth-century American mining industry, which involved Irish, English, and Welsh mineworkers. See Wallace, *St. Clair*, 133–38.

62. Respondent #3, personal interview, July 6, 1997.

63. Respondent, #7, personal interview, July 9, 1997.

64. Respondent #64, personal interview, Sept. 1, 1997.

65. Respondent #98, personal interview, June 1, 1998.

66. Respondent #30, personal interview, Aug. 4, 1997.

Chapter 5

1. For an argument that losing control over the work process results in a sense of powerlessness and self-estrangement, see Blauner, *Alienation and Freedom*.

2. Respondent #93, personal interview, May 25, 1998.

3. Respondent #102, personal interview, June 16, 1998.

4. Respondent #98, personal interview, Aug. 16, 2004.

5. Respondent #2, personal interview, May 5, 1998.

6. Ibid.

7. Respondent #10, personal interview, Aug. 11, 2004.

8. Respondent #2, personal interview, Aug. 3, 2004.

9. Respondent #42, personal interview, Aug. 18, 2004.

10. Respondent #129, personal interview, Aug. 17, 2004.

11. Respondent #113, personal interview, July 8, 1998.

12. Respondent #2, personal interview, May 5, 1998.

13. Respondent #2, personal interview, Aug. 3, 2004.

14. Respondent #130, personal interview, Aug. 16, 2004.

15. Ibid.

16. Respondent #10, personal interview, Aug. 11, 2004.

17. Ibid.

18. Respondent #29, personal interview, Aug. 14, 2004.

19. Respondent #131, personal interview, Aug. 16, 2004.

20. Ibid.

21. Respondent #18, personal interview, Aug. 6, 1997.

22. Respondent #6, personal interview, Sept. 5, 1997.

23. Respondent #2, personal interview, Aug. 3, 2004.

24. Respondent #29, personal interview, Aug. 9, 2004.

25. Respondent #29, personal interview, Aug. 29, 2004.

26. Respondent #11, personal interview, Aug. 5, 2004.

27. Respondent #10, personal interview, Aug. 11, 2004.

28. Respondent #29, personal interview, Aug. 14, 2004.

29. Respondent #2, personal interview, Aug. 3, 2004.

30. Respondent #10, personal interview, Aug. 11, 2004.

31. Respondent #10, personal interview, May 8, 1998.

32. Respondent #114, personal interview, July 7, 1998.

33. Respondent #42, personal interview, Aug. 18, 2004.

34. Respondent #129, personal interview, Aug. 17, 2004.

35. Respondent #127, personal interview, Aug. 12, 2004.

36. Respondent #29, personal interview, Aug. 21, 1997.

37. Respondent #94, personal interview, Aug. 11, 2004.

38. Respondent #42, personal interview, Aug. 18, 2004.

39. Respondent #123, personal interview, Aug. 5, 2004.

40. Granovetter, "The Strength of Weak Ties."

41. Respondent #110, personal interview, June 30, 1998.

42. These data are drawn from Jupiter's 1997 internal reports on its workforce.

43. Nee, "Organizational Dynamics of Market Transition."

44. Respondent #85, personal interview, Apr. 28, 1998.

45. Wank, *Commodifying Communism*, esp. 68–92.

46. Respondent #2, personal interview, Aug. 3, 2004.

47. Respondent #29, personal interview, Aug. 4, 2004.

48. Respondent #94, personal interview, May 27, 1998.

49. Walder, *Communist Neo-traditionalism.*

50. Respondent #36, personal interview, Aug. 12, 1997.

51. Respondent #85, personal interview, Apr. 28, 1998.

52. Respondent #21, personal interview, Aug. 5, 2004.

53. Respondent #128, personal interview, Aug. 12, 2004.

54. Respondent #132, personal interview, Aug. 17, 2004.

55. Respondent #87, personal interview, Aug. 7, 2004.

56. Respondent #21, personal interview, July 28, 1997.

57. Respondent #21, personal interview, Aug. 5, 2004.

58. Respondent #42, personal interview, Aug. 18, 2004.

59. Ibid.

60. Respondent #29, personal interview, Aug. 14, 2004.

61. Respondent #125, personal interview, Aug. 10, 2004.

62. On *danwei* practices, see Lü and Perry, eds., *Danwei.*

63. Respondent #93, personal interview, Aug. 10, 2004.

64. Respondent #104, personal interview, June 19, 1998.

65. Respondent #36, personal interview, Aug. 12, 1997.

66. Respondent #21, personal interview, July 28, 1997.

67. Respondent #21, personal interview, Sept. 5, 1997.

68. Respondent #104, personal interview, June 19, 1998.

69. Ibid.

70. Respondent #87, personal interview, May 8, 1998.

71. Respondent #21, personal interview, Aug. 5, 2004.

72. Respondent #128, personal interview, Aug. 12, 2004.

73. Respondent #109, personal interview, June 30, 1998.

74. On the moral economy perspective, see James Scott, *The Moral Economy of the Peasant.*

75. Respondent #113, personal interview, July 2, 1998.

76. Respondent #44, personal interview, Aug. 16, 1997.

77. Respondent #105, personal interview, July 13, 1998.

78. Respondent #87, personal interview, Aug. 7, 2004.

79. Respondent #11, personal interview, Aug. 5, 2004.

80. Respondent #10, personal interview, Aug. 11, 2004.

81. For a comparative-historical analysis of trade unions in post-Soviet Russia and post-Mao China, see Calvin Chen and Rudra Sil, "Communist Legacies."

82. Respondent #21, personal interview, Aug. 5, 2004.

83. Respondent #19, personal interview, July 27, 1997.

84. Respondent #81, personal interview, Sept. 6, 1997.

85. Schurmann, *Ideology and Organization,* 231–35.

Chapter 6

1. Gladwell, *The Tipping Point,* 9.

2. Thelen, *How Institutions Evolve,* 293.

3. Schurmann, *Ideology and Organization.*

4. See Gutman, *Work, Culture, and Society in Industrializing America*; and Cantor, ed., *American Workingclass Culture.* For an excellent overview, see Licht, *Industrializing America.*

5. Classic studies include Dore, *British Factory, Japanese Factory*; and Bendix, *Work and Authority in Industry.*

6. See Perry, "Trends in the Study of Chinese Politics."

7. Piore and Sabel, *The Second Industrial Divide,* esp. 28–35.

8. This issue is systematically analyzed in Han Chaohua et al., "Chuan qinshu haishi pin zhuanjia," 57.

9. See Saxenian, *Regional Advantage.*

10. Gladwell, *The Tipping Point,* 183–92.

Bibliography

Amsden, Alice. *Asia's Next Giant: South Korea and Late Industrialization.* New York: Oxford University Press, 1989.

Barnard, Chester. *The Functions of the Executive.* Cambridge: Harvard University Press, 1938.

Bendix, Reinhard. *Nation-Building and Citizenship.* Rev. ed. Berkeley: University of California Press, 1977.

————. *Work and Authority in Industry: Ideologies of Management in the Course of Industrialization.* New York: John Wiley and Sons, 1956.

Blauner, Robert. *Alienation and Freedom: The Factory Worker and His Industry.* Chicago: University of Chicago Press, 1964.

Bramall, Christopher. "The Wenzhou 'Miracle': An Assessment." In Peter Nolan and Dong Fureng, eds., *Market Forces in China: Competition and Small Business. The Wenzhou Debate.* New Jersey: Zed Books, 1990.

Braverman, Harry. *Labor and Monopoly Capital.* New York: Monthly Review Press, 1974.

Brown, George. "Budgets, Cadres and Local State Capacity in Rural Jiangsu." In Flemming Christensen and Zhang Junzuo, eds., *Village Inc.: Chinese Rural Society in the 1990s.* Honolulu: University of Hawai'i Press, 1998.

Brugger, William. *Democracy and Organisation in the Chinese Industrial Enterprise, 1948–1953.* Cambridge: Cambridge University Press, 1976.

Burawoy, Michael. *The Politics of Production: Factory Regimes Under Capitalism and Socialism.* London: Verso, 1985.

Byrd, William, and Lin Qingsong. "China's Rural Industry: An Introduction." In William Byrd and Lin Qingsong, eds., *China's Rural Industry.* Oxford: Oxford University Press, 1990.

Cantor, Milton, ed. *American Workingclass Culture: Explorations in American Labor and Social History*. Westport, CT: Greenwood Press, 1979.

Chan, Anita; Richard Madsen; and Jonathan Unger. *Chen Village Under Mao and Deng*. 2d ed. Berkeley: University of California Press, 1992.

Chandler, Alfred. *Strategy and Structure: Chapters in the History of the American Industrial Enterprise*. Cambridge: MIT Press, 1962.

Chen, Calvin. "Leninism, Developmental Stages, and Transformation: Understanding Social and Institutional Change in Contemporary China." In Vladimir Tismaneanu, Marc Morjé Howard, and Rudra Sil, eds., *World Order After Leninism*. Seattle: University of Washington Press, 2006.

Chen, Calvin, and Rudra Sil. "Communist Legacies, Postcommunist Transformations, and the Fate of Organized Labor in Russia and China." *Studies in Comparative International Development* 41, no. 2 (Summer 2006): 62–87.

Chen, Chunlai; Christopher Findlay; Andrew Watson; and Zhang Xiaohe. "Rural Enterprise Growth in a Partially Reformed Chinese Economy." In Christopher Findlay, Andrew Watson, and Harry Xu, eds., *Rural Enterprises in China*. New York: St. Martin's Press, 1994.

Chen Huixiang. *Zhongguo qiye de pipan* (A critique of Chinese enterprises). Beijing: Beijing daxue chubanshe, 1998.

Chen Weixin, ed. *Su, Zhe, Yue: xiangzhen qiye chenggong zhi lu* (Jiangsu, Zhejiang, Guangdong: the road to township and village enterprise success). Guangdong renmin chubanshe, 1985.

Child, John. *Management in China During the Age of Reform*. Cambridge: Cambridge University Press, 1994.

Coase, Ronald. "The Nature of the Firm." *Economica* 4, no. 4 (Nov. 1937): 386–405.

Cole, Robert. *Japanese Blue Collar: The Changing Tradition*. Berkeley: University of California Press, 1971.

Coleman, James. *Foundations of Social Theory*. Cambridge: Harvard University Press, 1990.

Cyert, Richard, and James March. *A Behavioral Theory of the Firm*. 2d. ed. Cambridge, MA: Blackwell Publishers, 1992.

Demsetz, Harold. "Towards a Theory of Property Rights." *American Economic Review* 57, no. 2 (May 1967): 347–59.

Deutsch, Karl. "Social Mobilization and Political Development." *American Political Science Review* 55, no. 3 (Sept. 1961): 493–502.

Deyo, Frederic. *Beneath the Miracle: Labor Subordination in the New Asian Industrialism*. Berkeley: University of California Press, 1989.

———. *The Political Economy of the New Asian Industrialism*. Ithaca: Cornell University Press, 1987.

Dong Fang. "Wenzhouren fujia yifang de aomiao" (The mystery of Wenzhou natives' prosperity). In Chen Junxian and Zhou Xingzeng, eds., *Wenzhou tanmi* (Exploring the secrets of Wenzhou). Beijing: Renmin ribao chubanshe, 2002.

Dore, Ronald. *British Factory, Japanese Factory: The Origins of National Diversity in Industrial Relations*. London: Allen and Unwin, 1973.

Eberhard, Wolfram. "Chinese Regional Stereotypes." *Journal of Asian Studies* 15, no. 12 (Dec. 1965): 596–608.

Edwards, Richard. *Contested Terrain: The Transformation of the Workplace in the Twentieth Century*. New York: Basic Books, 1979.

Fayol, Henri. *General and Industrial Management*. London: Pitman, 1949.

Fei Xiaotong. "Jiadishi chuangxinye: zaifang Wenzhou" (Real resources create new businesses: revisiting Wenzhou). In Zhang Xu and Zheng Dajiong, eds., *Wenzhou shicang: gaige kaifang de shuoguo* (The Wenzhou market: the rich fruits of reform). Beijing: Zhonggong dangshi chubanshe, 1996.

Forster, Keith. "The Political Economy of Post-Mao Zhejiang: Rapid Growth and Hesitant Reform." In Peter T. Y. Cheung, Jae Ho Chung, and Zhimin Lin, eds., *Provincial Strategies in Economic Reform in Post-Mao China: Leadership, Politics, and Implementation*. Armonk, NY: M. E. Sharpe, 1998.

———. *Zhejiang Province in Reform*. Honolulu: University of Hawai'i Press, 1998.

Frazier, Mark. *The Making of the Chinese Industrial Workplace: State, Revolution, and Labor Management*. New York: Cambridge University Press, 2000.

Friedman, Raymond, and Darren McDaniel. "In the Eye of the Beholder: Ethnography in the Study of Work." In Keith Whitfield and George Strauss, eds., *Researching the World of Work: Strategies and Methods of Studying Industrial Relations*. Ithaca: Cornell University Press, 1998.

Fruin, W. Mark. *Kikkoman: Company, Clan, and Community*. Cambridge: Harvard University Press, 1983.

Geertz, Clifford. *The Interpretation of Cultures*. New York: Basic Books, 1973.

Gereffi, Gary, and Donald Wyman, eds. *Manufacturing Miracles: Paths of Industrialization in Latin America and East Asia*. Princeton: Princeton University Press, 1990.

Gerschenkron, Alexander. *Economic Backwardness in Historical Perspective: A Book of Essays*. Cambridge: Harvard University Press, 1966.

Gladwell, Malcolm. *The Tipping Point: How Little Things Can Make a Big Difference*. New York: Little Brown, 2000.

Glickman, Rose. *Russian Factory Women: Workplace and Society, 1880–1914*. Berkeley: University of California Press, 1984.

Gold, Thomas. "Guerrilla Interviewing Among the *Getihu*." In Perry Link, Richard Madsen, and Paul Pickowicz, eds., *Unofficial China: Popular Culture and Thought in the People's Republic*. Boulder, CO: Westview Press, 1989.

Gouldner, Alvin. *Patterns of Industrial Bureaucracy: A Case Study of Modern Factory Administration*. New York: Free Press, 1954.

Granovetter, Mark. "Economic Action and Social Structure: The Problem of Embeddedness." *American Journal of Sociology* 91, no. 3 (Nov. 1985): 485–510.

———. "The Strength of Weak Ties." *American Journal of Sociology* 78, no. 6 (May 1973): 1360–80.

Guthrie, Doug. *Dragon in a Three-Piece Suit: The Emergence of Capitalism in China*. Princeton: Princeton University Press, 1999.

Gutman, Herbert. *Work, Culture, and Society in Industrializing America: Essays in American Working-Class and Social History*. New York: Alfred Knopf, 1976.

Hamilton, Gary, ed. *Asian Business Networks*. New York: Walter de Gruyter, 1996.

Han Chaohua, Chen Ling, and Ying Lifen. "Chuan qinshu haishi pin zhuanjia: Zhejiang jiaju qiye jieban wenti kaocha" (To hand off to kin or to hire experts: a study of the succession problem in a Zhejiang family enterprise). *Xiangzhen qiye, minying jingji* (May 2005): 54–65.

Hershatter, Gail. *The Workers of Tianjin, 1900–1949*. Stanford: Stanford University Press, 1986.

Hirschmann, Albert. *Exit, Voice, and Loyalty: Responses to Decline in Firms, Organizations, and States*. Cambridge: Harvard University Press, 1970.

Ho, Ping-ti. *Studies on the Population of China, 1368–1953*. Cambridge: Harvard University Press, 1967.

Ho, Samuel. *Rural China in Transition: Non-agricultural Development in Rural Jiangsu, 1978–1990*. New York: Oxford University Press, 1994.

Homans, George. *The Human Group*. New York: Harcourt Brace, 1950.

Hunt, Lynn. *Politics, Culture, and Class in the French Revolution*. Berkeley: University of California Press, 1984.

Inkeles, Alex, and David Smith. *Becoming Modern*. Cambridge: Harvard University Press, 1974.

Janos, Andrew. *Politics and Paradigms: Changing Theories of Change in Social Science*. Stanford: Stanford University Press, 1986.

Johnson, Chalmers. *MITI and the Japanese Miracle: The Growth of Industrial Policy, 1925–1975*. Stanford: Stanford University Press, 1982.

Jowitt, Ken. *New World Disorder: The Leninist Extinction*. Berkeley: University of California Press, 1992.

[Jupiter] jingsheng, [X] ren (The spirit of Jupiter, the people of X). Beijing, 1996.

Kaple, Deborah. *Dream of a Red Factory: The Legacy of High Stalinism in China*. New York: Oxford University Press, 1994.

Katznelson, Ira. "Working-Class Formation: Constructing Cases and Comparisons." In idem and Aristide Zolberg, eds., *Working-Class Formation: Nineteenth-Century Patterns in Western Europe and the United States*. Princeton: Princeton University Press, 1986.

Kerr, Clark; John Dunlop; Frederick Harbison; and Charles Myers. *Industrialism and Industrial Man: The Problems of Labor and Management in Economic Growth*. New York: Oxford University Press, 1964.

Kondo, Dorienne. *Crafting Selves: Power, Gender, and Discourses of Identity in a Japanese Workplace*. Chicago: University of Chicago Press, 1990.

Kornai, János. "The Hungarian Reform Process: Visions, Hopes, and Reality." In Victor Nee and David Stark, eds., *Remaking the Economic Institutions of Socialism: China and Eastern Europe*. Stanford: Stanford University Press, 1989.

———. *The Road to a Free Economy: Shifting from a Socialist System, the Example of Hungary*. New York: Norton, 1990.

———. *The Socialist System: The Political Economy of Communism*. Princeton: Princeton University Press, 1992.

Landes, David. *The Wealth and Poverty of Nations: Why Some Are So Rich and Some Are So Poor*. New York: Norton, 1998.

Latham, Richard. "The Implications of Rural Reforms for Grass-Roots Cadres." In Elizabeth Perry and Christine Wong, eds., *The Political Economy of Reform in Post-Mao China*. Cambridge: Harvard University Press, 1985.

Lee, Ching Kwan. *Gender and the South China Miracle: Two Worlds of Factory Women*. Berkeley: University of California Press, 1998.

Lee, Hong Yung. *From Revolutionary Cadres to Bureaucratic Technocrats in Socialist China*. Berkeley: University of California Press, 1991.

Lerner, Daniel. *The Passing of Traditional Society*. New York: Free Press, 1964.

Licht, Walter. *Industrializing America*. Baltimore: Johns Hopkins University Press, 1995.

Lin, Nan. "Local Market Socialism: Local Corporatism in Action in Rural China." *Theory and Society* 24, no. 3 (June 1995): 301–54.

Liu, Alan. "The 'Wenzhou Model' of Development and China's Modernization." *Asian Survey* 32, no. 8 (July 1992): 696–711.

Liu, Yia-Ling. "Reform from Below: The Private Economy and Local Politics in the Rural Industrialization of Wenzhou." *China Quarterly* no. 130 (June 1992): 293–316.

Lü, Xiaobo, and Elizabeth Perry, eds. *Danwei: The Changing Chinese Workplace in Historical and Comparative Perspective*. Armonk: M. E. Sharpe, 1997.

Ma Jinlong. "Wenzhou moshi yu Wenzhouren de gexing" (The Wenzhou model and the nature of Wenzhou people). In Chen Junxian and Zhou Xingzeng, eds., *Wenzhou tanmi* (Exploring the secrets of Wenzhou). Beijing: Renmin ribao chubanshe, 2002.

Ma, Rong. "Plastic Medical Products Factory." In John Wong, Rong Ma, and Mu Yang, eds., *China's Rural Entrepreneurs: Ten Case Studies*. Singapore: Times Academic Press, 1995.

Madsen, Richard. *Morality and Power in a Chinese Village*. Berkeley: University of California Press, 1984.

Martinelli, Alberto. "Entrepreneurship and Management." In Neil Smelser and Richard Swedberg, eds., *The Handbook of Economic Sociology*. Princeton: Princeton University Press, 1994.

Meisner, Maurice. *Mao's China and After: A History of the People's Republic*. New York: Free Press, 1986.

Meyer, John, and Brian Rowan. "Institutionalized Organizations: Formal Structure as Myth and Ceremony." In Paul Dimaggio and Walter Powell, eds., *The New Institutionalism in Organizational Analysis*. Chicago: University of Chicago Press, 1991.

Migdal, Joel. *Peasants, Politics, and Revolution: Pressures Toward Political and Social Change in the Third World*. Princeton: Princeton University Press, 1972.

National Bureau of Statistics of China, comp. *China Statistical Yearbook, 2004*. Beijing: China Statistics Press, 2004.

———. *China Statistical Yearbook, 2005*. Beijing: China Statistics Press, 2005.

Naughton, Barry. "China's Transition in Economic Perspective." In Merle Goldman and Roderick MacFarquhar, eds., *The Paradox of China's Post-Mao Reforms*. Cambridge: Harvard University Press, 1999.

Nee, Victor. "Organizational Dynamics of Market Transition: Hybrid Forms, Property Rights, and Mixed Economy in China." *Administrative Science Quarterly* 37 (Mar. 1992): 1–27.

Nelson, Daniel. *Managers and Workers: Origins of the New Factory System in the United States, 1880–1920*. Madison: University of Wisconsin Press, 1975.

North, Douglass. *Institutions, Institutional Change, and Economic Performance*. Cambridge: Cambridge University Press, 1990.

Nurkse, Ragnar. *Problems of Capital Formation in Underdeveloped Countries*. New York: Oxford University Press, 1962.

Oi, Jean. "Fiscal Reform and the Economic Foundations of Local State Corporatism in China." *World Politics* 45 (Oct. 1992): 99–126.

———. *Rural China Takes Off: Institutional Foundations of Economic Reform*. Berkeley: University of California Press, 1998.

———. *State and Peasant in Contemporary China: The Political Economy of Village Government*. Berkeley: University of California Press, 1988.

Organisation of Economic Co-operation and Development. *Economic Survey of China*. Paris, 2005.

Pan, Wei. "Politics of Marketization in Rural China: The Coalition Between Grassroots Authorities and Rural Industries." Ph.D. diss., University of California at Berkeley, Department of Political Science, 1996.

Parris, Kristen. "Local Initiative and National Reform: The Wenzhou Model of Development." *China Quarterly*, no. 134 (June 1993): 242–63.

———. "The Rise of Private Business Interests." In Merle Goldman and Roderick MacFarquhar, eds., *The Paradox of China's Post-Mao Reforms*. Cambridge: Harvard University Press, 1999.

Parsons, Talcott, and Edward Shils. *Toward a General Theory of Action*. New York: Harper and Row, 1951.

Perry, Elizabeth. *Rebels and Revolutionaries in North China, 1845–1945*. Stanford: Stanford University Press, 1980.

———. *Shanghai on Strike: The Politics of Chinese Labor*. Stanford: Stanford University Press, 1993.

———. "Trends in the Study of Chinese Politics—State-Society Relations." *China Quarterly*, no. 139 (Sept. 1994): 704–13.

Perry, Elizabeth, and Li Xun. *Proletarian Power: Shanghai in the Cultural Revolution*. Boulder, CO: Westview Press, 1997.

Pierson, Paul. *Politics in Time: History, Institutions, and Social Analysis.* Princeton: Princeton University Press, 2004.

Piore, Michael, and Charles Sabel. *The Second Industrial Divide: Possibilities for Prosperity.* New York: Basic Books, 1984.

Polanyi, Karl. *The Great Transformation.* Boston: Beacon Hill, 1944.

Pollard, Sidney. *The Genesis of Modern Management: A Study of the Industrial Revolution in Great Britain.* Cambridge: Harvard University Press, 1965.

Popkin, Samuel. *The Rational Peasant: The Political Economy of Rural Society in Vietnam.* Berkeley: University of California Press, 1979.

Price, Robert. *Society and Bureaucracy in Contemporary Ghana.* Berkeley: University of California Press, 1975.

Putnam, Robert. *Bowling Alone: The Collapse and Revival of American Community.* New York: Basic Books, 1998.

———. *Making Democracy Work: Civic Traditions in Modern Italy.* Princeton: Princeton University Press, 1993.

Putterman, Louis. "The Role of Ownership and Property Rights in China's Economic Transition." In Andrew Walder, ed., *China's Transitional Economy.* Oxford: Oxford University Press, 1996.

Ragin, Charles. *The Comparative Method: Moving Beyond Qualitative and Quantitative Strategies.* Berkeley: University of California Press, 1987.

Rankin, Mary. *Elite Activism and Political Transformation in China: Zhejiang Province, 1865–1911.* Stanford: Stanford University Press, 1986.

Rofel, Lisa. "Rethinking Modernity: Space and Factory Discipline in China." *Cultural Anthropology* 7, no. 1 (Feb. 1992): 93–114.

Rostow, Walt. *The Stages of Economic Growth: A Non-Communist Manifesto.* Cambridge: Cambridge University Press, 1960.

Sabel, Charles. *Work and Politics: The Division of Labor in Industry.* New York: Cambridge University Press, 1982.

Sachs, Jeffrey. *Poland's Jump to the Market Economy.* Cambridge: MIT Press, 1993.

Sachs, Jeffrey, and Wing Thye Woo. "Structural Factors in the Economic Reforms of China, Eastern Europe, and the Soviet Union." *Economic Policy* 18 (1994): 102–45.

Saxenian, AnnaLee. *Regional Advantage: Culture and Competition in Silicon Valley and Route 128.* Cambridge: Harvard University Press, 1994.

Schoppa, R. Keith. *Chinese Elites and Political Change: Zhejiang Province in the Early Twentieth Century.* Cambridge: Harvard University Press, 1982.

Schumpeter, Joseph. *Capitalism, Socialism, and Democracy.* New York: Harper and Row, 1976.

Schurmann, Franz. *Ideology and Organization in Communist China*. 2d ed. Berkeley: University of California Press, 1968.

Scott, James. *The Moral Economy of the Peasant: Rebellion and Subsistence in Southeast Asia*. New Haven: Yale University Press, 1976.

————. *Weapons of the Weak: Everyday Forms of Peasant Resistance*. New Haven: Yale University Press, 1985.

Scott, W. Richard. *Organizations: Rational, Natural, and Open Systems*. Englewood Cliffs, NJ: Prentice-Hall, 1992.

Scullion, Hugh, and P. K. Edwards. *The Social Organization of Industrial Conflict: Control and Resistance in the Workplace*. Oxford: Basil Blackwell, 1982.

Selden, Mark. *The Political Economy of Chinese Economic Development*. Armonk, NY: M. E. Sharpe, 1993.

Selznick, Philip. *Leadership in Administration: A Sociological Interpretation*. New York: Harper and Row, 1957.

————. *The Organizational Weapon: A Study of Bolshevik Strategy and Tactics*. New York: McGraw-Hill, 1952.

————. *TVA and the Grassroots: A Study in the Sociology of Formal Organization*. Berkeley: University of California Press, 1949.

Shih, Kuo-heng. *China Enters the Machine Age*. Cambridge: Harvard University Press, 1944.

Shue, Vivienne. *The Reach of the State: Sketches of the Chinese Body Politic*. Stanford: Stanford University Press, 1988.

Siegelbaum, Lewis. *Stakhanovism and the Politics of Productivity in the USSR, 1935–1941*. New York: Cambridge University Press, 1988.

Sil, Rudra. *Managing "Modernity": Work, Community, and Authority in Late-Industrializing Japan and Russia*. Ann Arbor: University of Michigan Press, 2002.

Simon, Herbert. *Administrative Behavior: A Study of Decision-making Processes in Administrative Organization*. New York: Macmillan, 1947.

Solinger, Dorothy. *Contesting Citizenship in China: Peasant Migrants, the State, and the Logic of the Market*. Berkeley: University of California Press, 1999.

Spencer, Herbert. *On Social Evolution*. Ed. J. D. Y. Peel. Chicago: University of Chicago Press, 1972.

Stark, David, and Laszlo Bruszt. *Postsocialist Pathways*. New York: Cambridge University Press, 1998.

Stark, David, and Victor Nee. "Toward an Institutional Analysis of State Socialism." In Victor Nee and David Stark, eds., *Remaking the Economic*

Institutions of Socialism: China and Eastern Europe. Stanford: Stanford University Press, 1989.

Steinfeld, Edward. *Forging Reform in China: The Fate of State-Owned Industry.* Cambridge: Cambridge University Press, 1998.

Surowiecki, James. *The Wisdom of Crowds.* New York: Anchor Books, 2004.

Taylor, Frederick. *The Principles of Scientific Management.* New York: Harper, 1911.

Thelen, Kathleen. *How Institutions Evolve: The Political Economy of Skills in Germany, Britain, the United States, and Japan.* New York: Cambridge University Press, 2004.

Thompson, E. P. *The Making of the English Working Class.* New York: Vintage Books, 1966.

————. "Time, Work-Discipline, and Industrial Capitalism." *Past and Present* no. 38 (1967): 56–97.

Tsai, Kellee. *Back-Alley Banking: Private Entrepreneurs in China.* Ithaca: Cornell University Press, 2002.

Wade, Robert. *Governing the Market: Economic Theory and the Role of Government in East Asia.* Princeton: Princeton University Press, 1990.

Walder, Andrew. "China's Transitional Economy: Interpreting Its Significance." In Andrew Walder, ed., *China's Transitional Economy.* Oxford: Oxford University Press, 1996.

————. "The Chinese Cultural Revolution in the Factories: Party-State Structures and Patterns of Conflict." In Elizabeth Perry, ed., *Putting Class in Its Place.* Berkeley: University of California, Institute of East Asian Studies, 1996.

————. *Communist Neo-traditionalism: Work and Authority in Chinese Industry.* Berkeley: University of California Press, 1986.

————. "Corporate Organization and Local Government Property Rights in China." In Vedat Milor, ed., *Changing Political Economies: Privatization in Post-Communist and Reforming Communist States.* Boulder, CO: Lynne Rienner Publishers, 1994.

————. "The County Government as an Industrial Corporation." In Andrew Walder, ed., *Zouping in Transition: The Process of Reform in Rural North China.* Cambridge: Harvard University Press, 1998.

————. "Local Governments as Industrial Firms: An Organizational Analysis of China's Transitional Economy." *American Journal of Sociology* 1, no. 2 (Sept. 1995): 263–301.

Wallace, Anthony. *St. Clair: A Nineteenth Century Coal Town's Experience with a Disaster-Prone Industry.* Ithaca: Cornell University Press, 1981.

Wank, David. *Commodifying Communism: Business, Trust, and Politics in a Chinese City*. Cambridge: Cambridge University Press, 1999.

Weber, Max. *Theory of Social and Economic Organization*. Ed. Talcott Parsons. New York: Free Press, 1947.

Weick, Karl. "Educational Organizations as Loosely Coupled Systems." *Administrative Science Quarterly* 21, no. 1 (Mar. 1976): 1–19.

Weitzman, Martin, and Chenggang Xu. "Chinese Township-Village Enterprises as Vaguely Defined Cooperatives." *Journal of Comparative Economics* 18, no. 2 (Apr. 1994): 121–45.

Wenzhoushi difangzhi bianzuan weiyuanhui (Wenzhou local gazetteer compilation committee). *Wenzhou shizhi* (Gazetteer of Wenzhou). Beijing: Zhonghua shuju, 1998.

Whiting, Susan. *Power and Wealth in Rural China: The Political Economy of Institutional Change*. Cambridge: Cambridge University Press, 2001.

Williamson, Oliver. *The Economic Institutions of Capitalism*. New York: Free Press, 1985.

———. "The Economics of Organization: The Transaction Cost Approach." *American Journal of Sociology* 87 (Nov. 1981): 548–77.

———. *Markets and Hierarchies*. New York: Free Press, 1975.

X shizhi (Gazetteer of X). Shanghai, 1993.

Xiangzhen qiye nianjian (Township and village enterprise yearbook). Beijing: Zhongguo nongye chubanshe, 1997.

Yang, Minchuan. "Reshaping Peasant Culture and Community: Rural Industrialization in a Chinese Village." *Modern China* 20, no. 2 (Apr. 1994): 157–79.

Yeh, Wen-hsin. *Provincial Passages: Culture, Space, and the Origins of Chinese Communism*. Berkeley: University of California Press, 1996.

Zhang Yi. *Zhongguo xiangzhen qiye jianxin de licheng* (The painstaking course of China's township and village enterprises). Beijing: Falü chubanshe, 1990.

Zhejiang nianjian (Almanac of Zhejiang). Hangzhou: Zhejiang renmin chubanshe, 1999.

Zhongguo shehui kexueyuan. Jingji yanjiusuo, ed. *Zhongguo xiangzhen qiye de jingji fazhan yu jingji tizhi* (The economic development and economic system of China's township and village enterprises). Beijing: Zhongguo jingji chubanshe, 1987.

Zhongguo xiangzhen qiye nianjian (China's township and village enterprise yearbook). Beijing: Zhongguo nongye chubanshe, 2004.

Zhou, Kate Xiao, and Lynn T. White III. "Quiet Politics and Rural Enterprise in Reform China." *Journal of Developing Areas* 29, no. 4 (July 1995): 461–90.

Zhu, Ding Yuan. "Fishing Gear Enterprise." In John Wong, Rong Ma, and Mu Yang, eds., *China's Rural Entrepreneurs: Ten Case Studies*. Singapore: Times Academic Press, 1995.

Index

Agriculture, 1, 28–33 passim, 37, 41, 56, 66, 71–72, 78, 94, 171; collectivization vs. household production, 31, 41, 44–45, 81–82

Anhui, 61, 71, 121

Automation, see under Rationalization

Banqian hui, 141

Beijing, 33, 41, 146, 171

Bendix, Reinhard, 79

Bramall, Christopher, 32

Bruszt, Laszlo, 10

Burawoy, Michael, 112

Bureaucratization, see under Rationalization

Capital, social, 5–6, 19, 26, 50, 54, 59, 73, 89, 123, 125–26, 167. See also Networks, social

Capital formation, see under Networks, social

Chen Yun, 81

Chiang Kai-shek, 29, 39–40, 42–43

Collective enterprise, see Enterprises, collective

Commune and brigade enterprises, see Enterprises, commune and brigade

Communist Party: role of local cadres, 9, 40, 54–55, 57, 61n, 82–87, 94, 170, 178; role in rural enterprises, 18, 23, 26, 29, 39–40, 127, 146, 167, 174, 188; global, 33, 131, 169, 182; influence in Wenzhou and Jinhua, 39–48; competition, 66, 88, 97, 123, 142, 173, 182–85, 190; Communist Youth League, 148–51, 157, 160–61

Conflict, social, 5, 14, 17, 74, 87, 89, 125–26, 159, 180, 187; insider vs. outsider, 68, 90, 116, 119–26, 142–45, 174

Cultural Revolution, 33, 42, 48–49, 56–57, 81

Customer outreach strategies, 63–66, 91, 179, 183. See also under Networks, social

Customer service, 97, 107, 112, 181

Harvard East Asian Monographs
(*out-of-print)

203. Robert S. Ross and Jiang Changbin, eds., *Re-examining the Cold War: U.S.-China Diplomacy, 1954–1973*

204. Guanhua Wang, *In Search of Justice: The 1905–1906 Chinese Anti-American Boycott*

205. David Schaberg, *A Patterned Past: Form and Thought in Early Chinese Historiography*

206. Christine Yano, *Tears of Longing: Nostalgia and the Nation in Japanese Popular Song*

207. Milena Doleželová-Velingerová and Oldřich Král, with Graham Sanders, eds., *The Appropriation of Cultural Capital: China's May Fourth Project*

208. Robert N. Huey, *The Making of 'Shinkokinshū'*

209. Lee Butler, *Emperor and Aristocracy in Japan, 1467–1680: Resilience and Renewal*

210. Suzanne Ogden, *Inklings of Democracy in China*

211. Kenneth J. Ruoff, *The People's Emperor: Democracy and the Japanese Monarchy, 1945–1995*

212. Haun Saussy, *Great Walls of Discourse and Other Adventures in Cultural China*

213. Aviad E. Raz, *Emotions at Work: Normative Control, Organizations, and Culture in Japan and America*

214. Rebecca E. Karl and Peter Zarrow, eds., *Rethinking the 1898 Reform Period: Political and Cultural Change in Late Qing China*

215. Kevin O'Rourke, *The Book of Korean Shijo*

216. Ezra F. Vogel, ed., *The Golden Age of the U.S.-China-Japan Triangle, 1972–1989*

217. Thomas A. Wilson, ed., *On Sacred Grounds: Culture, Society, Politics, and the Formation of the Cult of Confucius*

218. Donald S. Sutton, *Steps of Perfection: Exorcistic Performers and Chinese Religion in Twentieth-Century Taiwan*

219. Daqing Yang, *Technology of Empire: Telecommunications and Japanese Expansionism, 1895–1945*

220. Qianshen Bai, *Fu Shan's World: The Transformation of Chinese Calligraphy in the Seventeenth Century*

221. Paul Jakov Smith and Richard von Glahn, eds., *The Song-Yuan-Ming Transition in Chinese History*

222. Rania Huntington, *Alien Kind: Foxes and Late Imperial Chinese Narrative*

223. Jordan Sand, *House and Home in Modern Japan: Architecture, Domestic Space, and Bourgeois Culture, 1880–1930*

224. Karl Gerth, *China Made: Consumer Culture and the Creation of the Nation*

225. Xiaoshan Yang, *Metamorphosis of the Private Sphere: Gardens and Objects in Tang-Song Poetry*

226. Barbara Mittler, *A Newspaper for China? Power, Identity, and Change in Shanghai's News Media, 1872–1912*

227. Joyce A. Madancy, *The Troublesome Legacy of Commissioner Lin: The Opium Trade and Opium Suppression in Fujian Province, 1820s to 1920s*

228. John Makeham, *Transmitters and Creators: Chinese Commentators and Commentaries on the Analects*

229. Elisabeth Köll, *From Cotton Mill to Business Empire: The Emergence of Regional Enterprises in Modern China*

230. Emma Teng, *Taiwan's Imagined Geography: Chinese Colonial Travel Writing and Pictures, 1683–1895*

231. Wilt Idema and Beata Grant, *The Red Brush: Writing Women of Imperial China*

232. Eric C. Rath, *The Ethos of Noh: Actors and Their Art*

233. Elizabeth Remick, *Building Local States: China During the Republican and Post-Mao Eras*

234. Lynn Struve, ed., *The Qing Formation in World-Historical Time*

235. D. Max Moerman, *Localizing Paradise: Kumano Pilgrimage and the Religious Landscape of Premodern Japan*

236. Antonia Finnane, *Speaking of Yangzhou: A Chinese City, 1550–1850*

237. Brian Platt, *Burning and Building: Schooling and State Formation in Japan, 1750–1890*

238. Gail Bernstein, Andrew Gordon, and Kate Wildman Nakai, eds., *Public Spheres, Private Lives in Modern Japan, 1600–1950: Essays in Honor of Albert Craig*

239. Wu Hung and Katherine R. Tsiang, *Body and Face in Chinese Visual Culture*

240. Stephen Dodd, *Writing Home: Representations of the Native Place in Modern Japanese Literature*

241. David Anthony Bello, *Opium and the Limits of Empire: Drug Prohibition in the Chinese Interior, 1729–1850*

242. Hosea Hirata, *Discourses of Seduction: History, Evil, Desire, and Modern Japanese Literature*

243. Kyung Moon Hwang, *Beyond Birth: Social Status in the Emergence of Modern Korea*

244. Brian R. Dott, *Identity Reflections: Pilgrimages to Mount Tai in Late Imperial China*

245. Mark McNally, *Proving the Way: Conflict and Practice in the History of Japanese Nativism*

246. Yongping Wu, *A Political Explanation of Economic Growth: State Survival, Bureaucratic Politics, and Private Enterprises in the Making of Taiwan's Economy, 1950–1985*

247. Kyu Hyun Kim, *The Age of Visions and Arguments: Parliamentarianism and the National Public Sphere in Early Meiji Japan*

248. Zvi Ben-Dor Benite, *The Dao of Muhammad: A Cultural History of Muslims in Late Imperial China*

249. David Der-wei Wang and Shang Wei, eds., *Dynastic Crisis and Cultural Innovation: From the Late Ming to the Late Qing and Beyond*

250. Wilt L. Idema, Wai-yee Li, and Ellen Widmer, eds., *Trauma and Transcendence in Early Qing Literature*

251. Barbara Molony and Kathleen Uno, eds., *Gendering Modern Japanese History*

275. Timothy J. Van Compernolle, *The Uses of Memory: The Critique of Modernity in the Fiction of Higuchi Ichiyō*

276. Paul Rouzer, *A New Practical Primer of Literary Chinese*

277. Jonathan Zwicker, *Practices of the Sentimental Imagination: Melodrama, the Novel, and the Social Imaginary in Nineteenth-Century Japan*

278. Franziska Seraphim, *War Memory and Social Politics in Japan, 1945–2005*

279. Adam L. Kern, *Manga from the Floating World: Comicbook Culture and the* Kibyōshi *of Edo Japan*

280. Cynthia J. Brokaw, *Commerce in Culture: The Sibao Book Trade in the Qing and Republican Periods*

281. Eugene Y. Park, *Between Dreams and Reality: The Military Examination in Late Chosŏn Korea, 1600–1894*

282. Nam-lin Hur, *Death and Social Order in Tokugawa Japan: Buddhism, Anti-Christianity, and the* Danka *System*

283. Patricia M. Thornton, *Disciplining the State: Virtue, Violence, and State-Making in Modern China*

284. Vincent Goossaert, *The Taoists of Peking, 1800–1949: A Social History of Urban Clerics*

285. Peter Nickerson, *Taoism, Bureaucracy, and Popular Religion in Early Medieval China*

286. Charo B. D'Etcheverry, *Love After* The Tale of Genji: *Rewriting the World of the Shining Prince*

287. Michael G. Chang, *A Court on Horseback: Imperial Touring & the Construction of Qing Rule, 1680–1785*

288. Carol Richmond Tsang, *War and Faith:* Ikkō Ikki *in Late Muromachi Japan*

289. Hilde De Weerdt, *Competition over Content: Negotiating Standards for the Civil Service Examinations in Imperial China (1127–1279)*

290. Eve Zimmerman, *Out of the Alleyway: Nakagami Kenji and the Poetics of Outcaste Fiction*

291. Robert Culp, *Articulating Citizenship: Civic Education and Student Politics in Southeastern China, 1912–1940*

292. Richard J. Smethurst, *From Foot Soldier to Finance Minister: Takahashi Korekiyo, Japan's Keynes*

293. John E. Herman, *Amid the Clouds and Mist: China's Colonization of Guizhou, 1200–1700*

294. Tomoko Shiroyama, *China During the Great Depression: Market, State, and the World Economy, 1929–1937*

295. Kirk W. Larsen, *Tradition, Treaties and Trade: Qing Imperialism and Chosŏn Korea, 1850–1910*

296. Gregory Golley, *When Our Eyes No Longer See: Realism, Science, and Ecology in Japanese Literary Modernism*